Sharing
Power

Sharing Power

Public Governance and Private Markets

Donald F. Kettl

The Brookings Institution
Washington, D.C.

About Brookings

*The Brookings Institution is a private nonprofit
organization devoted to research, education, and publication
on important issues of domestic and foreign policy. Its
principal purpose is to bring knowledge to bear on current
and emerging policy problems.*

*The Institution was founded on December 8, 1927, to merge
the activities of the Institute for Government Research,
founded in 1916, the Institute of Economics, founded in 1922,
and the Robert Brookings Graduate School of Economics,
founded in 1924.*

*The Institution maintains a position of neutrality on issues
of public policy. Interpretations or conclusions in Brookings
publications should be understood to be solely those of the
authors.*

Copyright © 1993

THE BROOKINGS INSTITUTION

1775 Massachusetts Avenue, N.W., Washington, D.C. 20036

Library of Congress Cataloging-in-Publication data:

Kettl, Donald F.
    Sharing power : public governance and private markets /
Donald F. Kettl.
      p. cm.
    Includes bibliographical references and index.
    ISBN 0-8157-4906-6 (cloth)
    1. Privatization—United States. 2. Public contracts—United
States. 3. Contracting out—United States. 4. Government
contractors—United States. I. Title.
    HD3888.K48   1993
    338.973—dc20   92-41705
                                                    CIP

9 8 7 6 5 4 3 2 1

The paper used in this publication meets the minimum
requirements of the American National Standard for
Information Sciences—Permanence of paper for Printed
Library Materials, ANSI Z39.48-1984.

Preface

Part way through the research on this book, I visited the Department of Energy's Rocky Flats Plant, near Denver. Staff members at the plant told me a tale that in many ways is a parable for the central problem of this book.

In 1991, neighbors of the plant discovered that thousands of prairie dogs were migrating from the plant's property onto their land. A large colony, in fact, was expanding into land being investigated for plutonium contamination. The suspected contamination had occurred, researchers believed, decades before when barrels containing plutonium waste leaked into the surrounding ground and the dirt blew off the plant site. Many of the plant's neighbors worried that with the spread of the prairie dogs from the plant came the risk of plutonium contamination as well. The prairie dogs naturally soon came to be known to residents as the "hot dogs."

The prairie dogs were breeding vigorously. To zoo visitors that might be cute, but for western ranchers they are a major pest. Prairie dogs often remain on the land until they defoliate it. In the process, they can spread disease and dig holes that can trip horses and cattle. By late 1991 more than 3,000 prairie dogs had settled into the area.

What to do about the prairie dogs thus became a major problem for the Department of Energy (DOE), which owned the plant; for Rockwell International, the contractor that operated the plant for DOE; and for the local governments around the plant. To control the pests, DOE and local officials considered several options. One was to create natural barriers, such as hedges, but prairie dogs can eat their way through vegetation and tunnel under fences. Another was to put a dark plastic barrier around the site, but that had failed elsewhere. Yet another suggestion was to use a big vacuum machine to suck the prairie dogs out of their holes, but that was very expensive and led to another question: where could the prairie dogs be relocated?

A local animal rights group, Prairie Dog Rescue, proposed trapping and moving the animals. The technique involved flushing the prairie dogs from their holes with soapy water, cleaning them, drying them, and powdering them to prevent the spread of insects. The dogs would then be moved to another site. The only site in the area licensed to receive prairie dogs, however, was the Defense Department's Rocky Mountain Arsenal. Jefferson County, which was leading this part of the planning, applied to the arsenal for permission to relocate the dogs there, but defense officials refused. If the prairie dogs in fact were contaminated with plutonium, their carcasses would become radioactive waste when they died. Having struggled with their own environmental problems, defense officials were not eager to attract new ones.

The last option was to exterminate the prairie dogs. The Environmental Protection Agency (EPA) had earlier approved a poisoning technique: tablets of aluminum phosphate were dropped into the burrows, and the burrows were then stuffed with newspaper and covered with dirt. Moisture in the burrows activated the tablets, formed a toxic phosgene gas, and killed the dogs. With the burrows already buried in dirt, so too were the carcasses. There were no effects on surrounding plants or animals, EPA concluded. The cost for extermination was relatively low, at only $7.50 per prairie dog (for a total of $22,500), compared with $82.00 per dog (for a total of more than $200,000) for the flush-and-relocate strategy.

One major problem was deciding whose responsibility the prairie dogs were. DOE had created the problem, but as part of an earlier remediation effort had turned over to Jefferson County the land from which they were spreading. The county officials, in turn, feared a public relations disaster no matter what they did. Extermination was a highly emotional issue; animal rights groups pressed for some way to save the prairie dogs. The residents whose property was becoming overrun demanded, meanwhile, that the dogs be dealt with, one way or another. County officials reluctantly decided that extermination was the only realistic alternative.

Before they could begin, however, EPA's regulations posed further hurdles. The agency's rules prohibited harming endangered species in the effort, and the endangered black-footed ferret feeds almost exclusively on prairie dogs. County officials had to ensure that there were no ferrets in the prairie dog holes. So, on three different evenings, when the ferrets would have been most active, the county's extermination contractor searched for signs of the ferrets. They found none. Finally, the extermination contractor, working slowly and quietly from an unmarked truck, began killing the prairie dogs over several weeks.

This tale is a parable in several parts. DOE struggled with surprising technical uncertainties. It had to observe the regulations of other federal and state agencies, and it had to join with local partners to get the job done. At each step of the way, DOE found itself in the middle of a political storm. Finally, in managing the project, it relied on private partners for virtually everything it did. Such technical uncertainties, legal complexities, political conflicts, and intricate administrative relationships have come to define much of governance in the United States.

The administrative aspect of the parable deserves special attention. To a growing but often unrecognized degree, the government depends heavily upon private contractors for producing its goods and services. The markets in which it purchases these goods and services, moreover, are often not very competitive; they tend, in the economists' language, to be highly imperfect. As market imperfections grow, the government's problems increase as well. The humble prairie dogs represent in microcosm the government's challenges in using market mechanisms for managing increasingly complex and politically charged programs.

For several decades, reformers have argued that more reliance on private markets would improve government's performance. In this book, I take a different approach to this old debate. I do not argue that contracting is inherently good or bad. In fact, contracting has become a fundamental and necessary element of governance in the United States. What I do argue in the book is that public reliance on private markets is far more complex than it appears on the surface. In these relationships, the government inevitably finds itself sharing power, which requires it to fundamentally rethink not only how it manages but also how it governs. How can the government meet these challenges? The answer, developed in the chapters that follow, is that the government must become a *smart buyer*, able to define what it wants to buy, to know how to get it, and to be able to recognize and judge what it has bought.

Given the seven years this book has taken to write, I am even more indebted than usual to many scholars and practitioners who have helped me figure out the pieces. A large number of public officials generously gave of their time to answer my questions, empty their files, read my drafts, and struggle to straighten me out. Colleen Prentice, Kristin Stout, Elise Jaffe, Andrew Diefenthaler, and Kristofer Frederick helped in the book's research. I am indebted to Robert H. Haveman, Todd R. La Porte, Bruce McConnell, and H. Brinton Milward, who read portions of the manuscript and supplied extremely helpful comments. John Karl Scholz and Michael L. Wiseman provided invaluable advice. I am deeply indebted to John J. DiIulio, Jr., Paul J. Quirk, and Bert A. Rockman, who read the manuscript in its entirety. They provided enough soothing words to allow me to enjoy meeting their vigorous challenge to sharpen the book's arguments.

I am also grateful for generous financial support I received from the Earhart Foundation, the University of Wisconsin Alumni Research Foundation, and the University of Wisconsin's Robert M. La Follette Institute of Public Affairs. Martha V. Gottron edited the book with a skilled hand, invariably discovering what I was really trying to say. At Brookings, Nancy D. Davidson nurtured this project and provided invaluable suggestions for improving it. The final product is infinitely better for her skilled eye.

Finally, my wife, Sue, showed uncommon grace in putting up with a husband who roamed the country poking into pieces of this puzzle and who turned a large part of the home into a warehouse for the piles of documents he collected. I wonder at her patience and cannot thank her enough for her support.

Although I have benefited immensely from countless sources of help, the views in this book are mine. They should not be attributed to the institutions who generously provided financial support, or to the trustees, officers, or staff members of the Brookings Institution.

DONALD F. KETTL

Contents

Tables

Figures

1

The Competition Prescription

Americans have long had a reverence for private markets to match their dislike of public power. Markets seek efficiency; government may not. Markets promise choice, in quality and price; government does not. Markets offer competition; government has a monopoly. The distinction between private liberty and public authority has always been a critical one in American society.

The most profound attacks on government, in fact, have come from comparisons with the market. Without the discipline of competition, critics contend, government develops lazy habits. Its workers have little incentive to innovate, control costs, or deliver services effectively. The market, these critics say, keeps the private sector lean and efficient. Government tends to grow and grow, without regard to the available resources. While competition focuses private marketers clearly on the bottom line, the argument goes, government bureaucrats tend to be rewarded, not for efficiency, but for increasing the size of their budgets; not for responsiveness, but for expanding their power.[1]

1. The literature on these arguments is voluminous; for a sample, see William A. Niskanen, *Bureaucracy and Representative Government* (Chicago: Aldine, Atherton, 1971); Gordon Tullock, *The Politics of Bureaucracy* (Washington: Public Affairs Press, 1965); Anthony Downs, *Inside Bureaucracy* (Little, Brown, 1967); Thomas Borcherding, ed., *Budgets and Bureaucrats: The Sources of Government Growth* (Duke University Press, 1977); Gary J. Miller and Terry M. Moe, "Bureaucrats, Legislators, and the Size of Government," *American Political Science Review*, vol. 77 (June 1983), pp. 297–322; and E. S. Savas, *Privatization: The Key to Better Government* (Chatham, N.J.: Chatham House Publishers, 1987). For a review and critical examination of the theory, see André Blais and Stéphane Dion, eds., *The Budget-Maximizing Bureaucrat: Appraisals and Evidence* (University of Pittsburgh Press, 1991).

The argument has always been a powerful one. It explains why government spending has grown and why public power is so hard to restrain. It explains why government sometimes seems indifferent to the needs of citizens and why elected officials struggle to control bureaucrats. Most of all, it explains why government just does not seem to work well. It is a theory consistent with many observations, an argument that matches the antigovernment mood of both the electorate and elected officials.

The theory of the market is at once an explanation of what is wrong and what can be done to make things right. If the problem is a set of perverse incentives, the key is to change them. Instead of encouraging government to grow and rewarding bureaucrats with ever-larger budgets, the fix is to replace the government's monopoly with the discipline of vigorous competition.

Remarkably similar prescriptions, in fact, have come from both the left and the right. Neoliberals call for "reinventing government" by inspiring a new entrepreneurial spirit. They seek a vigorous government driven by a new engine—nothing less than "an American *perestroika*" based on competition. "Entrepreneurial governments have discovered that when organizations must compete for funding, they keep their costs down, respond quickly to changing demands and strive mightily" to satisfy citizens, one observer wrote.[2] The problem, the entrepreneurialists contend, "is not too much government or too little government." Rather, the "fundamental problem is that we have *the wrong kind of government*. We do not need more government or less government, we need *better* government." And that, they argue, can come by promoting competition among service providers. Competition, they say, empowers citizens—now rechristened "customers"—by giving them the power of choice and creating inescapable incentives for government workers.[3]

Neoconservatives begin with a far simpler prescription. Government, they say, is simply too big and and should be made smaller.

2. David Osborne, "Ten Ways to Turn D.C. Around," *The Washington Post Magazine,* December 9, 1990, p. 21. See also David Osborne and Ted Gaebler, *Reinventing Government: How the Entrepreneurial Spirit Is Transforming the Public Sector, from Schoolhouse to Statehouse, City Hall to the Pentagon* (Reading, Mass.: Addison-Wesley, 1992).

3. David Osborne and Ted A. Gaebler, "Bringing Government Back to Life," *Governing,* vol. 5 (February 1992), p. 50.

"As every taxpayer knows, government is wasteful and inefficient; it always has been and always will be," policy analysts James T. Bennett and Manuel H. Johnson contend.[4] To "shrink government,"[5] neo-conservatives propose to remove government from as many programs as possible and to turn the functions over to the private sector. Programs that must remain in government's hands should be contracted out, they argue. The government, they conclude, must be disciplined by market competition.

Whether the aim is to reduce government or just to make it work better, reformers from very different ideologies have settled on a *competition prescription* that substitutes market for government control, that replaces command-and-control authority with competition. The fix for what ails government, they agree, is to change the way government does business and, in fact, to make it more businesslike. During the Reagan administration, a report issued by the Office of Management and Budget (OMB) stated the thesis clearly:

> Competition is the driving force behind quality and economy of operations in the private sector. Private sector managers are continually challenged by competitors who may force them out of business if they do not operate in the most efficient manner. This constant competitive pressure forces managers to be innovative and flexible as they promote performance-based management to serve their customers.
>
> Government managers, in normal operations, do not encounter the same pressures for efficiency that private sector managers do. They have few baselines for comparisons and do not face the constant threat of competition. Moreover, Government managers many times face legislative and fiscal constraints that force them to operate inefficiently. Competition with the private sector can highlight these inefficiencies and consequently help identify the changes necessary either to streamline the Government operation or to determine whether the private sector can more efficiently perform the service.[6]

4. James T. Bennett and Manuel H. Johnson, *Better Government at Half the Price: Private Production of Public Services* (Ottawa, Ill.: Caroline House, 1981), p. 19.

5. The phrase comes from the subtitle of E. S. Savas, *Privatizing the Public Sector: How to Shrink Government* (Chatham, N.J.: Chatham House Publishers, 1982).

6. Office of Management and Budget, *Enhancing Governmental Productivity*

The fundamental paradox in the calls to implement this prescription is that American government has long been pursuing it, for pragmatic reasons quite apart from the rhetoric. In fact, *every major policy initiative launched by the federal government since World War II— including medicare and medicaid, environmental cleanup and restoration, antipoverty programs and job training, interstate highways and sewage treatment plants—has been managed through public-private partnerships.* These partnerships have not solved government's problems; indeed, many of them have helped fuel the problems that procompetition critics have used to attack government.

Clear evidence comes in four different government studies, conducted between 1989 and 1992, that examined management in the federal government. Each study identified programs whose performance was threatened by management problems such as waste, fraud, and abuse. What these programs shared was a common base in public-private partnerships; many of the programs relied on contracts with private, profit-oriented organizations. In a 1989 study requested by the Senate Governmental Affairs Committee, OMB identified seventy-three federal programs at "high risk" for abuse. Nearly 80 percent of these involved substantial public-private sector ties, and almost half relied upon contractors.[7] A year later the General Accounting Office (GAO) released its own list of fourteen high-risk programs. Of these, a dozen involved public-private connections, and contractors participated extensively in six.[8] A 1991 study by the staff of the House Budget Committee reviewed ten programs that had suffered substantial management problems during the 1980s. All ten relied on public-private partnerships, and half were programs that the government had contracted out.[9]

Then, in 1992, OMB released its own study of contracting in civilian agencies. "SWAT teams" that OMB had sent into twelve civilian agencies found such abuses as contractors who leased equipment from

through Competition: A New Way of Doing Business within the Government to Provide Quality Government at Least Cost (August 1988), p. 1.

7. News Release, Senator John Glenn, December 5, 1989.

8. General Accounting Office, letter from Charles A. Bowsher to Senator John Glenn and Representative John Conyers, Jr., OCG-90-1 (January 23, 1990).

9. *Management Reform: A Top Priority for the Federal Executive Branch,* Committee Print, House Committee on the Budget, 102 Cong. 1 sess. (Government Printing Office, 1991).

their spouses at inflated rates and charged living expenses to corporate expense accounts. After having championed contracting for more than a decade as an important strategy for shrinking government, OMB self-consciously admitted that

> the civilian agencies by and large have not given sufficient management attention (e.g., guidance, training, resources) to contract administration. Emphasis is placed on the award of contracts, not on assuring that the terms of the contract are met or that the procurement regulations are followed after contract award.[10]

The staff of the House Committee on Government Operations, looking at the same data, was harsher.

> Ineptitude, poor planning and inadequate auditing on the one hand, and venality and corruption on the other cost taxpayers billions of dollars in faulty procurements each year. Procurement officials repeatedly fail to identify the government's needs and objectives and as a result spend billions of dollar on projects that cannot accomplish what is required.[11]

The irony is rich. Despite the enthusiasm for entrepreneurial government and privatization, the most egregious tales of waste, fraud, and abuse in government programs have often involved greedy, corrupt, and often criminal activity by the government's private partners—and weak government management to detect and correct these problems.[12]

If reliance upon private markets is the answer to the government's problems, and the government has been expanding its partnerships with the private sector, why have such problems endured and, indeed, multiplied? The answer in brief—and I will spend the rest of this book developing it—is that the competition prescription is not a magic

10. Office of Management and Budget, *Summary Report of the SWAT Team on Civilian Agency Contracting: Improving Contracting Practices and Management Controls on Cost-Type Federal Contracts* (December 3, 1992), pp. i–ii.

11. "Managing the Federal Government: A Decade of Decline," Report of the Majority Staff, House Committee on Government Operations (1992), p. 5.

12. Paul Staff, "The Limits of Privatization," in Steve H. Hanke, ed., *Prospects of Privatization* (New York: Academy of Political Science, 1987), pp. 60–73.

bullet. Government's relationships with the private sector are not self-administering; they require, rather, aggressive management by a strong, competent government. Although competition might advance efficiency, this is not always the case, as I will show. Efficiency, moreover, is one, but only one, goal of a government operating in the public interest. Competition does not capture—and, indeed, can slight—a vast array of other goals that have equal or sometimes greater priority.

The competition prescription, in fact, does not so much reduce government as fundamentally change its role. Government's manifest problems stem not so much from following the competition prescription but from being unable to follow it intelligently. In many cases the problems proponents of the competition prescription rail against are the *result* of government's growing reliance on the private sector and its lack of capacity to manage public-private relationships.

This book is neither an attack on nor a defense of the competition prescription, in either its entrepreneurial or privatization formulations. Rather, it is a searching examination of what the growing reliance on public-private ties requires of government if the partnerships are to work well. That requires, in turn, a far more sophisticated understanding of the nature of these relationships and of the often surprising array of problems they present.

The Hidden Growth of Public-Private Partnerships

Governments, of course, have always relied on private partners to provide key goods and services. As long as there have been governments, there have been armies; as long as there have been armies, governments have purchased weapons and supplies from private vendors. And as long as governments have bought such goods, they have encountered problems. When George Washington commanded colonial troops in the battle against Britain, he complained constantly about private suppliers. They were slow to deliver and often stole the highest quality supplies to sell again for their own profit. Too often American troops, instead of receiving the best, suffered with the worst.[13] Waste, fraud, and abuse in American defense contracts began even before the country did.

13. Erna Risch, *Supplying Washington's Army* (GPO, 1981).

Despite the problems, public-private partnerships continued in the new United States as in other nations. It simply made no sense for the government to produce all of its own goods and services when private suppliers stood ready to do business with the government. The suppliers ranged from naval "privateers"—nongovernmental agents who took in customs duties at sea for a commission—to the original Secret Service, which operated under a government contract with the Pinkerton detective agency. Until nearly 1900 the federal government contracted with state and local governments for the jailing of federal prisoners. These governments, in turn, often contracted with private companies for the prisoners' labor.[14]

From the Civil War until World War II the basic rules governing government contracts with the private sector remained virtually unchanged. Government contract managers were required by law to develop detailed specifications for the goods or services they wanted to buy. They then had to advertise for bids, open the bids publicly at a predetermined time and place, and award the contract to the lowest bidder who complied with the specifications. The approach provided standardized products, which reduced the government's need to train workers to use different versions of the same product and made controlling the inventory far easier. The stable rules and uniform products also encouraged businesses to compete in supplying these goods and services. The competition, as the privatizers would have predicted, helped reduce the government's cost. It also produced a useful side benefit: with many suppliers in the market, the government found that it could quickly increase its purchases in an emergency.[15]

This process also meant that the government played a passive role in designing the goods and services it purchased. For the most part, it bought products off the shelf, choosing among goods and services already developed and proven in the private market. Even for most military products, the government waited until ideas had been "thor-

14. Ronald C. Moe, "Privatization from a Public Management Perspective" (Congressional Research Service, 1989), pp. 25–26.
15. This discussion relies on the classic early study of government contracting, Clarence H. Danhof, *Government Contracting and Technological Change* (Brookings, 1968), especially chap. 2. See also John D. Hanrahan, *Government by Contract* (Norton, 1983); and Daniel Guttman and Barry Willner, *The Shadow Government: The Government's Multi-Billion Dollar Giveaway of Its Decision-Making Powers to Private Management Consultants, "Experts," and Think Tanks* (Pantheon Books, 1976).

oughly tested and proved in civilian use," noted Clarence H. Danhof, a historian of government contracting.[16] Whether buying saddles or pistols, paper or machinery, the government had an arm's-length relationship with its suppliers, behaving very much like a private player in the private market.

World War II Changes

The federal government's practice of relying on standardized goods already tested in the private sector proved satisfactory for peacetime, and even for World War I. But World War II rendered the old approach obsolete. Technological certainties and cost savings were no longer the prime goals. Winning the war was, and that made government officials far more willing to take risks with their procurement system. New technologies, from radar to munitions, were rushed to the battlefield before they were thoroughly tested. Manufacturers found themselves producing new weapons and then modifying them, sometimes substantially, in response to successes and failures in the field.

The contract arrangement that had endured since the Civil War gave way to the new realities. Instead of writing clear specifications that described existing products, military officials worked cooperatively with manufacturers to design new systems. If the government and the manufacturer agreed that a new technology had promise, they would collaborate in research, design, and production.

Such flexibility in determining the precise product to be bought required a similar flexibility in pricing. Instead of the traditional fixed-price contracts, in which suppliers agreed to produce a certain quantity of goods or services at a predetermined price, the government moved to cost-plus-fixed-fee contracts, in which producers were paid for the costs they incurred plus a predetermined fee as profit.

For the first time, moreover, the government played a critical role in promoting innovation. The arm's-length relationship between buyer and seller that had characterized the government's procurement was fast being replaced by a new relationship based on cooperative partnership. It was to be a permanent shift. The pent-up demand for new technologies, both military and domestic, and the nation's need to maintain a technological edge over its potential adversaries encour-

16. Danhof, *Government Contracting and Technological Change*, p. 19.

aged a continuation of the public-private collaboration that had been so successful during the war.

This was a partnership founded in pragmatism. As President Harry Truman noted in 1945, "During the war we have learned much about the methods of organizing scientific activity, and about the ways of encouraging and supporting its activities. The development of atomic energy is a clear-cut indication of what can be accomplished by our universities, industry, and Government working together. Vast scientific fields remain to be conquered in the same way."[17]

In space, agriculture, health, and natural resources, as well as in defense policy, the government began to rely on the private sector for new technological concepts and ideas as well as for the development and production of advanced goods.[18] Federal funding for research and development increased at a "phenomenal rate," a special commission on contracting reported in 1962. From just $100 million a year in the late 1930s, federal spending on research and development (R&D) increased to $10 billion a year by the early 1960s. Before the war nearly all R&D financed by the federal government was conducted through governmental institutions. By the early 1960s, 80 percent was conducted at nonfederal institutions. The result was "a highly complex partnership among various kinds of public and private agencies, related in large part by contractural arrangements," the special commission concluded.[19]

Branching Out

The war forever changed the federal government from a passive customer of technological change to an active player in shaping it. Postwar demands—strategic, technical, and pragmatic—broke down the prewar procurement system and replaced it with a far more flexible approach. As new challenges occurred, the federal government expanded its use of public-private partnerships to meet them.

---

17. *Public Papers of the Presidents, Harry S. Truman, 1945*, pp. 293–94.
18. Danhof, *Government Contracting and Technological Change*, p. 123.
19. Bureau of the Budget, *Report to the President on Government Contracting for Research and Development* (hereafter Bell Report), S. Doc. 87-94, 87 Cong. 2 sess. (GPO, 1962), p. 191; and Danhof, *Government Contracting and Technological Change*, p. 93.

Perhaps the most dramatic example has been the nation's space program, which has been a collaborative venture from its beginning. In the race for space, the National Aeronautics and Space Administration turned to private contractors to perform the research and development, build the spacecraft, and manage the systems that make them fly. Although the fact is rarely apparent on television news coverage, contractors dominate most of the ground-based operations of space missions.

Less dramatic, but equally important, examples of public-private partnerships can be found in every other policy area as well. In fact, the government's reliance on the private sector, with the blurring of public-private boundaries that accompanies it, has become the dominant administrative pattern of postwar policy. Consider the following policy areas.

SOCIAL POLICY. Although federal financial support for social programs, from job training to housing rehabilitation, has declined since the late 1970s, the management strategy has remained the same. Since the enactment of the Great Society legislation of the 1960s, most social programs have been managed through a two-step approach. The federal government has defined ambitious goals and then awarded grants to state and local governments to manage these programs. State and local governments have then contracted out most of the programs to local organizations, particularly nonprofit, community-based groups.[20] Governmental action is increasingly complex because it is increasingly joint, between the government and private or nonprofit organizations.[21]

HEALTH POLICY. In 1965 the federal government launched the medicare program to provide medical care for the elderly. Since then this most important and enduring legacy of Lyndon Johnson's Great So-

20. On federal job training programs, see Jeffrey L. Pressman and Aaron B. Wildavsky, *Implementation*, 2d ed. (University of California Press, 1979); and Martin A. Levin and Barbara Ferman, *The Political Hand* (Pergamon Press, 1985). On housing and community development programs, see Donald F. Kettl, *Managing Community Development in the New Federalism* (Praeger, 1980).

21. In fact, Pressman and Wildavsky's argument about "the complexity of joint action" is a recognition of the mixed administrative system on which the federal government has come to rely. See Pressman and Wildavsky, *Implementation*, p. 87.

ciety has become one of the fastest growing programs in the federal budget. Behind the supercharged politics of the program, however, is a subtle administrative reality consistent with the course of postwar public management. Although the federal government finances the program, the private and nonprofit sectors administer most of it. Health care is provided, not by government agencies, but by hospitals, clinics, and private physicians throughout the country. Private fiscal intermediaries such as Blue Cross and Blue Shield manage the program's paperwork and reimbursements. These intermediaries receive the bills, review the claims for compliance with federal guidelines and proper medical procedure, and make the payments.[22] The federal government's growing role in, and important influence over, national health policy thus occurs through complex and often unseen partnerships with private agents.

ENVIRONMENTAL POLICY. Governments have always regulated the private economy, but government regulation—especially to protect health, safety, and the environment—has expanded markedly since the 1960s. Particularly in environmental policy, the federal government has set broad standards and then monitored state and local governments' implementation of those standards. If state governments do not set adequate standards, the federal government can step in and regulate directly. To implement the standards, the states, in turn, have relied heavily on private partners, especially private contractors who have built and managed important treatment facilities.[23] This complex relationship has muddied intergovernmental relations and made it difficult to determine just who is responsible for overseeing which rules.

BAILOUTS. When the savings-and-loan industry collapsed in the late 1980s, the federal government came to the rescue. It paid off depositors, took over the management of many of the thrift institutions' failed assets—from junk bonds to apartment complexes—and then struggled to sell off the assets to minimize the drain on taxpayers. At

22. On the history, see Murray Weidenbaum, *The Modern Public Sector: New Ways of Doing the Government's Business* (Basic Books, 1969), especially pp. 107–10.
23. John G. Heilman and Gerald W. Johnson, *The Politics and Economics of Privatization: The Case of Wastewater Treatment* (University of Alabama Press, 1992).

every step of the way the federal government relied on a vast network of private contractors. Federal bailout managers contracted with appraisers to assess the value of properties; with facilities managers to operate the apartment complexes, hotels, and shopping centers which the government now owned; with real estate agents to sell properties; and with a huge number of private lawyers to handle the complex legal transactions surrounding the bailout. The federal government paid the bills and set the fundamental policies, but private contractors did most of the work. The success of the bailout—as well as its ultimate cost—will be as much the product of these private agents as of the government's policies.[24]

SUPPORT SERVICES. The federal government, meanwhile, has dramatically expanded its reliance on private contractors for a host of support services. Consultants and other contractors have helped the government plan programs, evaluate their results, answer citizens' inquiries, write congressional testimony for cabinet secretaries, organize logistics, make photocopies, and perform virtually every other service one can imagine. Some of these services were "inherently governmental" in nature, according to GAO, which meant that private contractors were exercising government's core powers and basic management decisions.[25]

The federal government began to contract out many of these fundamental services during the 1970s, when the civilian executive branch work force declined slightly while federal expenditures increased 195 percent. Private consultants and service contractors helped take up the slack. Federal outlays for such service contracts, even after adjusting for inflation, increased 28 percent through the decade.[26] Most of the increase came about because of congressionally mandated personnel ceilings and the huge demands of new federal programs.[27]

24. Donald F. Kettl, "The Savings-and-Loan Bailout: The Mismatch Between the Headlines and the Issues," *PS: Political Science and Politics,* vol. 24 (September 1991), pp. 441–47.

25. General Accounting Office, *Government Contractors: Are Service Contractors Performing Inherently Governmental Functions?* GGD-92-11 (November 1991). See also Guttman and Willner, *The Shadow Government.*

26. General Accounting Office, *Civil Servants and Contract Employees: Who Should Do What for the Federal Government?* FPCD-81-43 (June 19, 1981), p. ii.

27. GAO, *Civil Servants and Contract Employees,* p. ii; and General Accounting

Implications

From defense to nuclear weapons, social services to health programs, environmental regulation to the savings-and-loan bailout, the federal government has chosen to build administrative partnerships instead of doing the job itself. In fiscal 1991, the federal government spent more than $210 billion through contracts, out of a total of $1.4 trillion in spending.[28] Transfer payments to individuals and contracting constitute two of the federal government's most important policy tools.[29] Similar figures on the use of contracting by state and local governments are unavailable, but all of the evidence indicates that they have increased their reliance on the tool even more dramatically.

Government's growing reliance on its partners in the private and nonprofit sectors means that its success in many cases has come to depend in large part on how well those partners perform. That reliance also raises serious questions about governance and accountability. As GAO warned in a 1991 report, "When contracting out, agencies should not relinquish government control to contractors, as appears to have happened in some instances."[30] In its eager pursuit of the competition prescription, government has—for a remarkable variety of reasons—too often surrendered its basic policymaking power to contractors.

Moreover, to get the specific goods and services it needs, the government has actively promoted private research, development, investment, and the creation and coordination of markets and market relationships that did not previously exist. As a result the government is no longer a buyer dealing at arm's length with a seller but a partner in a virtually seamless, mutually dependent interrelationship. These growing public-private ties, including substantial links with the nonprofit sector for social services, have blurred the boundaries among the sectors, making it ever harder to distinguish between public and private accountability.

Office, *Federal Workforce: Inappropriate Use of Experts and Consultants at Selected Civilian Agencies*, GGD-91-99 (July 1991).

28. General Services Administration, *Federal Procurement Data System: Federal Procurement Report, Fiscal Year 1991 Through Fourth Quarter* (1992), p. 2.

29. Other policy tools are important as well—regulation, tax incentives, and loan programs, in particular—but they tend to pale in comparison with the use of contracts and transfers.

30. GAO, *Government Contractors*, pp. 6–7.

This blurring of boundaries in turn has produced a fundamental irony. Although many of government's critics have presented the competition prescription as a way to replace government's pathologies with the superior virtues of the market, the federal government's increasing relationship with the private sector has instead brought the two sectors closer together. Instead of *privatizing the public sector,* the federal government's management strategies have tended to *governmentalize the private sector.* For pragmatic, rather than ideological, reasons, the government has been following the competition prescription for decades, and in so doing, its power has grown, not diminished. Its reach into the private sector has increased, not declined, and its problems of performance have palpably not vanished. What, then, has gone wrong? Why has the competition prescription not worked as its advocates expected?

Private Markets

Answering these questions requires an understanding of the case made for the market. The simple version is that market competition is more efficient than monopolistic behavior by the government. The argument, however, is considerably more subtle than simply contending that the market is more virtuous than government. Market advocates contend that competition would discipline the government in the same ways that it disciplines the private sector. Without the discipline of the market, government is doomed to inefficiency. Competition would make government's provision of goods and services to citizens self-correcting, they say, in three ways.

First, exchanges among those who want to buy and sell set the *level of production.* The demand of buyers balances the supply of sellers. Transactions among them set an equilibrium for production. The result, privatization advocates argue, is efficiency. In government, however, demand and supply rarely balance. If agency officials do not spend all of their budgets, they must return the money to the Treasury—and they are likely to find their budgets cut the next year. Since their status and power are frequently measured by the size of the budgets they manage, their incentives are to spend every dime and then to ask for more. Taxpayers simply are billed for the steady upward spiral of spending that these incentives produce. Government therefore tends to produce too many goods and services, the argument goes, because there is nothing to balance the pressures for greater supply of services, except for eventual taxpayer outrage.

Second, advocates of privatization contend that markets *minimize costs.* Competition opens the door to suppliers who think they might be able to underprice goods or provide goods superior to those already in the market. Such competition keeps the market honest and restrains price increases. If introduced into government, competition might also reduce government's costs, they argue.

Third, privatization advocates argue that market forces *regulate quality.* Producers who sell inferior goods and services will soon find themselves losing business to competitors who make better products. For government's critics, this is the trump card. If government produces mediocre goods and services, it does not suffer. In the private sector, losers can go out of business. In the public sector, inefficient bureaucracies do not go out of business. They may even see their budgets and the number of their employees increase in a vain effort to solve the problems.

These diagnoses and prescriptions command broad support, but their critics are legion. Rarely do participants on either side of the debate, however, stop to consider the critical underlying assumptions. The competition prescription assumes that there *is* a competitive market for the goods and services that the government buys, or at least that one can be created. What does a competitive market require? A market depends on *arm's-length transactions* among *large numbers of buyers and sellers* for *relatively undifferentiated goods.* Government, because it is government, frequently cannot meet these conditions.

Government buys many standard goods. A pencil or a tablet is the same whether it is put to public or private use. Garbage is garbage, whether it is public or private, and must be hauled away to a landfill. For these standard goods and services, the government usually may choose from among many suppliers. For most other public goods and services, however, the government cannot simply shop in some sort of giant supermarket. From cleanup of toxic wastes to construction of complex weapons, the government is often the only buyer. Much of what government buys is custom-made, often to plug gaps in what the market cannot do, has failed to do, or has done badly. For many of these custom-made goods there may be only one or two suppliers. In many cases, government must stimulate and simulate competition for its goods and services. Without the government, there would be no production of many of them.

Because many public goods and services are highly differentiated, and because the government must itself often structure the market, buyers and sellers often do not operate at arm's length. Whether they are designing weapons systems or a health care delivery system, the government and the contractor work closely to decide what needs to be done and how it can be accomplished. Government and its suppliers are often close partners instead of independent buyers and sellers who meet in the marketplace. Cooperation, not competition, often characterizes these relationships.

This is not to say, of course, that all private market transactions are characterized by undifferentiated goods traded at arm's length among many buyers and sellers. When a major auto company buys steel, it often must choose among only a few suppliers. It works closely with those suppliers to obtain the kind of steel it believes will make the best cars. Food processors frequently create intimate partnerships with growers so that the tomatoes or peas they put into their cans meet their standards. If the public sector is often not characterized by truly competitive markets, neither is the private sector.

The further the government moves away from the basic assumptions underlying market competition, the harder the government must work to substitute other mechanisms if it is to obtain the benefits that market competition promises. Government has often found this part of the competition prescription the most difficult to fill. When competition does not supply market discipline—and often even when it does—buyers must behave intelligently if they are to get their money's worth. Centuries ago the Romans coined a term for this age-old observation: *caveat emptor,* or "let the buyer beware." Government must do the same.

Reliance on contracting out has not so much solved the problems of efficiency in American government as aggravated them. Private markets are efficient only when they are truly competitive. The markets in which the government has operated, however, have been plagued by imperfections, and the more imperfections accumulate in the market, the less the promise of efficiency is met.

This raises two critical questions for the government. First, if it is to be efficient and effective, to what degree can the government rely on the market to shape its transactions? Second, to the degree that the conditions required for competitive markets do not apply, does the government have the capacity to manage these contracts effectively? To the degree that it does not, the quality of public services will inevitably diminish and costs will rise.

These questions lead directly to the argument of the book: The higher the level of imperfections in the markets in which it buys, the greater the burden on the government to behave as a *smart buyer*. Government must know what it wants to buy. It must know how to buy its goods and services. And it must be able to determine what it has bought. If it does not act as a smart buyer, it inevitably sacrifices its sovereignty to the private markets on which it has come to rely. The lack of a smart-buyer capacity trades off important public interests for private interests. The smart-buyer problem thus is the critical challenge for contracting out.

Public Interests

Buried within the competition prescription is the assumption that competition will meet government's goals—if only the goals can be identified clearly enough. Market competition single-mindedly pursues one goal—efficiency—above all others. Efficiency, the achievement of a given level of output at the lowest possible price, is certainly desirable. Who wants to pay more than necessary for any good or service? Even government's harshest critics do not accuse it of such dark motives.

Efficiency, however, is not government's only goal; it pursues other, sometimes contradictory, goals at the same time. Government's fundamental challenge in serving the public interest is balancing the pursuit of efficiency with other goals that have equal, sometimes greater, importance. Five standards compete to shape the public interest.

EFFICIENCY. For many analysts and critics of government, efficiency is the philosopher's stone. A leading textbook in policy analysis, for example, tells students they would be fortunate if they had a philosopher-king as a client. "The analyst could prepare advice with the knowledge that it would be thoughtfully evaluated on its merits by a wise leader who placed the welfare of the kingdom above considerations of private or factional interest." Since "many cooks contribute to the policy broth," however, the welfare of the kingdom—for that read "efficiency"—is never the only criterion.[31] The complexities of politics might force philosopher-kings, and ordinary politicians, to compromise efficiency for other goals. Efficiency, however, is the star by which many analysts and critics alike set their compasses.

EFFECTIVENESS. For these analysts, there is a sense of the second-best, of the politically corrupt, about other principles. Nonetheless, even though nearly everyone advocates efficiency, many citizens and policymakers—by their actions, if not by their rhetoric—rank other interests higher. Residents who discover a toxic waste dump in their neighborhood want it cleaned up, and cleaned up immediately. They do not care that there might be more efficient uses of public money, that other, more dangerous toxic waste dumps might need to be cleaned up first, or that other citizens might consider other government programs to be more important. For the people living near any one dump, any amount of money would be well spent if it eliminates the threat to their families and homes. Citizens and policymakers alike frequently demand that government meet the goals of public programs—that is, that the government manage the programs effectively—regardless of economic efficiency. A goal is a goal, regardless of its cost.

CAPACITY. Government, furthermore, sometimes deliberately engages in inefficient purchasing to keep more than one vendor in business and thus ensure some semblance of competition for future contracts. The Pentagon, for example, has deliberately awarded some of its business to losing competitors in the procurement competitions for new submarines. Awarding all of a contract to a single winning bidder might prove cheapest in the short run, but such a strategy could prove very costly in the long run if the losing bidders are driven

---

31. David L. Weimer and Aidan R. Vining, *Policy Analysis: Concepts and Practice,* 2d ed. (Prentice-Hall, 1992), p. 15.

out of business. The government works hard to maintain the capacity of its private suppliers to produce its goods and services.

Perhaps more important than ensuring competition in any particular market, the government must maintain its own capacity to manage its contracts. As the government has turned to private contractors for more of its administrative and support services, worries about its capacity to manage these contractors have multiplied. It is one thing to hire outside concerns to supply goods and services. It is quite another to hire outside concerns to judge what the government ought to buy, how much it ought to pay, and how good the goods and services actually are. The more the government has contracted out its core functions, the more the government worsens its problem of building capacity.

RESPONSIVENESS. Just as important as *what* is done is *how* it is done. After long debating the location for a permanent nuclear waste repository, Congress voted simply to impose it on Nevada. Many analysts argued that Nevada was the most efficient and effective site because the federal government already owned thousands of square miles around the proposed site and because geologists said the site was the safest of all those studied. Nevadans objected furiously because they had no voice in the process. Many Nevada officials vowed to use every tool they had to delay the project at every turn. The Nevadans objected that they had been denied due process. They also complained that the government seemed simply not to care about them because it did not listen to their concerns. Responsiveness is essential to both due process and trust in the process. Even if a decision is the most efficient and effective, citizens will attack it if they feel it is being rammed down their throats.

TRUST AND CONFIDENCE. Another issue about the *how* of public policy is the sense of trust and confidence that citizens feel in their government. Lawsuits, negative publicity, and continuing guerrilla action against programs can lead to endless delays, complicate every administrative stage, and ultimately undermine political support for programs. Many program managers have learned the hard way that the pursuit of efficiency alone is not enough. If public trust and confidence in both the process and the product wanes, that trust is hard to rebuild. And once it ebbs away, the very foundation of public programs is threatened.[32]

The Myth of the Self-Governing Market

The fundamental irony of the competition prescription is that practice has galloped madly ahead of theory. The government's reliance upon the private sector has grown faster than its ability to manage it. To regain control government must pay heed to three critical lessons derived from its relationships with the market since World War II.

First, these relationships cannot manage themselves. To rely on the markets, without competition, is to risk placing private goals above public goals, and to sacrifice—perhaps unknowingly—some public interests to others. The government's ties with the markets must be managed, and managed aggressively.

Second, if the government is to manage the markets, it must have the capacity to do so. The most disturbing trend in public management since World War II, however, is the gradual but unmistakable erosion of the government's capacity to oversee its contractors. It is an *emptor* who cannot judge the *caveat*.

Third, the markets in which the government deals are not of one piece. The government as a buyer therefore engages in a remarkable range of relationships with its suppliers. Just as these relationships vary, so too must the government's sophistication in managing them. Government must have a substantial capacity not only to manage, but also to discriminate among the different problems that different kinds of markets present. It is to that issue I turn in chapter 2.

32. For one agency's attack on this problem, see Office of Civilian Radioactive Waste Management, *Draft Mission Plan Amendment* (Department of Energy 1991), chap. 7.

2

Government and Markets

The expansion of the government's partnership with private suppliers brings three important issues into focus. First, government is relying on *private* partners to do *public* work. The growth of this trend has created a new kind of public management. Second, the practice of this new public management is scarcely uniform. Public-private partnerships produce highly variable relationships. The government often enters very different markets, deals with radically different organizations, and frequently receives surprisingly different results. Thus, while the growth of public-private partnerships has reshaped the foundation of public management, the partnerships themselves have created wide-ranging problems. No one management approach can solve them all.

Third, government's role has changed. Government is less the producer of goods and services, and more the supervisor of proxies who do the actual work.[1] In more traditional programs, where government itself produces goods or services, top managers give orders, which they expect agency employees to follow. In reality, these expectations are frequently breached. The literature on public bureaucracy is filled with tales of self-serving bureaucrats who go their own way instead

---

1. Frederick C. Mosher, "The Changing Responsibilities and Tactics of the Federal Government," *Public Administration Review,* vol. 40 (November–December 1980), pp. 541–48; Lester M. Salamon, "Rethinking Public Management: Third-Party Government and the Changing Forms of Government Action," *Public Policy,* vol. 29 (Summer 1981), pp. 255–75; and Donald F. Kettl, *Government by Proxy: (Mis?)Managing Federal Programs* (Washington: CQ Press, 1988).

21

of following the path defined by superiors.[2] It is scarcely trivial that orders from the top of the bureaucracy often go awry before they reach the bottom. For purposes of this discussion, however, what matters is the presence of a hierarchical chain that links, whether well or poorly, those who shape policy with those on the front lines of service delivery.

In public-private partnerships, contracts replace hierarchy. Instead of a chain of authority from policy to product, there is a negotiated document that separates policymaker from policy output. Top officials cannot give orders to contractors. They can threaten, cajole, or persuade, but in the end, they can only shape the incentives to which the contractors respond. There is a gap in the chain of authority, which the contract fills. The gap does not necessarily indicate trouble. Gaps in electronic circuits quite literally supply the sparks that power most modern technologies. Gaps can also produce uncertain results—ask anyone whose car's spark plugs have fouled.

The argument here is not that the contractual relationship, which lies at the core of the competition prescription, is prone to breakdown, but that it entails a *different kind* of public management. And that raises the central question: What role must government play to fill the competition prescription?

The Contracting Relationship

To answer this question, one must first look at the issues contracting relationships raise. A sophisticated, formal theory—known as principal-agent theory—suggests common problems in the contracting relationship. What follows here is a somewhat eclectic extension of the theory.[3]

2. The critiques grow out of arguments that bureaucrats seek to maximize their own power at the expense of the agency's mission. For an assessment of this argument, see André Blais and Stéphane Dion, eds., *The Budget-Maximizing Bureaucrat: Appraisals and Evidence* (University of Pittsburgh Press, 1991).

3. Major works on principal-agent theory include Terry M. Moe, "The New Economics of Organization," *American Journal of Political Science,* vol. 28 (November 1984), pp. 739–77; John W. Pratt and Richard J. Zeckhauser, eds., *Principals and Agents: The Structure of Business* (Harvard Business School Press, 1985), especially Kenneth J. Arrow, "The Economics of Agency," pp. 37–51, and Harrison C. White, "Agency as Control," pp. 187–212; David E. M. Sappington and Joseph E. Stiglitz, "Privatization, Information and Incentives," *Journal of Policy Analysis and Manage-*

The basic management goal in any contracting relationship is a simple one: "inducing an 'agent' to behave as if he were maximizing the 'principal's' welfare," as economists Michael Jensen and William Meckling put it.[4] The government, as principal, must write a contract that induces the contractor, as agent, to behave as the government desires. In theory this task seems easy. The government decides what it wants, writes a contract that specifies the goals, finds a contractor willing to meet those goals at the lowest cost, and then signs an agreement.

Matters would be this simple in practice were it not for a critical problem—*the* problem, in fact, which has undergirded the study of organizations for two generations. In the real world, Nobel laureate Ronald Coase recognized in a pathbreaking 1937 article, competition is not perfect and information is often lacking.[5] Herbert Simon, another Nobel laureate, extended this argument in his 1945 book, *Administrative Behavior*, contending that "it is impossible for the behavior of a single, isolated individual to reach any high degree of rationality." Decisionmakers have only fragmentary knowledge of consequences and can, at best, consider only a few of the many possible alternatives facing them. If individuals cannot be highly rational, then the organizations in which they work can scarcely be rational either, Simon argued. Rationality is bounded at best.[6]

The central importance of the work by Coase and Simon was to define *information*—and the barriers to obtaining it—as the main problem that organizations must solve. Organizations exist to do

ment, vol. 6 (Summer 1987), pp. 567–82; and Daniel Levinthal, "A Survey of Agency Models of Organizations," *Journal of Economic Behavior and Organization*, vol. 9 (March 1988), pp. 153–85. This discussion does not follow principal-agent theory completely. Much of the theory is highly formal and mathematical. It also builds on rigorous assumptions that limit its application to the cases in this book. Some organizational theorists, moreover, have raised serious reservations about some of the assumptions underlying principal-agent theory. For a critique, see Charles Perrow, *Complex Organizations: A Critical Essay*, 3d ed. (Random House, 1986), especially pp. 229–36.

4. Michael Jensen and William Meckling, "Theory of the Firm: Managerial Behavior, Agency Costs, and Ownership Structure," *Journal of Financial Economics*, vol. 3 (October 1976), p. 309.

5. Ronald H. Coase, "The Nature of the Firm," *Economica*, vol. 4 (November 1937), pp. 386–405.

6. Herbert Simon, *Administrative Behavior: A Study of Decision-Making Processes in Administrative Organization*, 3d ed. (Free Press, 1976), pp. 79, 81.

things, and to do those things, they must make decisions. In making decisions, though, they cannot know all there is to know. "Economic man" might optimize, but "administrative man" must "satisfice," Simon argued, by searching for satisfactory, not the most efficient, results. This tenet guides organizations—and the individuals who work within them—toward highly patterned behavior. Stable and predictable patterns help reduce the many uncertainties that result from negotiating through difficult problems with limited knowledge.[7]

How do organizations achieve these patterns? They negotiate contracts. Within the organization, individuals agree to perform the tasks that the organization defines in return for their pay. Put differently, individuals receive inducements in exchange for their contributions.[8] In dealing with each other, one organization negotiates payments in return for goods and services from another. In both cases, the compact defines the incentives that the principal offers for the agent's performance.

Two further problems, however, undermine the apparent simplicity of such contracts. First, principals supply incentives to induce the agent's work, but agents always have additional interests that they seek to satisfy first. To one degree or another, *shirking* of duties is virtually inevitable in principal-agent relationships. Shirking may mean that the agent simply does not work as hard as the principal believes is essential. An agent may make free use of work time and the office photocopy machine to prepare a betting pool. Agents may even use the knowledge they learn on the job in ways that do not benefit the principal; going to work for a competitor is one example. Moreover, shirking tends to be asymmetrical: agents have more opportunities and incentives to shirk than principals have to control them. Conflicts of interest, from the minor to the major, are the result.

Second, principals seek to reduce shirking by their agents by *monitoring* their behavior. If principals could learn about agents' shirking, they could prevent it by shifting the incentives. Monitoring is costly, however. No matter how much monitoring a principal does, some shirking persists—and every dollar spent on monitoring is money

---

7. These assumptions led to the classic work by Richard M. Cyert and James G. March, *The Behavioral Theory of the Firm* (Prentice-Hall, 1963).

8. James G. March and Herbert A. Simon, *Organizations* (John Wiley & Sons, 1958).

diverted from the principal's basic mission. Principals must try to find a balance between the level of shirking they can tolerate and the amount they must pay in monitoring costs to achieve that level. A second asymmetry is thus created: agents always know more about their behavior than principals do. This asymmetry is a variation of what theorists call the "moral hazard" problem.

These two fundamental asymmetries in the principal-agent relationship put principals at a disadvantage. Given the uncertainties they face, principals have little choice but to contract with agents. Agents, however, always respond to incentives in addition to those established in the contract (the conflict-of-interest problem). Principals are never able to detect and deter all shirking (the monitoring problem).

When the government is the principal, these asymmetries create interesting puzzles. Contracting replaces traditional authority-based management, with all of the problems of government performance that its critics have long since identified. But contracting introduces new problems, which advocates of the competition prescription rarely stop to notice. For many of these advocates, simply replacing government authority with market competition is enough. Embracing the market without examining its underpinnings, however, makes no more sense than arguing that government should solve every societal problem. For the competition prescription to work, it must answer a series of questions that flow from the conflict-of-interest and the monitoring problems.

Defining the Contractor's Job

The keystone of the contract is an agreement between principal and agent on goals. On one level, these goals are instrumental. The contract defines what the principal wants the agent to accomplish. On a higher level, goals also help define what an organization is and what it is not, what it will do and what it will leave to other organizations. Goals establish where an organization's boundaries are. These boundaries, in turn, suggest areas of cooperation and conflict with other organizations.[9] Goals thus animate organizations and the contracts that link them.

9. James D. Thompson, *Organization in Action* (McGraw-Hill, 1967), pp. 127–28.

Public sector contracting is more complex, however. In the private sector, owners and managers frame the goals. In the public sector, however, the goals that managers must pursue are the outcome of the legislative process.[10] This inherently political process tends to produce goals that are complex, varied, and sometimes conflicting. Discerning congressional and executive intent behind any single bill is a daunting task, as is tracking the subtle changes in goals that occur as programs are managed. Furthermore, compared with the goals of private organizations, public goals have another critical distinction: they are the product of law.[11] This legal standing conveys important social and political legitimacy. Public managers have less discretion than private managers over their goals. They must be alert to a far more complex environment. And, in the end, they are held to a more varied, often more demanding, set of standards.

These complexities are only multiplied in the principal-agent relationship. When a government implements a program directly, through the bureaucracy, goals are defined and refined through trial and error. If problems emerge, goals can be adjusted. In a contracting relationship, however, goals must be specified far more clearly, in advance, and reduced to legally enforceable language. For the government principal, the job is difficult because public goals rarely stand still long enough to allow precise formulation. For the government contractor, such fuzzy and shifting goals make it hard to know what the government expects. And without legally enforceable goals specified clearly in the contract, there are no clear standards against which to measure the contractor's performance. Defining goals is thus at once the most important and the most elusive element of the principal-agent relationship.

Choosing the Contractor

The government naturally wants to hire only the best contractors. That task, however, is deceptively difficult. One element of the information asymmetry problem is what theorists call "adverse selection."

10. James G. March and Johan P. Olsen, *Rediscovering Institutions: The Organizational Basis of Politics* (Free Press, 1989), especially chap. 1.

11. James W. Fesler and Donald F. Kettl, *The Politics of the Administrative Process* (Chatham, N.J.: Chatham House, 1991), pp. 8–11.

The phrase originated in the insurance industry, where, because of information asymmetry, insurers might find themselves writing expensive policies to cover risky populations. Sick applicants know about their condition, but insurers have a hard time uncovering the information themselves. As a result, the risks of insurers increase because they face an increased likelihood of covering conditions that are costly to treat. In contracting similar problems occur. Principals want to hire the best agents. Agents, however, always know more about their qualifications than principals can ever discover. As a result, no matter how thorough the search, the government can never be sure that it has hired the best possible contractor.

The contractor that wins the bid, furthermore, is likely to have flaws that the government will only discover as time goes by. The government's selection of contractors can therefore never be perfect, and some loss of efficiency and effectiveness (or some loss of utility, as economists would more elegantly put it) is inevitable.

One of the greatest dangers of this adverse selection problem is the risk of serious conflicts of interest. Because the government can never know everything about its agents, it might not discover serious potential conflicts of interest until it is too late—if in fact they are ever discovered. In government contracting, such information asymmetry is endemic. The government frequently contracts out under the assumption that the contractor knows more and can perform better than the government could. That means the government might not know enough to choose the best contractor—and it also means that the contractor increases the opportunity to shirk. Regular newspaper reports testify to the frequency and gravity of this problem. Principal-agent theory suggests it is unavoidable.

Selecting Incentives and Sanctions

Once principals have defined the goals and selected the agents, they must then structure incentives and sanctions to induce the agents to perform as desired. Ideally, the incentives are high enough to reward good performance and the sanctions are tough enough to discourage poor performance.[12] Put together, the right balance of inducements

12. Levinthal, "A Survey of Agency Models of Organizations," pp. 177–78.

and sanctions can produce the most desirable behavior from agents at the lowest cost to principals.

Designing inducements and sanctions is the core of every relationship between principal and agent, including those between superiors and subordinates in a government agency. Because of the restrictions of government service, measuring and rewarding quality in government work is notoriously difficult.[13] The civil service system has long relied on fixed rules, not flexible rewards and punishments. In contract relationships, however, the incentives and sanctions tend to be far more substantial and more clearly spelled out. Government officials attempt to design payment and penalty clauses to get the contractor to deliver the desired product on time and at a mutually agreeable cost.[14] Finding the best balance of incentives and sanctions is anything but easy, but seeking that balance is a central focus of the contracting process.

Government, moreover, has a hard time making sanctions stick. Goals, as already noted, are frequently fuzzy. Unclear goals give contractors an always-ready defense against charges of poor performance. Contractors, moreover, often do not have complete control over outcomes. Technological uncertainties and plain bad luck can interfere with the achievement of goals. Contractors also often work in complex networks with governments at all levels of the American federal system, other contractors, and private citizens. Results of a program often are the product of all of their interactions. If the test version of a new jet fighter crashes, untangling responsibility—determining whether the problem stemmed from an error by any one of hundreds of different subcontractors or from a basic design flaw, itself the result of complex government-contractor negotiations—may be impossible. The government is often reluctant to punish contractors when responsibility cannot be firmly fixed. Contractors themselves are often reluctant to take on a job where risks are high and things may go awry despite their honest efforts—unless the government agrees to limit sanctions for problems.

13. Advisory Committee on Federal Workforce Quality Assessment, *Federal Workforce Quality: Measurement and Improvement* (Merit Systems Protection Board and Office of Personnel Management, 1992).
14. For an examination of these issues, see Kettl, *Government by Proxy*.

Monitoring Performance

The information asymmetries present in choosing the best contractor carry over even more significantly to monitoring performance. Principals must know what agents are doing, yet even if they receive reports and complaints, observe the work directly, and study the agents' general work habits, principals can never know the full story. As a result, agents can underperform, knowing that they will not be detected.

Monitoring problems are legion. Agents naturally have strong incentives to protect themselves—to pass on only the good news, to hide the bad news, and to discourage anyone from looking too closely at their work. Good monitoring systems, furthermore, are hard to design. Getting the right information about the agent's performance, without drowning the principal in paper, is difficult. So too is developing a feedback system that gives the principal the needed information without interfering with the agent's work. If principals stick their noses too deeply into agents' operations, the dividing line between principal and agent can disappear. If principals do not look deeply enough, scandals and potential disasters can go undetected.

The problems of asymmetry inherent in the principal-agent relationship thus pose significant problems for any government that contracts out. Contracting creates a gap in the direct chain of authority between decisionmakers and program results. It replaces old problems with new ones. It means that results are inevitably suboptimal. It imposes costs, especially in monitoring, that make the transaction more expensive. Such transaction costs, in turn, reduce the efficiency of the competition prescription.[15] The benefits of the competition prescription may be considerable. They are not, however, free.

Different Markets, Different Problems

Even beyond the arguments of principal-agent theory, economists have long recognized that markets often are not fully efficient mechanisms for allocating resources. The assumption that markets produce

15. See Oliver E. Williamson, *Markets and Hierarchies: Analysis and Antitrust Implications* (Free Press, 1975); and *The Economic Institutions of Capitalism: Firms, Markets, Relational Contracting* (Free Press, 1985).

efficient outcomes depends on preconditions that rarely exist: buyers and sellers operate at arm's length, so that there are no sweetheart deals; goods are undifferentiated, so that there is no overwhelming advantage in buying from one supplier instead of another; there are large numbers of buyers and sellers, so that no one buyer can dominate the market and sellers have incentives to produce goods and services at the lowest price. In short, the competition prescription assumes that the market will be competitive.

"Imperfections" often undermine these assumptions, however. When market imperfections spread, economists explain, there tend to be "market failures," which prevent markets from being competitive and therefore efficient. Market imperfections have long been a major justification for government intervention into free enterprise. For example, if monopolists choke competition and thereby drive prices up, government traditionally has stepped in to regulate them.

The competition prescription thus builds on an unsteady foundation. The prescription is effective only so long as the assumptions hold. Two observations about market failures can thus be made. First, where market imperfections occur, they establish the case for government intervention in the market. A critical question is thus not whether the public or private sector should perform a given job but rather, given the imperfections in the market, what the balance between public and private power should be to produce the most efficiency.

Second, market failures are likely to trouble some markets far more than others. Some markets are far more competitive than others—and some far less so. The balance between public and private power therefore needs to vary with the imperfections that different markets present. The central task is to determine how public management must vary to deal effectively with the variety of markets in which the government has come to operate.

To explore these variations, I sort market failures into two categories. First, consider the failures that result from imperfections in the markets that provide the government's goods and services. Sometimes these imperfections result from the behavior of private suppliers, and sometimes they flow from the very structure of the market itself. Because these problems come from the seller's side, let me christen them *supply-side imperfections.*

Second, consider failures that result from imperfections in the government's own behavior as a buyer. For the competition prescription to work well, government must be an intelligent consumer. A variety of imperfections in the government's own behavior, however, can lead to failures in the market. Because these problems come from the buyer's side, let me call them *demand-side imperfections.* Taken together, the supply- and demand-side imperfections provide a guide to the behavior of the markets in which the government has come to operate.

Supply-Side Imperfections

Imperfections on the supply side fall into three categories: whether a market exists for the goods and services the government wants to buy; the level of competition among sellers for the government's business; and the nature of externalities, or side effects.

EXISTENCE OF A MARKET. As noted in chapter 1, much of the time the government operates like any other consumer. If it wants to buy pencils or sanitation services, cars or computers, it bids in the same large private marketplace in which many other buyers are seeking the same goods and services. The government, however, also buys a wide range of goods and services for which there is no preexisting market. In fact, for many of these products, no market would exist if it were not for the government's demand. Consider nuclear weapons, aircraft carriers, and prisons. In other cases, such as pollution abatement, government regulations have created or increased the demand among private corporations for services. Without government intervention, the private market would unquestionably be far smaller.

When the government enters an existing competitive market to buy a product, it can act like any other consumer, negotiating the best deal for a new computer system or for cafeteria food. The market itself helps to define the product, and market competition helps ensure low prices. Competition also promotes high quality; whether in food service or pencils, manufacturers who produce poor-quality goods do not stay in business long.

When the government itself creates or shapes a market, however, the situation is different. Government, not the market, must define the product, determine reasonable prices, and set standards of quality.

If the Pentagon decides, for example, to build a new generation of "stealthy" aircraft, largely invisible to radar, it must decide what the airplane should do. How fast and high should the plane fly? What weapons should it possess? And just how stealthy should it be, since even the stealthiest airplane becomes visible to radar at some point? The market cannot help the Pentagon resolve these issues or tell it how much the aircraft ought to cost, as it can when the government buys writing pads or police cars. Nor can the market provide benchmarks for comparing quality. A high-quality airplane at the lowest price, moreover, is not the government's only goal. It also wishes to obtain a predictable supply, keep the technology secret, and, if members of Congress have their way, ensure that the contracts and subcontracts are spread around to the "right" congressional districts. Removing the evaluation of products from the market and putting it into the hands of government introduces the potential for major imperfections.

COMPETITION IN THE MARKETPLACE. Whether it already exists or is created, a market must be competitive if it is to be efficient. Some markets, however, produce a single seller, or monopolist, who experiences increasing returns and decreasing marginal costs. A monopolist can dominate such markets and dictate the price to purchasers. Critics, for example, charge that IBM has tended to monopolize the market for large-scale government data systems. Other companies have been unable to break the computer giant's grip on the government's business, and they have long contended that the government pays higher prices because of the lack of competition.

In other cases, the market is dominated by only a handful of suppliers. Only two suppliers, for example, build nuclear submarines for the federal government. That leaves the government two choices. It can award submarine contracts to the lower bidder, which risks putting the other submarine builder out of business, ending competition in the market, and subjecting the government to a monopolistic supplier. Alternatively, it can split the contracts and award the higher bidder a smaller share. That strategy keeps both builders in business but also guarantees that the government pays higher prices for its submarines. Because defense planners have been far more worried about the long-run costs, both economic and strategic, of allowing the market to become dominated by a single supplier, the Pentagon has chosen the latter course. The huge investments in expertise and capital required to enter the business prevent the market from being competitive and make such difficult choices inevitable.

Finally, markets can have significant barriers that prevent new suppliers from entering. Sometimes these barriers are technological. The radar-evading stealth technology, for example, is closely guarded, and few new companies could compete with the handful of aerospace firms that developed and control the know-how. Some barriers are policy-based, especially in national security. The federal government, for example, tightly controls access to the knowledge required for producing some goods, such as plutonium triggers for nuclear weapons. Some barriers arise from the high capital expense required to begin production. The huge cost of building the facilities required for the construction of nuclear submarines, in addition to the difficulty of assembling the expertise and security clearances, effectively keeps the submarine market closed to other competitors. Some barriers are political. The Pentagon's need to build support for its budget can steer contracts to some suppliers rather than others. Put together, these barriers to entry can severely limit competition among potential suppliers.

EXTERNALITIES. The market can also be affected by externalities, that is, by costs and benefits that the market does not capture. For example, for nearly a generation, the government relied on a private contractor to produce triggers for its nuclear weapons at its Rocky Flats, Colorado, plant. In the process, however, the contractor also produced huge quantities of radioactive and toxic wastes that contaminated the surrounding ground and water. Public outcry is forcing the government to pay for cleaning up after its private contractor, at a cost of more than $1 billion. Perhaps more costly to the government is the loss of public trust and confidence in its operations. In purchasing goods and services in the private market, the government might get what it pays for. It might also get related problems that it did not intend and that, as principal, it could not control through its relationship with its private agent.

Demand-Side Imperfections

A different set of problems plagues the demand side of the market. In its role as a purchaser of goods and services, the government sometimes behaves in ways that undercut a competitive market. It sometimes cannot define the product clearly, so it has a hard time writing good contracts. It frequently cannot obtain good information about the behavior of its contractors, and it is often subject to internal problems that also hinder the effective digestion and transmission of information.

DEFINING THE PRODUCT. A market cannot be competitive unless the buyer can define what it wants to buy. The federal government must have the capacity to define products ranging from the purchase of office supplies out of a catalog to projects beyond the bounds of existing technology. In some cases the government cannot define precisely what it wants in advance. No one knows with certainty, for example, what toxic wastes a cleanup might uncover or, in some cases, how best to treat them. In these and other contracts, the final product often is not so much a market response to the buyer's demands as it is a cooperative alliance between the government and its suppliers. This sort of collaborative venture destroys the arm's-length relationship between buyer and seller that makes for a competitive market.

INFORMATION ABOUT THE PRODUCT. In a competitive market, the market itself provides at least some information about the quality of goods and services available. Suppliers are usually only too happy to point out the advantages of their own products and the flaws in the products manufactured by their competitors. Buyers can shop, compare, and choose the products that are most appealing.

In many government programs, however, the market is not a good source of information about performance. Many programs are huge with unclear goals. Many are at the edge of the technologically possible, so risks are great. Moreover, when budgets are tight, government units that monitor contractors' performance are often the first casualties. Declining morale, low salaries, and better opportunities in the private sector have often led technical experts to leave government service. The government has gradually become less expert, less able to make independent judgments about the quality of the goods and services it is buying, and thus less able to act as an intelligent consumer.

GAMESMANSHIP AND INTERNALITIES. Gamesmanship within government worsens its problems as a buyer. In a provocative study of "government failures" that mirror market failures, Charles Wolf, Jr., calls these games "internalities." A host of internal pressures, Wolf argues, distort the contractual relationship in the same way that externalities distort the behavior of other markets.[16]

The biggest force contributing to internalities is bureaucratic politics. The struggle for power within agencies can sometimes become more important than what the agencies are buying. In uncertain political environments, agencies sometimes concentrate their energy on building political support rather than on managing their programs. Communications barriers between political appointees, charged with running the agency, and career officials, who manage the details, can also muddy internal management.[17] A communications gap between technical workers—who deal with the details of programs and the government's agents—and higher-level managers—who are responsible for overall program performance—can likewise complicate management. Agencies that must tackle programs with high technical complexity have had the most problems in bridging the gap between the technical and the general.

Thus, on the demand side, the government's own behavior generates substantial market imperfections. The government often cannot define the nature of the product clearly enough to induce competition. It suffers from frequent and significant information failures, which means that the government cannot always determine if it is getting what it paid for. Finally, it endures substantial "internalities" in its own behavior that deflect attention from its policy goals.

16. Charles Wolf, Jr., *Markets or Governments: Choosing Between Imperfect Alternatives* (MIT Press, 1988), p. 66.

17. See, for example, Charles H. Levine and Rosslyn S. Kleeman, "The Quiet Crisis of the Civil Service," in Patricia W. Ingraham and Donald F. Kettl, eds., *Agenda for Excellence: Public Service in America* (Chatham, N.J.: Chatham House, 1992), pp. 208–73; and Patricia W. Ingraham and David H. Rosenbloom, "Political Foundations of the American Federal Service: Rebuilding a Crumbling Base," *Public Administration Review*, vol. 50 (March–April 1990), pp. 210–19.

Implications for Public Management

If the markets in which the government operates were more nearly perfect, the government could indeed rely on them to produce quality goods and services at the lowest cost. Market imperfections, however, mean that the government must assert strong control over the markets.

This market-based analysis of public management offers two important insights. First, *the variety of market failures helps explain why the expansive promises of public-private partnership have often been elusive.* Although advocates of contracting out have long argued that reliance on public-private partnerships can improve government efficiency and reduce the role of government, many of the government's most nettlesome problems have occurred in programs that have been contracted out. These problems have tended to be concentrated in markets with the most imperfections, such as the manufacture of nuclear weapons. Government has been singularly slow to develop new approaches to manage the variety of markets in which it is operating.

Second, *because the markets vary, so too do the tasks of public managers.* Market imperfections, on both the supply and demand sides, combine in interesting ways. In general, as market imperfections increase, so too do the government's management burdens and transaction costs. The four case studies that follow illustrate the different kinds of market imperfections (figure 2-1).

First, some markets are indeed relatively competitive, on both the demand and the supply side, and they thus present relatively few market imperfections. Under Circular A-76, for example, the Office of Management and Budget requires federal agencies wherever possible to contract out for goods and services available in the commercial market. Purchase of goods and services under A-76 guidelines, therefore, places the government in rather conventional, relatively competitive markets. Chapter 3 explores the A-76 contracting-out program.

Second, some of the markets in which the government deals are near-monopolies, with high imperfections on the supply side but more moderate imperfections on the demand side. The markets for data processing and telecommunications services fall into this category. Competition among potential suppliers in such oligopolistic markets is often very limited, and the government's ability to bargain

FIGURE 2-1. *Market Imperfections and Problems in Governance*

	A-76 contracting-out program	FTS-2000 telecommu- nications system	Superfund	DOE nuclear weapons complex
Supply-side imperfections	Low	High	Moderate	Very high
Demand-side imperfections	Low	Moderate	High	Very high

hard over prices is therefore limited. Chapter 4 examines the federal government's efforts to contract out the development of a massive new telecommunications system.

Third, some markets are characterized by moderate imperfections on the supply side but relatively high imperfections on the demand side; the Environmental Protection Agency's Superfund program is one example. In such markets, there are many contractors, but the government must negotiate with them to define what the goals are and when and how they will be achieved. Chapter 5 surveys the Superfund case.

Fourth, some markets have very high imperfections on both sides, as the Department of Energy's production of nuclear weapons so amply illustrates. In this market, the government was the only buyer, and it worked closely with a handful of suppliers in a virtually seamless partnership to define and produce the products. There would have been no market were it not for the government, and a competitive market was never even contemplated. Chapter 6 examines the DOE's management of its nuclear weapons complex.

In short, it is not possible to frame a single model that will serve all of the government's relations with its contractors equally well. Effective management of privatized programs must meet the challenges that different market imperfections present. The case studies in the succeeding chapters will examine these challenges.

Sharing Power

Deep worries among economists and critics of government have produced an enduring movement toward downsizing government and transferring, wherever possible, government's functions to the private sector. This relationship, however, is nettlesome and contradictory. Market imperfections, on the one hand, strengthen the case for governmental power; government imperfections, on the other hand, strengthen the case for market power. From a rhetorical point of view, strong arguments can be made for both market and government power—and for limiting each of their roles. From a practical point of view, the question is far more complex. Relying on either the government or the market imposes sometimes staggering burdens on the other.

The real issue thus is not how to choose between the market or government. It is, rather, how to strike the best balance between them—and how to manage the problems that this balance creates. The growing complexity of government programs, the pragmatic pressures of fiscal stringency, the adaptation to the ideology of privatization, and the search for expertise wherever it can be found have all led inexorably to a growing role for these public-private partnerships. In the process these partnerships have created new burdens and imposed new costs. Balancing public and private interests, as economist Coase pointed out long ago, requires everyone to "have regard for the total effect"—to pay attention to the effects the partnerships have on efficiency and accountability.[18]

The growth of science and technology, and of mixed public-private power, has transformed the existing role of government and has reassembled political power in very different ways, as political scientist Don K. Price has noted.[19] The sharing of administrative responsibility necessarily means the government shares its power and authority in society with those upon which it relies. This relationship is not one of equals, however, and the problem of finding the right mix in this arrangement is not simply one of establishing the best administrative balance between governmental control and private flexibility. Nor is it a matter of seeking a trade-off between accountability and efficiency,

18. Ronald H. Coase, "The Problem of Social Cost," *Journal of Law and Economics*, vol. 3 (October 1960), p. 44. Wolf makes a related argument in *Markets or Governments*.

19. Don K. Price, *Government and Science: Their Dynamic Relation in American Democracy* (New York University Press, 1954), p. 3.

because they are not substitutes for each other. Rather, the issue hinges on the government's management of private agents to pursue the public interest.

Even as the sharing of responsibilities between the public and private sectors blurs the boundaries between them, the separate interests of each sector remain. The most important issue is whether the sharing of public and private power endangers the public interest that the government is obliged—by the Constitution, by law, and by public will—to pursue.[20] Many of the major scandals that have afflicted government in the last generation have revolved around private abuse of the public interest. Simply turning over government's work to the private sector is no nostrum for government's ills.

This leads in turn to four broad conclusions. First, given society's demands and the growing complexity of the nation's problems, public-private ties are inevitable, necessary, and desirable. The days when the government could assemble the world's best experts on every conceivable subject are long gone. Only by relying on the private sector can government procure the expertise it needs to manage its complicated programs without itself growing to unacceptable proportions. Second, the dilemmas that emerge in all principal-agent relationships are magnified in markets with substantial imperfections. Careful public management thus requires meticulous attention to the variations of administrative problems, as well as to the enduring core issues. It requires as well zealous public oversight, particularly of the public-private relationships that are most likely to be troublesome—the relationships with the greatest market imperfections.

Third, the basic principal-agent problems and the various market imperfections caution against a too enthusiastic embrace of the argument for privatization. Privatization works best where markets are lively, where information is abundant, where decisions are not irretrievable, and where externalities are limited. It works worst where externalities and monopolies are abundant, where competition is limited, and where efficiency is not the main public interest.[21] Privatiza-

20. Ronald C. Moe, "Exploring the Limits of Privatization," *Public Administration Review*, vol. 47 (November–December 1987), pp. 453–75.

21. John R. Chamberlin and John E. Jackson, "Privatization as Institutional Choice," *Journal of Policy Analysis and Management*, vol. 6 (Summer 1987), p. 602.

tion is no magic cure that fits all situations; its advocates rarely have tried to match the solution to the problems it best solves. Finding the right balance between public and private power is deceptively difficult.

Fourth, in the search for this balance, seeking the public interest is paramount. The government, after all, is not just another principal dealing with just another agent. In most markets, the search for compromise between buyer and seller is the central activity. The government is more than an automobile manufacturer buying steel or glass, or a corporation buying new computer or telephone equipment. It is a representative of the public and its goals must represent public goals as embodied in law. Pursuing those goals—and the sense of the public interest that lies behind them—is the central task of government.

The government's pursuit of public goals through the private sector thus creates a layered series of problems. In seeking to solve these problems, government faces a sometimes sharp tension between seeking accommodation through market-based compromise with its agents and pursuing without compromise the public interest that the law demands. Critical issues cascade in uncommon complexity from the ideological and pragmatic imperatives that brought government into these growing relations with the private sector. Thus I turn to studies of federal government contracting to examine these issues more carefully.

3

The A-76 Program: Logistics and Libraries

In the years following World War II government contracting expanded in a vast array of high-tech fields, such as space, aircraft, weaponry, and computers. Not all government contracting was high-tech, however. As government grew, it needed a broad range of support services, such as cafeterias and libraries, maintenance and transportation, printing and foreign-language translation, security and laundry services, and systems engineering and manufacturing. Many of these items were ordinary services widely available in the private market. In 1955 the Eisenhower administration promulgated a formal policy stating that "the Federal government will not start or carry on any commercial activity to provide a service or product for its own use if such product or service can be procured from private enterprise through ordinary business channels."[1]

The basic thrust of the policy was simple. Where the private sector could do the job, it should do the job. The government would not compete with the private sector by independently producing goods or services. The government would deviate from this policy only when necessary to preserve the public interest, such as in cases involving national security. The policy followed the basic competition prescription long before it had been formulated: market competition would keep goods and services cheap and of high quality.

A decade later, however, the government was still producing a host of goods and services that could potentially be supplied by the private

1. Bureau of the Budget, Bulletin 55-4 (1955).

sector. In 1967 the Bureau of the Budget issued Circular A-76, which required federal agencies to review their commercial activities, to examine how much the government was paying for them, and to transfer to the private sector those activities the private sector could perform at a lower cost. On one level, A-76 retreated from the 1955 policy by suggesting that the government ought to engage in commercial activities in some cases. On a more basic level, however, A-76 promoted the use of contracts by introducing the use of cost comparisons.

Circular A-76, however, lacked much guidance on how federal agencies were to conduct the cost comparisons, and the comparisons were thus often haphazard. More important, the lack of clear instructions signaled the absence of a clear policy. To remedy that failure, the Carter administration revised Circular A-76 in 1979. Issued by the Office of Management and Budget (OMB), the successor to the Bureau of the Budget, the revised circular began with an unmistakable reaffirmation of the principles first outlined in 1955:

> In a democratic free enterprise system, the Government should not compete with its citizens. The private enterprise system, characterized by individual freedom and initiative, is the primary source of national economic strength. In recognition of this principle, it has been and continues to be the general policy of the Government to rely on competitive private enterprise to supply the products and services it needs.[2]

The revised circular then added muscle to the policy by prescribing a detailed methodology that agencies were to follow in conducting cost comparisons. Finally, the new version of A-76 ordered federal agencies to concentrate on *what* had to be done, not *who* was to do it or *how* it was to be done. The result, OMB hoped, would be "a balanced and disciplined management system that will produce consistency, predictability, and equity for affected workers, agencies, and contractors."[3]

2. *Federal Register* 44 (April 5, 1979), pp. 20557–58.
3. *Federal Register* 44, p. 20556.

The Reagan administration took the process one step further by providing an even more elaborate methodology for comparing costs and by requiring federal agencies to conduct efficiency studies as part of the cost comparisons. The administration characterized its revised A-76 not as a "contracting out" initiative but as a management improvement program. Under the new procedures, federal agencies and interested private contractors would prepare bids to do a particular job, and the low bidder would win. In the spirit of the competition prescription, federal workers performing tasks that could be contracted out were forced to bid for their own jobs.

The A-76 process as it operated during Reagan's presidency thus makes a good case with which to begin the assessment of the competition prescription. Committed to buying goods and services already available in the private market, the government would be one buyer among many, in a relationship that minimized supply-side problems. The real questions were how the government would behave as a buyer, and whether the market would impose discipline on the government, as the competition prescription asserted it would.

Devising a Competitive Process

The A-76 process as it was revised in 1983 was a complex affair (figure 3-1).[4] The circular required agencies to develop an inventory of all operations that potentially could be performed by private contractors. Activities that were determined to be "inherently governmental in nature," that is, activities "so intimately related to the public interest as to mandate performance only by Federal employees," were not to be contracted out. This phrase was exceptionally vague and was to lead to continual disputes over where the boundary line ought to be drawn. For a vast array of commercial activities, however, the A-76 circular established a review process to determine whether public or private workers could do the job more efficiently. The key, in concert with the competition prescription, was the creation of a competition between the government and contractors.

4. An excellent summary of the process, from which this description is drawn, is General Accounting Office, *Federal Productivity: DOD's Experience in Contracting Out Commercially Available Activities*, GGD-89-6 (November 1988), pp. 11–14.

FIGURE 3-1. *The A-76 Process*

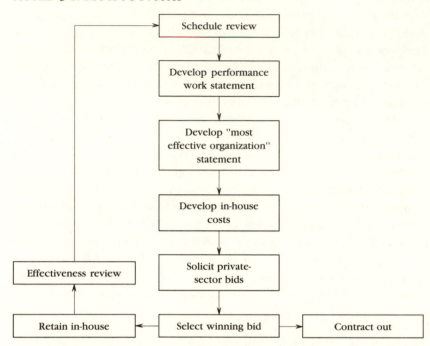

SOURCE: Derived from General Accounting Office, *Federal Productivity: DOD's Experience in Contracting Out Commercially Available Activities*, GGD-89-6 (November 1988), p. 12.

Once an agency scheduled a commercial activity for a full review, the most critical and complex phase of the A-76 process began—the development of a "performance work statement" (PWS). Agencies had to define precisely what work was needed, set deadlines for completion of the work, and establish work quality standards of quality. All of these performance standards were then to be converted into a PWS, which Reagan's OMB viewed as its new plan for managing the federal government. The PWS became the fundamental guidance for the rest of the process: it told government employees what they must accomplish, it gave government officials a standard by which to judge private bids for a contract, and it provided standards for ultimately judging performance.

The government employees currently providing the good or service then had the opportunity to compete for the job. The "in-house work force," as the group of employees working on the task were known, conducted a management study on how most efficiently to meet the objectives spelled out in the PWS. The organizational structure and method they chose—known in the A-76 process as the "most efficient organization," or MEO—became the basis for determining the government's cost of providing the good or service. These cost projections then became the government employees' bid for the project.

Meanwhile, the PWS defined the specifications for a competition conducted among private contractors interested in the project. These private bids were then compared with the government's projections for the costs of doing the job itself. A private bidder could win the contract if government reviewers concluded that the contractor was able to meet the standards set in the PWS, if the contractor's bid was less than the government workers' bid, and if the contractor produced a bid at least 10 percent lower than the government's personnel costs. The circular set the 10 percent margin to account, in part, for the short-term disruptions that any change in service providers would cause as well as any for other unexpected risks that might develop.

A-76 did not provide any oversight of private contractors to ensure that the promised cost savings materialized. The assumption was that the initial market competition would produce continuing good performance at cheap prices. The circular did require, however, a review of the effectiveness of government employees who won competitions. The activity, moreover, was put back in the inventory of commercial products for a future round of A-76 reviews. Here, the assumption was that the absence of market competition could not guarantee that the employees' winning bid would remain the lowest. This sharp distinction in the way OMB treated different kinds of winners in the process created significant problems as the A-76 process evolved.

The competition theme fit neatly with the Reagan administration's broader privatization agenda and its efforts to downsize the federal government.[5] As revised by the Reagan administration, A-76 sought to

5. The President's Private Sector Survey on Cost Control, known as the Grace commission, concluded in its 1983 report that the government had "expanded to its present size because of the assumption that it is the only capable producer of the services it needs to provide its citizens." The result of this assumption, the commission said, was duplication and the "lack of incentive for efficiency." President's Private Sector Survey on Cost Control (Grace Commission), *Report on Privatization* (Spring–Fall 1983), p. ii.

provide an incentive for efficiency by using "the competitive market-place to change the way the Government manages," as OMB put it. Through A-76,

> quality service and reduced cost are emphasized in two ways: (1) by providing an incentive to Federal agencies to clearly define their performance standards and to reduce the cost of Government operations in order to compete with private industry; and (2) by offering the commercial sector an opportunity to meet these Government needs when they can do so more economically. In either case, the American public are the true beneficiaries, since costs are reduced whether the government or industry 'wins' the competition.[6]

A-76 offered great promise to privatization advocates. More than 380,000 federal employees worked at commercial activities in the Department of Defense alone, and about one-fourth of the entire federal work force performed commercial or industrial activities that could be contracted out.[7] To the Reagan administration, A-76 was a keystone of its broader privatization movement. To many federal employees, employee unions, and members of Congress who represented them, however, A-76 loomed as a huge threat.

The Fruits of Competition

The Reagan and Bush administrations praised A-76 for producing impressive savings. OMB proudly claimed total savings of nearly $696 million from fiscal 1981 to fiscal 1987, with the equivalent of 45,737 full-time positions freed to perform higher-priority missions (table 3-1). The government saved an average of 30 percent from original costs, OMB reported—20 percent savings when government employees won and 35 percent savings when private contractors won. Gov-

6. Office of Management and Budget, *Enhancing Governmental Productivity through Competition: A New Way of Doing Business within the Government To Provide Quality Government at Least Cost* (August 1988), p. 15, introduction.
7. Congressional Budget Office, *Contracting Out: Potential for Reducing Federal Costs* (June 1987), p. 1; and General Accounting Office, *Civil Servants and Contract Employees: Who Should Do What for the Federal Government?* FPCD-81-43 (June 19, 1981), p. 15.

TABLE 3-1. *Cumulative Savings from A-76 Reviews, Fiscal Years 1981–87*

Department	Dollar savings (millions)	Positions saved[a]
Defense	611,445	37,064
General Services Administration	37,287	2,151
Transportation	12,769	2,117
Commerce	8,375	552
Interior	6,987	560
Veterans Administration	4,773	132
Health and Human Services	4,459	232
Energy	4,220	392
Agriculture	2,234	666
Treasury	568	542
Other	2,585	224
Agency for International Development	60	12
Federal Emergency Management Agency	0	886
Housing and Urban Development	0	56
Labor	0	5
National Aeronautics and Space Administration	0	0
Environmental Protection Agency	0	0
Office of Personnel Management	0	147
Education	0	0
Small Business Administration	0	0
State	0	0
Justice	0	0
U.S. Information Agency	0	0
Total	695,852	45,737

SOURCE: Information supplied by Office of Management and Budget, *Commercial Activities Contracting Act of 1987*, Hearings before the Senate Committee on Governmental Affairs, 100 Cong. 1 and 2 sess. (Government Printing Office, 1988), pp. 136–37.

a. Positions are full-time equivalents.

ernment workers won the competition about 45 percent of the time, while private contractors won about 55 percent.[8]

Problems in Performance

Not everyone viewed the program with enthusiasm. Critics condemned the program for upsetting patterns of government and for

8. OMB, *Enhancing Governmental Productivity through Competition*, pp. 3–4; and Office of Management and Budget, *Management of the United States Government, Fiscal Year 1990* (1989), pp. 3-118–19.

creating serious morale problems among government employees. They charged that the savings were ephemeral and that private contractors often performed more poorly than the government workers had. Although these claims were exaggerated, OMB's claims were also overstated. Five major problems emerged in the A-76 process: (1) implementation of A-76 varied widely among federal agencies; (2) OMB set unrealistic goals; (3) the steps required for the A-76 process were lengthy and disruptive; (4) agencies had great analytical difficulty in producing the studies, especially the critical "performance work statement," which led decisionmakers to award jobs without adequate information; and (5) legislative restrictions limited the application of A-76.[9]

UNEVEN IMPLEMENTATION. The biggest message from table 3-1 is not the overall size of the savings, but their unevenness. Just four agencies—the Department of Defense (DOD), the General Services Administration (GSA), the Department of Transportation (DOT), and the Department of Commerce—accounted for 96 percent of all dollar savings and 92 percent of all the positions saved.[10] The high concentration of savings in just a few agencies can be explained in part by the high concentration of commercial activities in them. From aircraft maintenance to cafeterias, DOD operates a vast array of activities that contractors can perform. GSA is the government's supplies and logistics expert, so much of its work is also readily contracted.

OMB, however, had set savings targets for each agency according to the number of its commercial activities, and these four agencies accounted for only 61 percent of those goals. Many of the other federal agencies simply saw little value in the A-76 process and resisted undertaking the cost studies it mandated. Some agency officials considered the program to be a "millstone around their neck" and suggested that it was "counterproductive." Others said that A-76 was "not a

---

9. *Contracting Out and Its Impact on Federal Personnel and Operations,* Hearings before the House Committee on Post Office and Civil Service, 101 Cong. 1 and 2 sess. (Government Printing Office, 1990), Statement of L. Nye Stevens, pp. 104–09.

10. *Contracting Out and Its Impact on Federal Personnel and Operations,* Hearings, p. 104.

major concern" for them.[11] Sixteen agencies met less than 10 percent of the goals OMB set, and many accomplished nothing.[12]

Several reasons explain why the Defense Department accounted for most of OMB's claimed savings. DOD employed more than one-third of all federal civilian workers and nearly half of all federal civilian workers outside the Postal Service. In its vast network of bases, it conducted far more commercial activities—from laundries to maintenance—than any other agency or department. Most important, to sweeten the pot, from 1981 to 1988 OMB allowed DOD alone to keep all of the savings A-76 produced. The Defense Department thus had unique incentives to pursue A-76 aggressively.[13]

UNREALISTIC GOALS. The administration's enthusiasm for the A-76 program, coupled with the hope that it might yield substantial budget savings, led OMB to set goals that federal agencies could not achieve. In the early years, no one—not even the Defense Department—had sufficient trained staff to conduct the complex cost comparisons that A-76 required. Even after DOD geared up its process, however, it still managed to achieve only 56 percent of its goals from 1984 to 1988. The other federal agencies met only 14 percent of their goals.[14]

In an attempt to force all agencies to pursue A-76 comparisons more aggressively, President Reagan in 1987 issued Executive Order 12615, which required federal agencies to review at least 3 percent of all agency positions annually until all possible commercial activities had been uncovered.[15] OMB for a while also reduced agency budgets by the amount that it expected A-76 cost comparisons to save. Despite these heavy pressures, no one ever believed that the quotas could or would be met. A General Accounting Office (GAO) survey released in

11. *Review of OMB Circular A-76 and Contracting Out,* Hearings before the House Post Office and Civil Service Committee, 98 Cong. 2 sess. (GPO, 1984), Statement of Walter F. Peters, p. 58.

12. General Accounting Office, *Managing the Government: Revised Approach Could Improve OMB's Effectiveness,* GGD-89-65 (May 1989), p. 57.

13. GAO, *Managing the Government,* p. 57.

14. "Inefficiency and Mismanagement: OMB's Contracting Out Program," Staff Report for the Senate Committee on the Budget (April 1990), p. 2.

15. *Public Papers of the Presidents of the United States: Ronald Reagan, 1987,* book II (July 4, 1987–December 31, 1987) (1989), pp. 1356–57.

1990 found that nineteen of twenty-one agencies questioned believed that the goals were unrealistic.[16]

DISRUPTIVE PROCESS. Although the basic concept of A-76 was simple—determine the cost of what the government does and allow private business to compete to do the job more cheaply—the process in practice proved enormously complicated. Federal managers, technical experts, and support workers suddenly found themselves in the position of management analysts. They had to figure out what their agencies' goals were—a process that fuzzy congressional language made deceptively difficult—and then develop innovative tactics for meeting them. As GAO pointed out, these were "tasks they often are not skilled in, may never do again, and are frequently given to do as extra duties."[17]

As a result, the time required to complete A-76 cost comparisons gradually lengthened. From 1978 to 1986, a typical cost comparison study took about two years. From 1987 to 1990 the time doubled, to an average of four years and three months. Some cost comparisons, in fact, had been under way for more than six years and were not close to completion. For many agency officials, other tasks had far higher priority. So many officials had a hand in the cost comparisons that delays inevitably crept in as A-76 staff struggled to move the paperwork along.[18]

ANALYTICAL PROBLEMS. The performance work statements were critical to the success of the entire A-76 process, but agencies rarely had sufficient expertise to write them. Employees detailed to write the statements frequently had many other tasks to contend with as well. Moreover, writing a good PWS was often a daunting technical challenge. The details had to be precise, for they guided the contracting activities and set the standards for judging performance. It was little

16. *Contracting Out and Its Impact on Federal Personnel and Operations*, Hearings, p. 108.

17. *Contracting Out and Its Impact on Federal Personnel and Operations*, Hearings, p. 105.

18. *Contracting Out and Its Impact on Federal Personnel and Operations*, Hearings, p. 105; and General Accounting Office, *OMB Circular A-76: Legislation Has Curbed Many Cost Studies in the Military Services*, GCD-91-100 (July 1991), p. 7.

wonder that performance work statements were frequently incomplete and their goal statements often vague.[19]

Underlying the problem of writing clear work statements was the poor quality of management information. Few government agencies had developed management reporting systems to pursue clearly defined goals. Objectives were fuzzy, data on current activity frequently were thin, and useful information on performance was often nonexistent. Federal workers often spent eighteen months or more assembling the basic historical and performance data needed to develop the government's bid.[20] Long delays and poorly drafted PWSs frequently resulted. With only fuzzy guidance to outline their work, contractors' costs often escalated once contracts were awarded, which further undercut support for the program.

LEGISLATIVE RESTRICTIONS. Congress also stepped in to restrict OMB's pursuit of its A-76 goals. In addition to holding hearings that publicized problems with and objections to A-76, Congress also passed two important pieces of legislation to restrain OMB. In the defense authorization act for fiscal 1988 and 1989, Congress gave military base commanders the authority to decide for themselves which activities would be subject to A-76 review. The Defense appropriations act for fiscal 1991 cut off funding for A-76 reviews of a single function (such as a laundry) that lasted for more than two years or of multiple functions (including combinations of services at a single facility) that lasted for more than four years. These measures seriously undercut OMB. Not only did base commanders win more flexibility in planning their A-76 reviews, but they were also allowed to ignore OMB's quotas. The 1991 appropriations act forced the Defense Department to cancel nearly 400 A-76 studies that were exceeding the time limit. The number of A-76 studies that DOD completed decreased from 1,200 in fiscal 1987 to just 115 by fiscal 1991, largely as a result of the legislation.[21]

---

19. *Contracting Out and Its Impact on Federal Personnel and Operations,* Hearings, pp. 109–11; General Accounting Office, *Federal Productivity: DOD's Experience in Contracting Out Commercially Available Activities,* GGD-89-6 (November 1988), p. 19; and General Accounting Office, *Synopsis of GAO Reports Involving Contracting Out under OMB Circular A-76,* PLRD-83-74 (May 24, 1983), p. 19.

20. GAO, *OMB Circular A-76: Legislation Has Curbed Many Cost Studies,* p. 8; and President's Council on Management Improvement, *Study of OMB Circular A-76: Performance of Commercial Activities* (GPO, December 1990).

21. GAO, *OMB Circular A-76: Legislation Has Curbed Many Cost Studies,* pp. 2–3.

Contracting Out for Defense Logistics

All of these problems led to harsh attacks on the program. "There is sad irony in this situation—a management improvement program trumpeted by the Administration for over a decade has become wasteful and ineffective," Senator Jim Sasser concluded in 1990. "This can only serve to undermine public confidence in Federal management and alienate Federal employees."[22] Fueling the fire were reports that some contractors, after submitting winning bids, produced far higher costs and much lower performance than the government employees they replaced.

At Fort Eustis, Virginia, for example, the Army conducted an A-76 cost comparison for logistics support functions: food, supply, transportation, maintenance, and laundry services.[23] In 1982 the Army accepted a bid submitted by Northrop Worldwide Aircraft Services, Inc., to provide the services for $13.9 million less than they could be provided by government employees.

In the final accounting, however, the contractor's operations cost the government $600,000 *more* than in-house operations would have. Some of the problem came from Northrop's huge underestimates of some important costs. For example, the company estimated that it could provide maintenance services for $600,000 when the existing maintenance contract cost $1.4 million a year. Ft. Eustis's employees had estimated that the work could not be done for less than $1.1 million. Northrop also estimated its administrative costs at far less than its historic costs and projected labor costs based on a substantially shorter workyear. Correcting these estimates would have added $6.4 million to Northrop's $28 million bid.

Under its contract Northrop was reimbursed for the higher costs even though they greatly exceeded its bid. In a fixed-price contract, in which the government agrees in advance to pay a set price for the work to be done, the contractor bears the risk for any increase in cost. In the cost-plus-award-fee contract that Northrop received, however, it was the government that bore the risk, because as Northrop's costs rose, so too did the government's reimbursement.

22. "Inefficiency and Mismanagement," cover letter.
23. The description of this case comes from General Accounting Office, *Army Procurement: No Savings From Contracting for Support Services at Fort Eustis, Virginia*, NSIAD-89-25 (October 1988).

On top of these higher costs, moreover, Northrop received substantial award fees for its performance. The fees were set as a percentage of the costs. The contractor's incentives were strong to bid low, win the contract, allow costs to rise (knowing that the government would pay them), and then win award fees based on the higher costs. That was precisely what happened at Fort Eustis. By this time, however, the government's work force had been disbanded, so there was no in-house competition to challenge Northrop at the end of the contract period. The government, meanwhile, had little data on Northrop's real costs, so it could not challenge the contractor to switch to a fixed-price contract in the next round. In this case, the fruits of competition were a loss of the government's in-house capacity and an inability to control the contractor's costs.

At Fort Sill, Oklahoma, an artillery training facility, another contract to Northrop produced even more serious problems.[24] In fiscal 1989 Northrop took over supply, maintenance, and transportation services that federal employees had previously provided. Following an eight-year A-76 study, the Army had determined that using the contractor would save $2.7 million over a five-year period. After just two years of the contract had elapsed, however, GAO calculated that Northrop's costs were going to exceed its bid by $14.8 million—not including award fees—and that government workers would have done the job for substantially less money.

The award fees also turned out to be costly. The contract was a standard cost-plus-award-fee version, which provided award fees based on the contractor's performance measured against contract standards. The standards were based on the government employees' previous work; if the contractor met the level of that work, it would receive 100 percent of the available award. Northrop's productivity was actually only 82 percent of the government workers'. Because of the contract's award fee structure, however, Northrop still won an award—$239,000 for fiscal 1989—for performance substantially lower than the workers they replaced. If, in the remaining four years of the contract, Northrop improved to meet the *minimum* standards set by the government workers, it stood to win $2.4 million in award fees, which would further increase the government's costs.

24. GAO, *OMB Circular A-76: Expected Savings Are Not Being Realized in Ft. Sill's Logistics Contract*, GGD-91-33 (February 1991).

The General Accounting Office was perplexed by these incentives. "Contrary to the Army's instructions to Ft. Sill, Ft. Sill's administration of the award fee provisions of the contract did not motivate the contractor to provide excellence in performance," GAO found. Instead, "the approach taken by Ft. Sill in administering the award fee was used solely to motivate the contractor to meet—not exceed—performance standards." GAO also concluded that Ft. Sill's level of readiness under Northrop's management failed to meet the Army's standards for a "fully deployable" unit—one ready for combat; and that, when the equipment was needed for Operation Desert Shield, performance was substandard. When government employees provided the services, the unit was consistently "fully deployable."[25]

Yet another contractor, Hawthorne Aviation, at the Dugway Proving Grounds in Utah, produced "disastrous" performance, according to one local government employee union, and was notified by the government that it was in breach of the contract. The contract was for five years at $4.2 million, but Hawthorne spent $8.6 million in the first three years alone.[26]

Contracting Out for Libraries

Among the government activities scheduled for A-76 review were the libraries operated in each federal agency. Representatives from the library community were surprised to find the government libraries included on the list. "Nowhere but in the federal government are libraries considered 'commercial activities,' " exclaimed a spokesperson for the American Library Association. She noted that corporations tend not to contract out their libraries, a fact she found surprising if substantial savings were possible.[27]

The American Library Association raised major objections in advance of A-76 reviews of government libraries. Because many of these libraries contained business trade secrets, the private contractor operating

25. GAO, *OMB Circular A-76: Expected Savings Are Not Being Realized,* pp. 7, 9, 12–13.

26. *Commercial Activities Contracting Act of 1987,* Hearings before the Senate Committee on Governmental Affairs, 100 Cong. 1 and 2 sess. (GPO, 1988), Statement of Mike LeFevre, pp. 91–94.

27. *Office of Management and Budget Circular A-76,* Hearings before the House Committee on Post Office and Civil Service, 99 Cong. 1 sess. (GPO, 1986), Statement of Patricia W. Berger, p. 138.

the libraries would have access to valuable inside information to use in competing for future government contracts and for business outside the government. Furthermore, because private contractors have to respond only to the provisions of the agreement, an agency might find itself unable to respond to emergency information needs, the association warned.[28] Critics were most concerned, however, that the government would lose its institutional knowledge and control of its data bases if it contracted out its agency libraries. It would then become even more a captive of the contractors, they feared. Contracting out could lead to "national amnesia," one association official warned.[29]

Representative Major R. Owens, who had worked for eight years as a librarian in the Brooklyn Public Library before his election to Congress, argued that A-76 reviews of government libraries posed serious risks. "A grave error would be perpetrated," he said, "if library and information services continue to be lumped together [for A-76 contract reviews] with clerical services."[30] Despite these objections, however, the government pressed ahead and contracted out the management of the libraries at the Department of Housing and Urban Development, the Department of Energy, and the Environmental Protection Agency.

The initial experience with contracting out library services confirmed the crtics' warnings. The American Library Association noted that contractors tended to hire relatively inexpensive workers, who often were not library professionals; made little effort to develop their employees' expertise; and counted on high turnover to keep their costs down. Many government employees complained that, just as the ALA had warned, the government's institutional knowledge had eroded. One government official complained that his library—now operated by a contractor—could not find a publication he needed "unless you give them the call number." He said that he had to use other federal libraries and work in a public library on his own time

28. *Office of Management and Budget Circular A-76*, Hearings, pp. 141–43; *Commercial Activities Contracting Act of 1987*, Hearings, Statement of Eileen D. Cooke, p. 82; and *Implementation of Circular A-76*, Hearings before the House Post Office and Civil Service Committee, 98 Cong. 2 sess. (GPO, 1985), pp. 288–93.
29. *Office of Management and Budget Circular A-76*, Hearings, p. 143.
30. *Office of Management and Budget Circular A-76*, Hearings, p. 91.

to find information he could not get from his own department's library.[31] OMB insisted that the government had saved money by contracting for library services, but the libraries' users openly questioned whether the savings were worth the inconvenience and problems they encountered in tracking down needed facts.

Assessing Savings from Contracting Out

OMB claimed significant cost savings from its A-76 process during the Reagan years, but the actual costs and savings of the program are difficult to assess. Investigations revealed, for example, that OMB's cost savings estimates did not take into account the cost of the A-76 process itself. At one congressional hearing in 1988, witnesses pointed out that a five-year A-76 review, costing $8 million to $10 million to conduct, saved just $480,000 and cost many federal workers their jobs.[32]

In 1990 Senator Sasser observed that in the Department of Defense alone, "over 1,700 people are continuously assigned to A-76 studies at an annual cost estimated at $150 to $300 million, far outweighing any estimated savings."[33] Despite the great effort made to total the cost savings from A-76, the best estimates of the annual cost to produce those savings in a single department had an error factor of 100 percent and a cost range of $150 million—compared with OMB's total estimated cost savings of $696 million over six years.[34]

In fact, the GAO found that no one really knows how much the A-76 review process cost. OMB and DOD officials said that it was too expensive to conduct cost-effectiveness studies on the program, and DOD planned to stop collecting information that would make even rough estimates possible. "Moreover," GAO noted, "OMB officials believe that doing reviews to determine the most effective way to accomplish operations is a management responsibility that should be carried out routinely and thus should not be counted as a cost against A-76 savings." GAO disagreed, arguing that more should be done to

31. *Commercial Activities Contracting Act of 1987*, Hearings, pp. 77–78; and *Office of Management and Budget Circular A-76*, Hearings, p. 137.
32. *Commercial Activities Contracting Act of 1987*, Hearings, p. 87.
33. "Inefficiency and Mismanagement," cover letter.
34. *Commercial Activities Contracting Act of 1987*, Hearings, p. 136.

determine how much A-76 studies cost and whether those costs exceeded the savings they were alleged to produce.[35]

Nor did agencies that issued contracts after an A-76 study routinely monitor the contracts' costs to see if the savings claimed in the bid were actually achieved. DOD's savings estimates, for example, came from standardized assumptions, not the best available cost data on the individual activity. The agencies did not comprehensively audit the contracts after they were issued, so the government did not know how effective the contractors' performance was. "DOD officials readily acknowledge that no one really knows what, if any *actual* savings have been achieved," and no one has the information to find out, the Senate Budget Committee pointed out in 1990.[36] GAO concluded:

> Accordingly, some of the controversy surrounding the A-76 program is understandable—Congress questions whether projected savings are real, and agencies are not sure of the benefits of implementing the program. . . . We could not determine, from the available data, the impact the program has had or whether the reported economies were overstated or understated. . . . Our principal message is that accurate A-76 savings figures are needed to address long-standing and growing congressional concerns about the A-76 program's value and achievements.[37]

The apparently hard numbers for cost savings that OMB produced, in fact, hid considerable debate over just how real they were—and whether the program justified the enormous efforts and disruptions it caused.[38]

Some members of Congress also wondered what happened to the millions of dollars of claimed savings. They pointed out that the agencies had neither returned the money to the Treasury nor notified Congress that it was available to be appropriated for another purpose. Senator David Pryor made the point to OMB and DOD officials this way:

35. General Accounting Office, *OMB Circular A-76: DOD's Reported Savings Figures Are Incomplete and Inaccurate*, GGD-90-58 (March 1990), p. 7.

36. "Inefficiency and Mismanagement," p. 5 (emphasis in original).

37. GAO, *OMB Circular A-76: DOD's Reported Savings Figures*, pp. 7, 9.

38. For a supporting view, see CBO, *Contracting Out: Potential for Reducing Federal Costs*, especially p. 12.

My wife's birthday is coming up pretty soon. If I gave my wife $50 and said, "I do not know what kind of dress you want; you go out and buy yourself a dress with this $50." I do not think that would buy much of a dress these days, but anyway, let's say she goes out and finds exactly what she wants for $30. She has $20 left in her pocket [not far from the alleged percentage savings under A-76 reviews]. Now, I would not ask her what she is going to do with that $20, but I think that Congress ought to ask you what you are doing with your savings. I think OMB has been very negligent in not monitoring these alleged savings.[39]

Contracting Out and Government Employees

Advocates of the competition prescription warned that government employees would strongly resist the A-76 process. Government administrators, they cautioned, did not always have noble visions of their role in the public service. Instead, "they were all too often concerned with expanding their area of responsibility, obtaining a larger number of subordinates, capturing greater privileges of office, and concentrating on other matters more related to the self-interest of the administrator than to the service of the public interest," the President's Commission on Privatization argued in 1988. Rank-and-file employees would worry about their benefits and seniority before they worried about their work. Managers would resist the loss of control that came with contracting out and would worry that, with fewer government employees to supervise, their grade level—and hence their pay—would decrease. Foot-dragging and obstruction might well result, the commission said.[40]

Although OMB tried to sell A-76 as a management-improvement program, government workers were always suspicious that the rhetoric was a cover for a strategy to increase contracting out and to eliminate their jobs. They had heard throughout Ronald Reagan's 1980 presidential campaign that they were part of the problem, that government programs were ineffective and inefficient, and that the only

39. *Commercial Activities Contracting Act of 1987*, Hearings, p. 37.
40. President's Commission on Privatization (Linowes Commission), *Privatization: Toward More Effective Government* (March 1988), pp. 243, 139, 136.

way to solve the problems was to hack the programs back. Government employees understood clearly that cutting government programs usually meant cutting government employment, since personnel costs accounted for a large share of the government's costs in commercially available activities. An official of the American Federation of Government Employees argued that the union was "sure that Federal employees can perform the services of Government more economically than private corporations. Our problem with Circular A-76 is that it is designed to promote reliance upon the private corporations for Government services regardless of how much more it will cost to contract out than to utilize Federal employees."[41]

Morale Problems

The result was low morale among workers subject to A-76 reviews. Government employees saw the threat and not the promise of A-76. As soon as government managers announced an A-76 review, attrition increased. Workers retired, left for other positions in government, or took private sector jobs. One DOD official discussed the morale problem bluntly:

> The major problem with A-76 is with the human spirit—it's a real downer. If you back away from the details, the concept of competition, what we're doing is taking 10,000 of our employees a year and threatening the hell out of them. . . . These [reviews]can drag on for years. There's a tremendous problem with morale, people leaving for other jobs.[42]

At one DOD installation, for example, an A-76 study was initiated in June 1981. By the time the contract was let four years later, so many employees had left that many maintenance jobs went undone. The problem grew so serious that the government had to ask the contractor to begin work before the official start of the contract simply to relieve the backlog. By one estimate, the problems caused by em-

41. *Review of OMB Circular A-76 and Contracting Out,* Hearings, p. 14.
42. *Office of Management and Budget Circular A-76,* Hearings, Statement of Bun B. Bray, Jr., p. 66.

ployee turnover during the A-76 process cost the government an extra $1.5 million.[43]

"Good employees leave, while others worry about keeping their jobs and do not do their jobs," one senior DOD official said. The official added, "While only a small percentage of employees lose their jobs—they all worry. . . . Good businesses do not threaten people with the loss of their jobs if they do a good job."[44]

Many government workers believed that the cost comparison process was a sham. They cited arbitrary cost figures applied to the government employees' bids. At one Army post seventy workers lost a bid and their jobs solely because OMB decided that fringe benefits ought to be calculated at 35.75 percent of wages instead of 27.3 percent.[45] Careful economic estimates in Washington went into the change, but to the affected employees the increase seemed an unjustified effort to load the process in favor of contractors' bids. At another facility OMB forced government employees to use a 7 percent pay increase in projecting their own salaries, when they actually received only a 4 percent increase. The three percentage point difference made the employees' bid higher than one submitted by a private contractor, and they lost the contract as a result.[46]

Critics also complained about "low-balling," the procedure in which contractors deliberately submit significantly understated bids to get the job and then allow costs to rise after winning the contract. One government official bitterly told a congressional hearing:

I guess the word that comes to mind is "frustration." When you consider a study that has taken years to complete, when you see contractors coming in low-balling and then six months later they default, when you see contractors come in and do shoddy work that the Government employees then have to go back behind them and redo, I can't say that it's an effective management tool.[47]

43. "Inefficiency and Mismanagement," p. 7.
44. *Contracting Out and Its Impact on Federal Personnel and Operations,* Hearings, p. 103.
45. *Office of Management and Budget Circular A-76,* Hearings, Statement of James Peirce, p. 27.
46. *Commercial Activities Contracting Act of 1987,* Hearings, pp. 91–94.
47. *Efficiency in Government Act,* Hearings before the House Committee on Post Office and Civil Service, 101 Cong. 2 sess. (GPO, 1990), Statement of Eddie Smith, p. 37. See also *Office of Management and Budget Circular A-76,* Hearings, pp. 66–67.

Other officials complained that A-76 was a deliberate strategy to break public employee unions.

Representative Ike Skelton was especially critical of an A-76 competition in his Missouri district, at the Fort Leonard Wood Army base. The base's employees won an award one year for maintaining the best post in the Army. The next year, because of decisions made by officials at higher levels, some of the post's commercial operations were contracted out. "Some of them [the post's employees] will be lucky enough to be hired by the contractor at a lower rate of pay and with fewer fringe benefits. The rest will lose their jobs completely," Skelton told a congressional hearing, adding that such treatment of award-winning workers demonstrated "insensitivity."[48]

Other officials, however, noted the obvious. "Any effort to reduce spending, by closing a base or contracting out, brings cries of outrage from affected employees," said a spokesman for the Contract Services Association of America, a lobbyist for government contractors. "There is no easy solution to this problem, but mandating life-time employment for the current Government work force is certainly not the right answer."[49]

Effects on the Federal Work Force

Government employees proved effective in price competitions, winning nearly half of all of the competitions. In the activities that were awarded to outside contractors, the vast majority of affected federal employees—86 percent—either obtained other jobs in the government or retired. About half of the remaining 14 percent obtained jobs with the contractor and about half went jobless. Slightly more than half of the workers who took other government jobs or who went to work for private contractors had to settle for positions paying less than they had been making. Nearly all employees who switched to the contractor's employment complained that the benefits were not

48. *Status of Major Issues Relating to the DOD Commercial Activities or Contracting Out Program,* Hearings before the Subcommittee on Investigations of the House Armed Services Committee, 100 Cong. 2 sess. (GPO, 1988), p. 4.

49. *Efficiency in Government Act,* Hearings, Statement of Gary D. Engebretson, p. 55.

as good as the government's and that the work was less satisfying than government work.[50]

It would be impossible to tell the workers who found their careers disrupted, their pay cut, their benefits diminished, and their satisfaction reduced that the A-76 process did not have harmful or painful consequences. Compared with the size of the federal work force, however, the number of employees adversely affected by A-76 reviews was small.

The Government as Buyer

Through all its revisions, the A-76 initiative remained attractive in numerous ways. It directly confronted the realities of postwar federal management in recognizing the growing dependence of government on the private sector. It recognized as well that government tends to drift into activities that the private sector could do more cheaply and more effectively. Every presidential administration since Eisenhower's has pursued a policy of encouraging federal agencies to contract out commercial activities. The logic was irrefutable: there simply was no need for the government to duplicate private sector businesses and to risk the rising costs and falling performance that occur without the incentives of market competition.

No administration embraced A-76 with more enthusiasm than the Reagan administration. In providing a diagnosis of at least part of what was wrong with government and a prescription for what could be done about it, A-76 was a perfect match for the ideological predisposition of many administration officials. For advocates of private competition, nothing made more sense than to have government workers compete with the private market for their jobs. As OMB's reports of savings mounted, the results seemed impressive. Despite the complaints of public employee unions and others, the underpinnings of A-76 were unarguably within the tradition of American government.[51]

50. GAO, *Federal Productivity: DOD's Experience in Contracting Out Commercially Available Activities,* pp. 15–23.

51. The unions' protests took the form of counterstudies that raised serious problems with contracting out. See, for example, American Federation of State, County, and Municipal Employees, *Passing the Bucks: The Contracting Out of Public Services* (Washington, 1983); and AFSCME, *When Public Services Go Private: Not Always Better, Not Always Honest, There May Be A Better Way* (Washington, 1987).

If there were problems, everyone knew that, at its core, the policy made sense.

The A-76 process under Reagan produced some unquestioned cost savings. Moreover, a much-cited study in 1984 noted that the competitive process—whether in the public or private sector—produced important improvements, with clearer organizational goals, better management, and happier workers.[52] Reagan's Commission on Privatization succinctly laid out the conditions necessary for contracting to work well:

Contracting is likely to be most successful where the terms and measurements of service delivery are clear and easily defined, where at least several firms have the capacity to perform the contract, where the contractor does not have to make large new capital expenditures, and where the contract can be subject to renewal and renegotiation regularly. When enough of these conditions are missing, the contractor may become an extension of the government, freed from many of the government personnel practices and other limitations that inhibit effective government management. In that case, contracting may offer significant benefits, but many of the problems of the American governing process identified by the public choice school and other critics will still be fully applicable.[53]

The commission's conclusions pointed just as clearly to the problems that underlay the A-76 process. The government struggled with substantial demand-side problems in defining the goals the contractors should pursue; in choosing the best contractors; in setting the right balance of incentives and sanctions; and in measuring what the contractors accomplished. Supply-side problems spread as well. With cost-plus-fee contracts, contractors had strong incentives to low-ball the costs and then collect even larger fees as contract costs rose. Having disbanded the government work force, the government committed itself to buying goods and services in the private market. When

52. John B. Handy and Dennis J. O'Connor, *How Winners Win: Lessons Learned from Contract Competition in Base Operations Support* (Bethesda, Md.: Logistics Management Institute, September 1984). The report was produced by a government contractor.
53. Linowes Commission, *Privatization*, p. 244.

the market presented government buyers with few choices, many of the advantages that the competition prescription promised evaporated.

OMB claimed substantial savings from the A-76 program but never measured the cost of producing those savings. Even after the program had been in place for several years, no one—not OMB, not GAO, not any of the federal agencies affected—really knew how well A-76 was working and how much, on balance, it had saved the American taxpayers. In the turbulent struggle between the program's adherents and its outspoken critics, the broad political issues quickly drove out the narrow analytical ones. Debates about the role and cost of government employees soon trumped management analysis—all the more because OMB saw little point in collecting the detailed information needed to produce hard numbers about the real results. Given the Reagan administration's ideological commitment to the program, OMB had little incentive to look any closer. The agency retreated instead to an old temptation, by substituting "conformity with administrative and fiscal procedures for evaluation of substantive performance," as President Kennedy's Bell commission on government contracting described the standard response a quarter of a century earlier.[54]

The heated struggles, however, hid a far more important issue: the government's program for contracting out commercial activities has been plagued with problems since it was first implemented by the Eisenhower administration in 1955. Federal agencies have not pursued contracting out aggressively because it upsets their routines and introduces additional uncertainty into their operations. It threatens the job security of government workers, and the savings it produces are hard to measure.

Most of all, though, the government's experience with the A-76 program points out just how difficult it is to introduce genuine contracting into government. As the Bell commission told President Kennedy in 1962, "In order for the contracting system to work effectively, the first requirement is for the Government to be a sophisticated buyer—that is, to know what it wants and how to get it."[55] Nothing

54. Bureau of the Budget, *Report to the President on Government Contracting for Research and Development,* (hereafter *Bell Report*), S. Doc. 87-94 , 87 Cong. 2 sess. (GPO, 1962), p. 229.

55. Bureau of the Budget, *Bell Report,* p. 228.

troubled A-76 more than the government's difficulty in defining the desired product and then trying to determine if private contractors were delivering satisfactorily.

If these problems proved troublesome in competitive markets, where imperfections on the supply and demand sides were relatively small, they were far more so in other markets in which the government operated. The market for telecommunications equipment, for example, offered little competitive discipline, as chapter 4 shows.

4

The FTS-2000
System: Federal
Telecommunications

On February 13, 1985, the General Services Administration (GSA) attracted widespread attention by announcing a competition for a contract to provide a new telephone system for the federal government. The government's existing telephone system, the largest in the free world, had an annual budget of $400 million. The new system, christened FTS-2000 (short for Federal Telephone System for the year 2000) was to be even bigger: the largest nondefense procurement in American history, worth perhaps as much as $25 billion over its life. Furthermore, whoever won the competition would gain an enormous customer base from which to launch a new generation of telecommunications for private buyers. The winner could develop new services, test new systems, and then market them to private companies as a proven winner. The huge contract was worth winning in its own right. It was even more valuable for the advantages it promised in winning the shakeout in the recently deregulated industry.

The existing federal telephone system had a venerable record. Built in the 1960s, it was the first to link together the various parts of the far-flung federal government. By the late 1950s government and its programs had grown significantly. At the same time, government officials had begun worrying about the survivability of government op-

I am grateful to Bruce McConnell for invaluable comments and suggestions in this chapter.

erations in the event of nuclear war. Defense planners wanted to ensure that the command-and-control apparatus for the military would be able to survive an attack. Civilian managers were concerned about restoring civilian operations as quickly as possible after a nuclear exchange. Those concerns became more urgent after the Cuban missile crisis of 1961, when messages overloaded the government's communications system. Government officials had to fall back upon the civilian telephone system, which compromised security. The federal government had already begun making plans for a new system, but the missile crisis made plain that the new system had to have much greater capacity and far more security than the existing one.

In response GSA in 1963 developed a single, dedicated network that linked thousands of government facilities through central switching centers. Representative Jack Brooks, the first person to use the new system, was amazed to be able to pick up a telephone in GSA's headquarters and reach a Federal Aviation Administration manager in Los Angeles—in just thirty-seven seconds. "The service was fast," he noted at the time, "and the cost was about one-half the former commercial rate." In its first two decades, the FTS—Federal Telephone System—served 1.3 million subscribers through 60,000 circuits and 11 millions miles of transmission cables. It was bigger than the seventeen largest private telephone systems in the United States combined.[1]

The Problem of Competition

As the original FTS matured into the late 1970s, however, two major events occurred: deregulation of the telecommunications industry, and the rapid change in telecommunications technology. Both raised very difficult questions as GSA began planning for the next generation of government telecommunications.

New Competitors

Before the mid-1970s AT&T (American Telephone and Telegraph) had virtual control of the government's phone business, as it had over

---

1. Bernard J. Bennington, "Appendix A: FTS2000 Case Study," in *Beyond FTS2000: A Program for Change* (Washington: National Research Council, 1989), pp. 1–4.

all other telecommunications, both private and commercial. Long a traditional monopoly, AT&T was allowed to dominate the market in exchange for government regulation of its prices and the quality of its service. In the late 1960s, though, an upstart company called Microwave Communications, Inc. (MCI) won permission from the courts to begin long distance telephone service between Chicago and St. Louis. In 1976 MCI further broke into AT&T's monopoly by winning permission from the Federal Communications Commission (FCC) to buy bulk telephone service from AT&T at the same deeply discounted rates that the federal government paid for its service and then to resell the service to the public. MCI established a technological point—that companies other than AT&T could provide long distance service—and an economic point—that competitive long distance service might well produce lower rates for consumers. MCI reinforced both arguments when, in 1977, it won a contract from GSA to replace the government's AT&T long distance circuits between Washington and New York City.

These events fundamentally changed the government's telephone business.[2] After the FCC ruling, AT&T saw its monopoly, based on special "Telpak" rate tariffs, begin to slip away. MCI's successful challenge raised a harsh trade-off for AT&T. If it retained the Telpak rates, and thereby the government's business, it would be forced to sell telephone service to MCI at the same cheap government wholesale rates, and then find MCI undercutting AT&T's prices in the retail market. If it canceled Telpak it risked losing the government's business, but at least it would not feed MCI's growth with cheap rates. AT&T, not surprisingly, chose the latter strategy and canceled Telpak in 1976. The government, eager to keep its prices low and its service stable, fought AT&T for five years to force the company to honor the agreement. In 1981 AT&T finally won government permission to withdraw Telpak. Without AT&T's favorable tariffs, and with a competitive long distance market still years away, the federal government's bills for long distance service doubled almost immediately, with an increase of $100 million a year. The costs of access to the system stayed about the same, but the per-minute costs of long distance service soared from thirteen cents a minute to twenty-six cents a minute.[3] Four years

2. This section draws heavily upon Bennington, "FTS2000 Case Study," pp. 4–9.
3. Judith Haveman, "For Phone Contacts, a Busy Signal," *Washington Post*, August 26, 1987, p. A21.

later, when the telecommunications industry was deregulated, consumers had to pay not only for long distance service but also for access through local telephone companies to long distance lines. The federal government's costs went up again, this time to about thirty-one cents a minute, and the government's total telephone bill went up by $95 million. Furthermore, because local telephone companies set the local access charges, the federal government faced different charges, on different schedules, every place it did business.[4]

Deregulation of the telecommunications industry upset federal agencies as much as it did private consumers. The rapid increase in prices scrambled agency budgets, and for the first time agency officials were having to make decisions about the kind of telecommunications systems their agencies needed. Many of them were unprepared for the task. Like other consumers, they suddenly found they had a series of unfamiliar choices to make: what equipment and services to buy, how to buy them, and how to manage the process.

New Technologies

GSA was of little help. Its managers still had a Telpak mindset. They were used to thinking in terms of economies of scale, to buying large quantities of service from AT&T's network, and to working at the margins to produce better services at lower prices. Where possible, that meant replacing human operators with electronic switchboards and putting switching centers and long distance circuits out to bid. It did not mean thinking strategically about the new telecommunications world the government was facing. To be sure, GSA was not the only consumer confused by the bewildering array of options generated by deregulation of the telecommunications industry. Like many others, GSA found itself constantly running just to keep up with changes and challenges that were multiplying on the technical side.

The old FTS was a voice-based long distance service: federal workers used it to talk with other government officials and with agency clients around the country. By the early 1980s, however, telecommunications was far more than just voice communications. The Department of Energy (DOE), for example, was developing a system for high-speed, computer-to-computer transfer of information about the nation's nu-

---

4. Haveman, "For Phone Contacts, a Busy Signal," p. A21.

clear stockpile. Meanwhile, emerging technologies produced new services: facsimile transmission of documents, which would soon simply be shortened to fax; electronic mail, far faster than regular mail service, soon to be simply E-mail; video conferencing, in which people at opposite ends of the country could, with the help of special equipment, "meet" with each other without every leaving their own cities; and a vast array of data transmission through computer modems.

Confronted with this myriad of options, GSA decided to treat deregulation as an opportunity: in the new telecommunications world, competition among many new companies would provide the government with new technological options at lower prices. GSA officials made two strategic errors, however. First, they greatly underestimated how quickly the large field of new long distance carriers would shake out into a small number of competitors. Instead of presenting them with a full range of market choices, the industry produced only a handful of companies capable of handling the government's business. Furthermore, these new companies were not playing on a level field; AT&T continued to dominate the market. There was more competition than in the past, but the market remained far closer to a quasi-monopoly than to a fully competitive market.

Second, GSA officials went into the FTS-2000 project imagining the market would rush to present them with choices. They badly underestimated just how active they would have to be in shaping those choices. Buying the government's telecommunications services turned out to be a very different proposition from buying standardized goods or services in a competitive market. Instead of engaging in a series of arm's-length transactions in an exciting new telecommunications bazaar, GSA had to develop a close working partnership between the government and its suppliers for highly differentiated goods. GSA needed to be a far smarter buyer than it had anticipated; its attempts to fill that role led to numerous problems.

Thus this case illustrates what can happen when major imperfections exist on the supply side. The market was an oligopoly, with just a few companies dominating the market—and with AT&T dominating all of them. Market imperfections, inherent in the technology of telecommunications, had long been the basis for government regulation of the industry. Traditionally, vast economies of scale in constructing and operating telephone systems had created natural monopolies, which the government allowed to operate in exchange for careful regulation of quality and price. GSA hoped that the growth of new telecommunications companies, coupled with the new technologies, would allow greater market competition. These hopes were dashed. Supply-side imperfections quickly reasserted themselves, and with that came a renewed need for government to manage the market for its own telecommunications.

Competition in Contracting

When GSA began sketching plans for FTS-2000, it found that it had three options.[5] First, it could do nothing. Telecommunications technology was evolving rapidly, but its direction was uncertain. Agency requirements, meanwhile, were also developing, but most of the new features were, in 1984, little more than a "will-o'-the-wisp in the minds of most federal managers," according to some critics.[6] If GSA sat back for a while, its officials could watch these new technologies take shape before investing heavily in them. An iterative process that made moderate changes incrementally was attractive. Neither the industry nor its government customers knew what possibilities might be available even a few years later. Neither could predict well just what uses the government would find for the new possibilities. Neither could even be sure that each was talking clearly to the other, so great was the pace of innovation. The chances for getting out in front of this trend seemed remote.

For GSA, however, delay in shaping a new policy meant losing control over both the costs and the structure of the government's telecommunications system. Federal agencies, led by DOE and several of the armed services, were already planning to drop out of the FTS, a move that threatened GSA's traditional approach of seeking economies of scale through central coordination and procurement of the government's telecommunications business. If agencies contracted for their own telecommunications services, furthermore, costs would be less predictable, and centralized budget control would be reduced.

5. See Bennington, "FTS2000 Case Study," pp. 10–11, for a discussion of these options.
6. J. B. Miles, "Teamwork Is the Key to FTS Competition," *Government Computer News,* January 16, 1987, p. 101.

Rising telecommunications costs had already caught OMB's attention, and support for GSA within and outside the administration would surely erode if costs continued to climb rapidly. GSA's calculus of political risk ensured that this first option never received much consideration.

Second, GSA could design, engineer, and buy a new system of switches and circuits. The original FTS had been handled this way, with the government prescribing the requirements for its telecommunications system and AT&T delivering them. GSA planners argued that this approach might have made sense at a time when the government had few options, but new realities—on both sides of the AT&T-GSA partnership—discouraged them from pursuing this option. GSA itself did not have the staff, in numbers or expertise, to design its own system,[7] and the salary and recruitment limits of the federal personnel system made it impossible for GSA to hire the talent it needed. Moreover, the Reagan administration's OMB was exerting heavy pressure on GSA to pursue the route of competition.

AT&T, for its part, had not yet begun to think competitively. The company had little incentive to move aggressively, since the longer the government remained with the old FTS, the longer AT&T retained almost all of the government's telecommunications business. Any change in the existing service might reduce AT&T's share of the government's business and would reduce the prices it could charge for whatever share it retained. Therefore, when AT&T proposed its own alternative to FTS-2000, it was scarcely more than a new version of Telpak, christened "Software Defined Network," that would be proprietary to AT&T.

GSA had a third option, to purchase services through a competitive process from private suppliers. This option had a host of advantages. It fit the Reagan administration's procompetition privatization strategy. It avoided the necessity that GSA itself would have to design the new system. The agency could instead go shopping in the promising new telecommunications supermarket and buy the most attractive package of services at the lowest available cost—or so GSA officials envisioned. This option would also let GSA retain its control over the government's telecommunications business and stop the movement

7. Bennington, "FTS2000 Case Study," p. 11.

toward decentralized planning that threatened to unravel the government's established telecommunications policies.

Best of all, this option seemed the simplest of the three. With many companies competing for price, quality, and service, the government could act as an ordinary consumer, allow the industry to develop a marketplace of prices and services, and then choose the best product. As one congressional staff member explained, "The intent was to get GSA out of the business of telecommunications management, and into the business of contract management. The goal was to let the private sector meet the government's requirements."[8] That philosophy set the stage for FTS-2000.

Once GSA opted for a competitive process, it prepared a three-part strategy.[9] First, it planned a winner-take-all competition. By dangling the bait of the government's huge business, GSA officials believed that they could entice all of the nation's long distance companies—AT&T as well as the new upstarts—to bid in a competitive procurement. Given the big government market and the important advantages the winner would gain in the private market, GSA was confident it would obtain the lowest price possible.

Second, GSA proposed to make the winning supplier responsible for all implementation and operation of the system. Instead of the close working relationship the AT&T monopoly had forced on GSA, the agency now planned simply to buy the services at an agreed-upon price. How the winning supplier designed the system would be up to that supplier. Indeed, GSA officials hoped that leaving the *how* questions up to competing companies would give them powerful incentives to produce the most imaginative system that made the best use of emerging technologies.

Third, GSA proposed to oversee the service on behalf of the users: government officials and their agencies. With government oversight, individual agencies would not find themselves taken advantage of as they might if suppliers could deal with them one-on-one. The agencies, in fact, would be in about the same position as they were in the old FTS. They would buy services—from a vastly larger menu, to be sure—from the winning supplier, while GSA would ensure that the

8. Interview with Charles Wheeler, January 8, 1992.
9. Miles, "Teamwork Is the Key to FTS Competition," p. 101.

services would be of the highest quality and at the lowest prices. In the process, of course, the federal government (and GSA) would keep centralized control of the costs and the technology.

All three of the elements in GSA's strategy were predicated on one critical assumption: that a large number of companies would compete for the government's business. When GSA began planning, that seemed a safe assumption. Five new long distance companies had joined AT&T in the marketplace—MCI, GTE Sprint, Satellite Business Systems, US Telecom, and US Transmission Service (a subsidiary of ITT)—and none of them could afford to ignore the huge government market. A competition for the FTS-2000 contract seemed certain.

Two big problems, however, undermined GSA's strategy. Within three years a major shakeout in the industry reduced the number of long distance carriers to three: MCI, Sprint, and AT&T. What looked at first like a freewheeling battle now was a far more limited competition.

It was becoming apparent, furthermore, that the new system would be far more complicated technologically than GSA had initially realized. Putting voice, data, and video simultaneously over a single network would require vastly more planning and entail far more risk than had the earlier voice-only system, which had relied primarily on off-the-shelf technology.

Pushing the Envelope

In short, GSA was boldly pushing where no organization had gone before. With FTS-2000 the agency was proposing to do nothing less than replace the largest telephone system in the free world with a new system, full of unproven technologies, developed and priced in a market in which few companies had much experience. The risks were enormous.

To be successful GSA had to define a system that was at, perhaps beyond, the state of the art: a system that would have to perform reliably for millions of government customers—and that would also have to meet special requirements for national security and confidentiality. Just installing the new system presented problems. Any misstep risked major disruptions in the government's business. Everything from defense procurement to operation of the federal bond markets to citizen hot lines might be temporarily crippled by snags in the transition.

The very nature of this option, in turn, demanded far more of GSA than the old system did. The General Accounting Office (GAO) observed that

> the changing telecommunications environment requires a new degree of central management if the goals of cost economy, national security and emergency preparedness, and system compatibility are to be achieved. The central managers need to guide the individual agencies and establish methodologies for evaluating telecommunications alternatives. Similarly, these central managers need to identify areas where coordination and cooperation among the agencies is required and to implement procedures to achieve federal telecommunications objectives.[10]

GAO doubted that GSA was up to the job. In early 1987 GAO found that GSA had "no overall plan" to define the government's telecommunications strategy. GSA's proposal was little more than "a summary compilation of proposed agency procurements," GAO said, and "the absence of meaningful government planning has left the government open to the risk of serious problems in the development of new or replacement telecommunications systems."[11]

So serious, in fact, did GAO believe GSA's problems to be that it recommended postponement of the FTS-2000 procurement. By August 1987 GAO found that GSA had made improvements and grudgingly suggested that the agency might move ahead with FTS-2000 as an interim solution. The risk, however, was that the "interim solution could easily lapse into a *de facto* long-term commitment." GAO continued to question "whether FTS-2000 is optimal technically, economically, or contractually." With billions of dollars hanging on the decision, GAO argued that "no long-term commitment to this program should be made without further study."[12]

Although GSA maintained that it would manage the new system, GAO asserted that no one in GSA had the expertise to solve technical

10. General Accounting Office, *Information Management: Leadership Needed in Managing Federal Telecommunications*, IMTEC-87-9 (May 1987), pp. 13–14.

11. GAO, *Information Management: Leadership Needed*, p. 3.

12. General Accounting Office, *Information Management: Status of GSA's FTS 2000 Procurement*, IMTEC-87-42 (August 1987), p. 6.

problems. Because of the complexity of the system and its own limitations, GSA had little choice but to rely on other contractors for virtually every procurement task, from system design and selection of the contractor to system monitoring. GSA, in fact, was "depending on private vendors to manage the procurement" itself, GAO found. To draw up the technical standards for the new system, GSA had turned to a private contractor, who not only prepared the "request for proposal" but also developed a model for evaluating the competing bids. GAO also found that GSA planned to hire other contractors to monitor the price and quality of the winning contractor's services.[13]

Having created the game, GSA was not on its own smart enough to play it. One federal telecommunications manager, in fact, saw GSA's FTS-2000 procurement request "as almost a plea to industry for help because the government just can't manage a project of this scale. It's as if GSA has just thrown up its hands in the face of an inability to manage the system in any defensible way, and so it has invited private industry to do it for them."[14] Interlocking imperatives—ideological, technical, organizational, and political—drove GSA ahead, despite GAO's warnings. The warnings, however, were to prove on the mark.

Winner-Take-All or Continuing Competition?

On January 7, 1987, GSA held a press conference to announce the opening of bidding on the new system. GSA Administrator Terence E. Golden excitedly told reporters that "the federal government will have in its hands, once it's complete, the most advanced telecommunications systems in the world." The deputy GSA commissioner for telecommunications services, Bernard J. Bennington, added, "When you compare the two systems, you're literally looking at the difference between horses and jet planes."[15]

Perhaps the most striking feature of the competition was that none of the competing long distance telephone companies, not even AT&T, felt it had enough expertise to enter the lists alone. AT&T joined with Boeing to form a team that clearly was the one to beat. As the gov-

13. GAO, *Information Management: Leadership Needed,* p. 30.
14. Miles, "Teamwork Is the Key to FTS Competition," p. 101.
15. Deborah Mesce, "GSA Opens Data Network Bid Process," *Washington Post,* January 8, 1987, pp. E1, E10.

ernment's current provider of most long distance service, AT&T had decades of experience in working with GSA and in operating the world's largest telephone network. From its defense contracts, Boeing had decades of experience in managing huge government procurements. It also had developed substantial know-how in "systems integration," a skill critical to ensuring that the various components of the technologically advanced system would work together. Boeing had won a contract from the National Aeronautics and Space Administration (NASA) to develop a package of voice and data telecommunications services similar to the FTS-2000.

The second team was a coalition made up of Martin Marietta, Northern Telecom, MCI, and the regional Bell operating companies (the local companies spun off from AT&T in the industry's deregulation, which were also known as the "Baby Bells"). Martin Marietta took the lead on this team, investing $50 million to draw up the bid. Like Boeing, Marietta had substantial project management experience. It had also won telecommunications contracts from the Department of Defense, NASA, and the Federal Aviation Administration, including a ten-year contract to upgrade the nation's air-traffic control system. Northern Telecom, a major manufacturer of telephone switches, was to provide the design of the network as well as technical support and development of the complex computer software required to make the new system work. MCI had a network of advanced fiber optic lines, which provided clear signal quality and simultaneous transmission of voice and data communications. The Baby Bells stood to get a substantial share of the business no matter which team won the competition, since government offices would have to use local telephone lines for access to long distance service. In the newly deregulated environment, however, the Baby Bells were worried that their former parent, AT&T, would devour them if they did not establish substantial independent business. Far more complex than the AT&T–Boeing team, this coalition was much younger, and none of its members had any substantial long-term telecommunications experience or expertise in managing anything as large as the FTS-2000. Nevertheless, the team was competitive with the AT&T group.

The third team was composed of Sprint and Electronic Data Systems (EDS). FTS-2000 was expected to generate substantially more traffic than the old FTS, and EDS was a logical competitor because much of the growth in government telecommunications was expected to be on the data side. A leader in data processing for federal agencies, EDS had won contracts with the Defense, Agriculture, Justice, and Energy departments, the Customs Service, and the Postal Service. Furthermore, EDS was at the time a subsidiary of IBM and could call on the computer giant for help in designing and managing data integration. Sprint was a small long distance carrier, with substantially less experience than AT&T and MCI in working with the government. The upstart was also experiencing serious management problems, especially in its billing operations, that were enraging customers and cutting into its revenues. Sprint had suffered a $700 million loss in 1986, and analysts expected the hemorrhage of red ink to continue.[16] To many observers, this team appeared the weakest.

A great deal was at stake for each of the three teams. For its part AT&T needed to win the contract to maintain both its market share and its profit base. Industry analysts pointed out that 90 percent of AT&T's business revenues came from just 10 percent of its business customers. The largest share of its business service profits came from its top 300 accounts—and the largest of these was the federal government.[17] If AT&T lost the government's business, it would lose not only substantial profits, but perhaps many other accounts that might turn to the winner of the FTS-2000 competition.

For MCI and Sprint, winning was crucial to their survival, which would be threatened if they could not demonstrate that they could take business from AT&T. Sprint, for example, had just 6.5 percent of the nation's long distance minutes, while AT&T had 77.8 percent.[18] A victory would give either MCI or Sprint a huge increase in business as well as an important toehold for cutting into AT&T's virtual monopoly of business customers. "It will give them the credibility that they don't have with large corporate users," one analyst observed. "It's more than revenues, it's prestige and capabilities. If the government feels confident enough, AT&T competitors will use this as an affidavit to penetrate other camps."[19]

16. Bennington, "FTS2000 Case Study," p. 39.
17. Bennington, "FTS2000 Case Study," p. 38.
18. Bennington, "FTS2000 Case Study," p. 39.
19. Elizabeth Tucker, "Teaming Up to Win Pact for Federal Phone System," *Washington Post*, February 2, 1987, p. E22.

For the defense-based contractors who teamed up with the long distance companies, FTS-2000 was important for other reasons. They saw clearly that rising deficits were likely to reduce future defense spending. For companies heavily dependent on the Pentagon—85 percent of Martin-Marietta's business was defense-related in 1986— survival lay in diversification. One Marietta official called it an "opportunity of a lifetime."[20] Robert Polutchko, president of Marietta's Information and Communication Systems Company, put it bluntly: "FTS-2000 is a must-win program for us."[21]

Despite the initial enthusiasm of the three teams, the prospect of real competition for the contract quickly diminished. On June 9 EDS pulled out of its bidding partnership with Sprint. The potential for endless litigation of the contract was one major concern, but so too were the company's continuing difficulties in building a working partnership with Sprint.[22] Without EDS, Sprint's position was gravely weakened, and a month later, on July 8, Sprint itself withdrew from the bidding. Some analysts once had expected as many as seventy vendors to bid on the FTS-2000 package. By mid-summer in 1987 only two competitors remained, AT&T and Marietta, and AT&T was beginning legal action to eliminate Marietta, claiming that MCI's plan to use the Baby Bells would violate the rules of the AT&T divestitute agreement. GAO official Thomas Giammo worried that "there are only two viable competitors left, and that's pretty risky, because what happens if one drops out."[23]

GSA's top officials had envisioned the winner-take-all process as one in which it could shop, in marketplace fashion, among rival proposals and choose the least expensive. To pursue this course, it surrendered from the beginning its cooperative, regulated relationship with AT&T. Now, its shrinking choices meant that the government might again be tied to AT&T, this time without the protection of government regulation of either quality or price.

20. Tucker, "Teaming Up to Win Pact for Federal Phone System."
21. Michael Schrage, "Marietta Seeks Golden Federal Phone Contract," *Washington Post*, March 24, 1986, Business section, p. 3.
22. Leslie Cauley, "Electronic Data Pulls Out of FTS Bidding," *Washington Times*, June 10, 1987.
23. Calvin Sims, "Federal Phone Plan Is Disputed," *New York Times*, August 3, 1987, p. D1.

GSA's decision to award the whole contract to a single bidder, in fact, had given AT&T a huge advantage from the very beginning, private consultants had warned. "The size, scope and restrictions" of the proposed system, one report cautioned, "overwhelmingly favor the position of the entrenched FTS service provider"—AT&T.[24] OMB was recommending that the FTS-2000 contract be awarded to a single vendor, but that government agencies be allowed to acquire their own telecommunications systems. In contrast GSA's consultant urged that all government agencies be required to use the FTS-2000 system and that at least two vendors be awarded parts of the contract. Competition that continued throughout the life of FTS-2000, GSA's consultant argued, was superior to a single winner-take-all competition. GSA officials worried that dealing with multiple vendors and developing a strategy for dividing the contract among the vendors would prove far too complicated. Top GSA managers therefore rejected the proposal and stuck with their winner-take-all approach.[25]

A Passion for Competition

It was at this point that Jack Brooks, chairman of the House Government Operations Committee, got involved in the contract debate. Brooks had long been an established power in the government's information technology issues; that he was chosen to make the first call on the new FTS system in 1963 was not surprising. James Tozzi, a former official at OMB, said, "To win an argument in Washington, there are two questions you have to answer. How good is someone's substantive position? And how much elbow grease can be put behind that position? Jack Brooks always scores in the 90s on both counts."[26]

For two decades Brooks had championed a hard-headed view of competition in the government's purchase of information technology. As Charles Wheeler, long one of Brooks's principal staff members on the committee noted, "Over the years, we have felt that the best way for government to seek what it needs at reasonable prices is to ensure

24. Christine Bonafield, "AT&T Has Held the Edge in FTS Bid All Along, Coveted Study Declares," *Communications Week*, August 31, 1987, pp. 1, 45.

25. GAO, *Information Management: Leadership Needed*, p. 29.

26. Bob Davis, "Texan Wants Last Word on U.S. Contract," *Wall Street Journal*, September 4, 1987, p. 4.

competition."[27] In 1965 Congress passed a bill, known as the Brooks act, that promoted competition in the government's purchase of data processing equipment. Brooks was concerned that, in the fledgling data processing industry, IBM would come to monopolize the government's computer business. Under the act the government first had to define what it needed. Then every qualified company was allowed to bid on the job. The goal, in the phrase the Brooks act made famous, was "full and open competition." IBM continued to win a huge amount of the government's business, but the Brooks act "was the salvation of several companies, including Control Data Corp., Honeywell and Burroughs," one Virginia computer consultant said.[28] The share of the government's business they won kept them in business; without the Brooks act—and Brooks's aggressive oversight of the act and therefore competition in the business—the companies would have fallen on hard times indeed. Every major data processing contract, in fact, came to Brooks for review before GSA let the contract.

Brooks also championed the Competition in Contracting Act of 1984, which ensured full and open competition for a far broader range of government procurements. The act established a procedure for contesting contract awards, which allowed administrative law judges to stay a contract until a challenge was settled. Compared with old protest procedures, in which complainants succeeded less than 10 percent of the time, contract appeals under the new system were sustained about two-thirds of the time, and far more quickly at that. "The agencies have grown to hate this," Government Operations Committee staff member Wheeler explained.[29] Brooks also sponsored the 1988 amendments to the Competition in Contracting Act, which further tightened the government's procurement process, in response to defense contracting scandals during the Reagan administration.

Brooks operated from the belief that the very structure of competitions for large, high-tech, information management procurements tended to promote the chances of the largest businesses in the field. He also believed that once established, big companies were very hard to displace. Brooks therefore was sure that a winner-take-all procure-

27. Wheeler interview.
28. Davis, "Texan Wants Last Word," p. 4.
29. Wheeler interview.

ment for FTS-2000 spelled trouble. In an August 1987 letter to GSA Administrator Golden, Brooks asked the agency to divide the contract between two vendors.

> I recognize that after two years of working on the project, it is difficult for you and your staff to be faced with the problem of having to restructure this procurement. However, I believe a multi-vendor award with continuing competition throughout the life of the contract will greatly reduce the risks inherent in the project and will ensure that the future telecommunications needs of the government are met economically and efficiently.[30]

Golden countered that splitting the contract would be more expensive. To give the second lowest bidder a substantial piece of the contract would surely increase prices above those that the low bidder would charge. Splitting the contract, furthermore, would impose significant new management challenges on GSA. If the government had to deal with two long distance companies, GSA not only would have to act as a buyer of services, but also would have to manage systems integration. As anyone who has ever attempted to set up a desktop computer can testify, making the different pieces of a high-tech system interrelate is not always an easy matter. The complexity of the new FTS-2000 multiplied the systems integration problem, and GSA resisted having to take that on. Any change in the procurement, finally, would certainly require GSA to push back the September deadline for the bids, perhaps by as much as a year or two, Golden explained. Delays might entangle the procurement with the 1988 presidential election contest and, perhaps, push the award into a new president's administration, and a new GSA administrator's tenure. Golden therefore dug in to resist Brooks's pressure.

Behind the scenes, the competitors lined up behind the two positions. If the contract were to be split, EDS and Sprint said they might reenter the competition. Marietta, however, threatened to withdraw if the contract were split, for it had all along been aiming for a winner-take-all victory. Marietta officials warned against the eighteen-

30. Judith Haveman, "Marietta: Don't Split Phone Work," *Washington Post*, August 6, 1987, p. E3.

month delay that might result. That, they said, "is a long time to be pregnant."[31]

AT&T confidently supported the idea of competition. "We have competition now as a fact of life, we are used to it and we feel we can be very successful in a competitive situation," a spokesman told the press. Industry analysts pointed out that AT&T also needed to demonstrate that it could succeed in a deregulated market. "If that means taking less of a contract," a PaineWebber analyst argued, "they'll do it. They still get some of the business and make their political point." But AT&T urged that that competition be delayed. "Why should we lay our cards on the table when the dealer hasn't decided what the game is?" a top official complained. AT&T pursued virtually every opportunity for delay, since the longer it took to field the new system, the longer it reaped the benefits of the old FTS. Marietta complained that AT&T was "drawing several million dollars" in revenue for each month that the competition went uncompleted. "The time factor is crucial," a Marietta official pointed out. "AT&T can afford to wait it out. We can't."[32]

Despite GSA opposition, Brooks and his colleagues persisted. At the end of September Representative Glenn English, chairman of the committee's Subcommittee on Government Information, wrote GSA saying that the procurement should be stopped, pending a congressional review of all of the documents in the procurement. The subcommittee gave GSA just three days to produce the mountain of documents. "The history of the procurement, and the twists and turns of the agency's actions and attempted actions, have seriously undermined confidence in the soundness and integrity of the program," English wrote. The subcommittee would be satisfied only if the contract were split, he said.[33]

Golden and GSA finally surrendered, postponing the procurement—and agreeing to split it into two. The decision opened the door

31. Calvin Sims, "Marietta Threatens to End Phone Bid," *New York Times,* August 6, 1987, p. D6.

32. Steve Coll and Judith Haveman, "Dispute Threatens U.S. Phone Contract," *Washington Post,* July 31, 1987, p. B1; Haveman, "Marietta: Don't Split Phone Work," p. E1; Steve Coll, "Federal Phone Contract May Be Split in Two," *Washington Post,* September 24, 1987, p. E1; and Davis, "Texan Wants Last Word," p. 4.

33. Leslie Cauley, "Hill Calls for Halt to FTS 2000," *Washington Times,* September 24, 1987, p. A1.

for the Sprint-EDS team to reenter the competition, which in Brooks's view was critical to creating a truly effective competition. The plan, as it began emerging, was to give the low bidder 60 percent of the contract and the second lowest bidder 40 percent. Making that work, however, was to prove anything but easy. New bids were due March 31, 1988, with the winner to be announced by September 30.

In the meantime a minor scandal on a much smaller contract erupted that spilled over into AT&T's relations with GSA. In October 1987 a group of Baby Bells, competing with AT&T for the operation of twelve computerized switching centers for the existing telephone network, submitted lower bids than AT&T in seven of the competitions. AT&T was upset that its offspring won more than half of the contracts, but it was infuriated by reports that a GSA employee had leaked information about its bid to the Baby Bells. Senior GSA managers, furthermore, knew that the reports were true but proceeded with the contract award anyway.

One of the Baby Bells later admitted that "our bid may have been influenced improperly by information passed to the company."[34] Although there was no evidence that the disclosure materially affected the competition, it did raise doubts—among many independent experts as well as with AT&T—about GSA's ability to conduct a fair bidding process for FTS-2000. AT&T, always apprehensive about the procurement, demanded that GSA remove from the FTS-2000 process any employee who had anything to do with the switching contract. A congressional staff member added, "Until they [GSA] get rid of those individuals involved in the switch contracts, the agency is nothing more than a rotten tooth with half the decay removed and a filling placed on top."[35] As a result of this incident AT&T developed a profound distrust of GSA that was to color its relations with the agency for years.

Administering the Contract

The decision to split the contract had delayed the procurement almost a full year. GSA had to redraft its procedures, each of the

34. John Burgess, "BellSouth Finds Signs of Wrongdoing, Offers to Give Up Federal Contract," *Washington Post*, January 23, 1988, p. C1.
35. Calvin Sims, "Agency Jumps Hurdles in Rush to Award Pact," *New York Times*, March 21, 1988, p. A16.

competitors had to refocus its proposal, Sprint had to catch up after having dropped out of the race for a time, GSA had to clean house after the switching scandal, and the agency had to rebuild its relations with Capitol Hill. Meanwhile GSA Administrator Golden resigned, so the agency had to establish new top leadership as well.

The bids from the three competitors finally arrived in May 1988. Sprint filed a 7,000-page bid. EDS had once again left the team, but Sprint officials said they were prepared to subcontract some of the work if it proved necessary later on. AT&T used a truck to deliver the ten required copies of its twenty-volume proposal. Marietta submitted a 3,000-page bid on behalf of its complex team.[36]

In reviewing the massive bids, GSA had a pair of immediate problems. First, the agency did not itself have the technical capacity to assess them. It was as if GSA had decided to buy a car but did not have the capability to define what a car looked like, what it ought to do, or what it ought to cost. GSA split its review into four pieces—technical, management, transition, and cost issues—and then hired the MITRE Corporation, a major consulting firm, to help it evaluate the proposals.

Second, to minimize concerns about leaks raised by the earlier scandal, GSA moved the review process out of its Washington offices to MITRE's headquarters across the Potomac River in McLean, Virginia. MITRE had performed extensive consulting work for the Defense Department, had regularly been audited by the Defense Investigative Service for security leaks, and knew how to create "a secure, self-contained bubble" in which the proposals could be reviewed without compromising the process. MITRE required document safes, receipts, and double-wrapped bags for transferring any part of any proposal from one office to another, and established secured destruction of trash, central alarms, security badges, and tight restrictions on visitors and phone usage. Agents regularly swept the facility for bugs.

AT&T distrusted even this process and sent a team to test the security by trying to gain access. The team failed. When congressional staff members arrived to inspect security, they were refused admission. It is a safe bet that no civilian operation in American history ever had

36. "Voluminous FTS2000 Proposals Filed by Three Contenders; US Sprint Forms New Division," *Telecommunications Reports,* May 2, 1988, p. 13.

tighter security.[37] GSA also created a blue-ribbon advisory committee, chaired by the president of the National Academy of Public Administration, Ray Kline, to oversee the review process.

Reviewing the proposals was a massive job. The paperwork alone was enough to fill a room thirty feet long, ten feet wide, and nine feet high to the ceiling. Simply separating the documents for the four different review panels took a week of full-time work. AT&T supplied a computer with software to run its cost model. Between April, when preliminary work on the review process began, and December, when the winner was announced, GSA and MITRE officials working on the bids took off only Thanksgiving Day. Staff members regularly stayed at a nearby hotel, as did the evaluation board's chairman. Some workers even bought liability insurance to protect themselves from possible lawsuits once the process was finished.[38]

Winners and Losers

In December GSA asked AT&T officials to come to a meeting at MITRE's McLean offices to iron out a problem in the review process. When they arrived, GSA officials surprised them with the announcement that AT&T would be awarded 60 percent of the FTS-2000 contract. The AT&T group was then locked into a room for an hour, without a telephone, while GSA contacted Sprint officials to tell them that they had won the remaining 40 percent. Marietta got nothing.[39]

When the bids were revealed, observers were surprised at the great differences among them. Perhaps the biggest surprise of all was the strength of AT&T's bid: it was far cheaper, with far fewer technical problems, than either the Marietta or the Sprint proposal. Sprint offered a system that was managed through sophisticated software, but that was little more than "a foot in the door," one observer suggested. Sprint was playing catch-up, both because it had to work its way back into the competition and because EDS had left the Sprint team just two months before the bid was submitted. For its part, Marietta had proposed that GSA assume its old role of integrating services in a predominantly private network. Marietta itself had little

37. Bennington, "FTS2000 Case Study," pp. 56–58.

38. Bennington, "FTS2000 Case Study," pp. 59–60.

39. John Burgess, "AT&T Federal Systems Proves It Can Win Major Contracts," *Washington Post,* January 9, 1989, Business section, p. 5.

experience in telecommunications and, because of its extensive reliance on its partners, the elements of its system were far less coordinated and sophisticated than those offered by Sprint and AT&T. In fact, Marietta proposed using magnetic tape or paper to move some information among members of its team. Magnetic tape lagged well behind the state of the art; using paper was, by the technical standards of the mid-1980s, prehistoric. Moreover, Marietta's prices were higher than the other competitors.[40]

The proposals were competitive, but they scarcely were equal. The evaluators ranked Marietta's proposal below Sprint's and both far below the AT&T bid.[41] The quality of AT&T's proposal, the company's answers to questions raised along the way, the design of its system, and its low price made the basic decision far easier for the review panels than anyone had anticipated.

The huge difference in the proposals, in fact, raised for some observers the same questions that had dogged the Golden-Brooks duel. By forcing GSA to split the contract into two pieces, Brooks had guaranteed that the federal government would pay significantly higher prices than if the contract had remained winner-take-all. Because the gap in the bids was far larger than expected, so too was the government's premium for maintaining a two-company system. On the other hand, the split procurement also guaranteed that at least two major companies would be in business to serve the government. Given the shakeout in the telecommunications system, GSA believed that keeping at least two companies in business was an advantage for the deal it had announced.

AT&T was the big winner. It had won the lion's share of the business and had proved as well that it could shake off its old monopoly culture and compete effectively in the newly deregulated industry. To have come in second would have been devastating for AT&T, its own officials admitted later. To go from the vast majority of the government's business to just 40 percent would have been a loss, both economically and psychologically. Sprint was also a winner. Its share of the contract established it as a major player in the deregulated telecommunications industry.

40. Bennington, "FTS2000 Case Study," pp. 60–62.
41. Bennington, "FTS2000 Case Study," pp. 60–62.

The big loser was Marietta, which lost not only its $50 million investment but a chance to diversify from its shrinking defense base. Another big loser was EDS, which had spent $30 million before withdrawing. IT&T, the second largest supplier in the old FTS with slightly more than a third of the circuits, now was shut out of the business completely.

AT&T could not rest on its laurels, however. Under the agreement GSA had struck with Representative Brooks, the competition would be reopened in the fourth and seventh years of the ten-year contract. Only the winners—AT&T and Sprint—would be involved, but they would be allowed to rebid on the services and, if Sprint's offer were superior, the 60-40 allocation could be reversed. Meanwhile, the losers, especially MCI, began to work hard to convince GSA that future bidding should not be restricted only to AT&T and Sprint.

Splitting the Business

The awarding of the contract did not end GSA's problems with managing FTS-2000. GSA quickly discovered that getting out of telecommunications management was impossible and that getting into contract management was far more complicated than anyone had thought. Marietta and MCI immediately tried to reopen the bid contest by taking several issues to court. MCI had originally nudged its way into the government's telecommunications business through the courts and had a reputation as an aggressive litigator. AT&T had not publicly disclosed its rates for FTS-2000, citing vestiges of the divestiture agreement that allowed it to keep its tariffs confidential. MCI challenged AT&T's position in court, asking how there could be competition if the prices were not public and demanding that the courts reopen the bidding. AT&T eventually replied by making public a collection of its FTS-2000 rates, buried in seven volumes of complex and inscrutable charts.

MCI also contested GSA's "mandatory-use" provision, which required all federal agencies to join FTS-2000. Mandatory use was an economic precondition for the 60-40 award. By forcing all federal agencies into the system, even the smaller share was well worth winning. If agencies had the option of buying their own systems, however, the contract would have had little value for its winners. Before the award, MCI had aggressively begun picking federal agencies out of the FTS and worked hard to outfit them with individual systems. After the award, MCI told agencies that it could provide them with better and cheaper service than the system that GSA was forcing them to buy. MCI's marketing confirmed GAO's worries that GSA had moved to mandatory use without adequately studying whether that approach was truly best for the agencies.[42]

Attacks from losers were not the only problems facing GSA. The agency was also finding it extremely difficult to achieve the promised 60-40 split. Almost from the outset Sprint began earning far more than the 40 percent share of FTS-2000 revenues that it had been awarded.[43] Four factors—"levelizing" prices, estimating the service volume in the new system, aggressive marketing of services by Sprint, and setting rates comparable to those charged private customers for similar services—accounted for the difficulty.

LEVELIZATION. Because the two vendors charged different prices for their services, GSA's own costs varied. But GSA could not charge different government agencies different prices. No agency manager would tolerate paying more for a service than another manager in another agency was paying. GSA therefore developed a formula to "levelize" AT&T's prices up, by charging the agencies assigned to AT&T more than the company's contract rate, and to "levelize" Sprint's prices down, by charging the agencies assigned to Sprint less than the contract rate. Through this process, GSA hoped, all agencies would end up paying equivalent prices for the same services. GSA planned to set the "levelization" factors as required to produce the 60-40 revenue split.[44] The agencies assigned to AT&T, however, knew that they were paying more than they would have if they had been dealing directly with the company. The agencies assigned to Sprint knew that they were getting a bargain, and that encouraged them to sign up for the company's new services. Levelization proved extraordinarily complicated to develop and disruptive to apply.

42. GAO, *Information Management: Leadership Needed*, p. 30.
43. General Accounting Office, *General Services Administration's Management of FTS 2000*, T-IMTEC-91-9 (April 19, 1991), Statement of Milton J. Socolar, pp. 6–8.
44. GSA ended levelization in the fall of 1991 when it negotiated roughly comparable prices from both Sprint and AT&T.

ESTIMATING SERVICE VOLUME. To achieve the 60-40 revenue split GSA also had to estimate how much service each agency would use and then factor that estimation into the levelization formula. GSA, however, had to base its estimates on usage under the old FTS system. This network almost entirely served voice traffic, while the new FTS-2000 system transmitted voice, data, fax, video-conference, and other traffic as well. The old system, therefore, proved a poor guide for demand under FTS-2000.

AGGRESSIVE MARKETING. Sprint's aggressive marketing made those projections even more outdated. Eager to promote its business, Sprint convinced many agencies to sign up for new services. As a result, its business grew more rapidly than AT&T's, making it even more difficult for GSA to maintain the 60-40 split.

COMPARABLE RATES. GSA also had trouble with what seemed the most straightforward provision in the contract—the clause stipulating that neither company could charge the government more than it charged the general public for comparable services. The reason for the provision was obvious: prices were constantly dropping because of rapid changes in technology, and the government wanted to be sure that it paid market prices for its services. What no one anticipated was that the contract's initial low rates would very quickly be higher than the rates available to the public. After just the first year GSA found that both AT&T and Sprint were violating the price cap. In fiscal 1991 and 1992, GAO estimated, FTS-2000 prices exceeded commercial rates by $148 million.[45]

GSA therefore pressed for refunds and reduction in future rates. AT&T agreed to a reduction, but Sprint refused, threatening not only to go to court, but to "turn out the lights" at its government operations center and shut down its service rather than cave in to the government's demands.[46]

After intense lobbying by Sprint officials, GSA withdrew its demands for a refund. For its part, Sprint agreed to reduce its prices over the

45. General Accounting Office, *FTS 2000: GSA Must Resolve Critical Pricing Issues*, IMTEC-91-79 (September 1991), p. 1.
46. Jay Mallin, "AT&T Will Ring Most Government Phones—GSA," *Washington Times*, April 19, 1991.

next two years in return for being assigned an agency whose telecommunications business was worth $20 million; the Navy was its choice. Despite AT&T's objections, GSA agreed to make the change. In the long run GSA stood to save millions of dollars because Sprint agreed to accept the price caps. In the short run, however, savings would be minimal because, as a concession to Sprint, GSA gave up the right to enforce the price cap until the fourth year of the contract. The haggling over the agreement, moreover, took a year, during which GSA lost the chance to enforce the price cap for both companies.

Whither the Navy?

Even worse, the Sprint agreement fed AT&T's already justified paranoia that GSA was not dealing with it straightforwardly. GSA negotiated with Sprint in secret and did not tell AT&T about the deal until four months after it was signed. AT&T never had the chance to offer a better deal than Sprint. Reassigning the Navy to Sprint distorted the 60-40 revenue split even more. In the first year of FTS-2000, the revenue split was 57-43 in favor of AT&T. By the third year, fiscal 1991, Sprint actually had 52 percent of the business, and that was before it was assigned the Navy. In classic understatement, GAO officials concluded, "Clearly, these estimates suggest that, in total, GSA's efforts will not come close to achieving a 60-40 revenue split."[47]

AT&T officials were not the only ones angered by GSA's decision to assign the Navy to Sprint. Brooks, who by this time was serving as chairman of the Judiciary Committee, was enraged: "The ones that bid the most are getting the most out of the contract," he told one reporter "and the ones who bid the least are getting the least; that's just not fair."[48] To another reporter, he complained, "GSA conducted a race where AT&T won by a large margin, but Sprint got the medal."[49]

The House Government Operations Committee, now chaired by John Conyers, demanded that GSA suspend the transfer of the Navy's business from AT&T to Sprint. "It's one thing that GSA's incompetent management is threatening this important program, but quite another that GSA refuses to take even rudimentary corrective actions once

47. GAO, *General Service Administration's Management of FTS 2000*, p. 9.
48. Edmund L. Andrews, "Loss of Millions Seen in U.S. Phone Contract," *New York Times,* April 19, 1991, p. D7.
49. Mallin, "AT&T Will Ring Most Government Phones."

these deficiencies have been pointed out to them," Conyers said.[50] New GSA Administrator Richard Austin refused Conyers's request, and Sprint defended the reassignment. Sprint officials claimed they were offering the "most efficiency and most effective service possible" and would not apologize for their success. They argued that AT&T had little incentive for pressing ahead with the new FTS-2000 system since it was currently providing service under the old system to several agencies, including the Navy, at higher prices than would be applicable under FTS-2000.[51]

In May 1991 Conyers resorted to the approach his predecessor had found successful in the earlier struggle to split the contract. Unless GSA suspended the Navy transfer, Conyers threatened, he would bring GSA to a virtual halt with requests for tons of documents and personal interviews with a score of top GSA officials. GSA capitulated, and Conyers and GSA Administrator Austin then reached a formal agreement under which GSA suspended the Navy's transfer from AT&T to Sprint and agreed to "make every effort possible to achieve a cumulative 60-40 split (AT&T versus Sprint) by year 4."[52] At Conyers's insistence, Austin also agreed to appoint a new assistant GSA administrator to manage FTS-2000. Conyers worried that Sprint had found too eager an audience in the GSA officials who were handling the contract. A fresh face, coupled with a special office to manage FTS-2000, would, he hoped, both short-circuit special interest pleading and improve GSA's competence.

The struggle over the Navy assignment was a reprise of old notes familiar in the FTS-2000 saga. Once again, AT&T felt that GSA had given favored treatment to its competitor. As Charles Wheeler of the House Government Operations Committee's staff put it, "They [AT&T] came into the process feeling that if they were going to deal with GSA, they were going to get screwed."[53] Sprint believed that AT&T was dragging its heels in the transition to the new system so that the industry giant could enjoy the higher prices of the old service. Sprint aggressively marketed its business and claimed it should not

50. News Release, House Committee on Government Operations, May 3, 1991.
51. Jennifer Richardson, "GSA Cries Uncle, Halts Navy FTS Trade," *Federal Computer Week*, May 13, 1991, p. 4.
52. News Release, House Committee on Government Operations, May 8, 1991.
53. Wheeler interview.

be penalized if agencies signed up for a broader range of services faster than other agencies signed up with AT&T. The House Government Operations Committee, meanwhile, remained highly suspicious of GSA's commitment to full competition and its ability to manage the market it had created. Chairman Conyers called it a " 'stealth agency,' free from the regular Congressional authorization process," controlling "a vast array of hundreds of billions of dollars of government property."[54] Special interest pleading coupled with poor oversight had resulted in the government paying rates that were 20 percent higher than commercial rates.[55]

Managing Market Competition

Despite these problems, FTS-2000 was a huge success in many important respects. First, the new telecommunications system worked. The exceptionally difficult job of designing the new system, putting it into operation, and switching over millions of telephones to the new system was accomplished with surprising smoothness. Second, FTS-2000 saved the federal government money. In just the first three years the new system cost $346 million less than the old FTS system would have cost.[56] Third, quality was improved. The new system could handle more calls more quickly and provide better sound quality. Fourth, federal agencies had a far greater range of telecommunications options at their disposal than ever before, even though after four years nearly all of the traffic was still traditional voice communication. With lower prices, better service, and the end—if temporarily—to GSA-Sprint-AT&T-Government Operations Committee haggling, FTS-2000 was working well.

Many federal agencies, however, believed that they had been disadvantaged by being forced into the system. Agencies assigned to AT&T knew that they could get a lower price—a substantially lower price, in fact—if they were allowed to deal with AT&T directly. And although prices under the new system were significantly lower than

54. News Release, House Government Operations Committee, October 28, 1991.
55. GAO, *FTS 2000: GSA Must Resolve Critical Pricing Issues*, p. 3.
56. *GSA Implementation of FTS2000: Bad Connections and No Operator Assistance*, Opening statement, John Conyers, chairman, Committee on Government Operations, press release, April 18, 1991.

they had been in the old system, they were still significantly higher than commercially available rates. In struggling to manage the contract, and thereby manage the market, GSA found itself lagging behind the explosive changes in the private telecommunications world.

MCI, meanwhile, continued to tempt government agencies with promises of wonderful service at even lower prices if only a way could be found to break the FTS-2000 mandatory-use requirement. In March 1992 it made a major breakthrough when it won a ten-year, $558 million contract to supply long distance service to the nation's air-traffic control system. Thus it seemed that the government's problems in managing its future telecommunications business were only beginning.

In abandoning the old FTS system, GSA also abandoned the traditional way it had done business with the telecommunications industry. The old, regulated system had been, if nothing else, predictable. AT&T's monopoly combined with Federal Communication Commission regulation not only limited choices about service and price but also made managing the chosen system comparatively easy. GSA had spent a generation working cooperatively with the AT&T monopoly, designing the system and collaborating on its management. Indeed, GSA had hoped and assumed that the advent of competition would allow it to establish an arm's-length, businesslike relationship with its telecommunications suppliers. GSA would not design; it would only buy. It would not set prices, but it would allow sellers to compete on costs. It would not manage the system, but it would demand that sellers provide good service; otherwise, the government would take its business elsewhere. The switch seemed logical and fit neatly into the Reagan administration's procompetition, privatization agenda.

Having opted for this competitive process, GSA found itself in a terrible position. It could have awarded the contract to the bidder that provided the best services at the lowest price, which turned out to be AT&T. This approach would have secured, at least in the short run, the lowest cost, but it risked driving the few other competitors out of business in the long run and minimizing the competition for future procurements. It also risked, in the long run, making GSA dependent on AT&T, this time without the protection of the FCC's regulations.

GSA could have negotiated the best possible deal for a cutting-edge system and then allowed agencies to join or not at their option. This strategy was risky for all concerned. Vendors would have been leery about setting prices before they knew how much business they would get. GSA, for its part, did not want to surrender control over telecommunications decisions to the agencies, for that would have undercut its power within the federal establishment. Agencies were eager for more choice, but many of them discovered that they did not have sufficient expertise in-house to buy smart.

GSA retreated, therefore, to a third option, splitting the contract among two vendors. In pressing this option on GSA, Representative Brooks was following his data processing model: by ensuring continuing competition over prices, the government would pay more in the short run but guarantee itself a wider range of choices in the long run.

The central lesson of the FTS-2000 contract saga is how extraordinarily difficult it was for the federal government to manage the market problems it faced. The structure of the market did not accommodate the Reagan administration's assumptions about how the market would restore competition to government procurement. On the supply side, instead of a strongly competitive market, GSA found itself wrestling with an oligopoly where a few competitors were still dominated by AT&T. Keeping even three long distance companies in the game proved difficult for GSA.

On the demand side, the government had difficulty defining just what the new telecommunications system ought to accomplish. The technological options were staggering, but deciding how far out in front of existing technology—and how heavily to bet on competing visions of the future—proved much more complex than GSA had anticipated. In hiring contractors both to help it select vendors and to manage the contract after it was awarded, GSA increased its dependence on outsiders to tell the government what it needed. In the bargain, GSA increased its vulnerability to conflict-of-interest problems, undue external pressure, and the kinds of fraud that had plagued several of the government's other high-tech contracts. Designing incentives for the vendors likewise proved difficult. Awarding 60 percent of the business to the low bidder seemed clear enough, but implementing the contract split was quite another matter.

GSA was never able to shop in a telecommunications bazaar as its planners had once hoped. Even had such a bazaar existed, GSA would not have been an ordinary shopper. The very size of the government's contract made it unlike any other player in the market. Moreover, the government insisted on a number of special requirements that made it unique: special network services and management requirements; an indefinite-delivery, indefinite-quantity contract; national emergency requirements, including dedicated network features and a special hardened site for use in emergencies; and government billing, testing, oversight, and auditing requirements. Both AT&T and Sprint cited these special requirements to justify charging the government more than commercial rates. The absence of a real market made it impossible to settle this dispute.

A state-of-the-art design, custom-made for a single purchaser, the FTS-2000 procurement was very much like a defense procurement for a cutting-edge weapons system. "Big government systems that are custom [made] are more similar to defense systems than [to] commercial systems," one defense electronics analyst explained.[57] As in defense work, contractors can learn a great deal that can then be translated into commercial products, but the procurement itself is a one-of-a-kind deal. In such procurements, the relationship between buyer and seller can only be collaborative and cooperative, never arm's length.

GSA struggled with every step of the process, from structuring the procurement and reviewing the proposals to managing the 60-40 split and overseeing system prices. Along the way it committed the government to higher costs than were necessary. It tested the patience of Congress, it discouraged government agencies, and it lost the confidence of a major vendor. Most of all, it learned a critical lesson. GSA officials started out believing that they could simply create a market and then do their shopping. The complexity of the product and the structure of the market, however, required them to manage the arena in which they were buying. They were sucked into a role they did not want and were unprepared, with either staff or capacity, for the role they were forced to play.

57. Schrage, "Marietta Seeks Golden Federal Phone Contract."

5

Superfund: Red Ice and Purple Dogs

During the late 1970s public health officials around the nation uncovered a series of hazardous waste dumps. Researchers were discovering that many of the chemicals found in these dumps were potent
carcinogens that posed health risks to humans who came into even
minimal contact with the chemicals. Some of these chemicals were
leaching into drinking water. Children returned home after playing
near one of the dumps to report that ice some days turned blue, some
days red. Their pet dogs came home purple from the sludge.[1] First in
New York's Love Canal, then in Missouri's Times Beach and Kentucky's
Valley of the Drums, and eventually in hundreds of other sites around
the country, citizens demanded that someone clean up the hazardous
wastes that were fouling their neighborhoods and threatening their
health.

The logical "someone" was the company that had dumped the
waste in the first place. Some manufacturers and waste haulers had
been careless in their disposal of the chemicals; others had followed
appropriate disposal procedures only to find years later that those
procedures were not adequate. Simple justice required that, whether
the pollution was intentional or not, the polluters pay to clean up
the mess. Analysts contended that it was both socially unfair and
economically inefficient to allow companies to externalize their pol-

1. Carl E. Van Horn, ed., *Breaking the Environmental Gridlock: The Report on a
National Conference* (New Brunswick, N.J.: Eagleton Institute of Politics, 1988), Statement of John Powell, p. 73.

lution costs by leaving them to others, including future generations, to pay. Economists argued, moreover, that if the polluters were forced to assume the costs for the mess they had created, they—and other industrialists—would have strong incentives to avoid creating new problems.

This solution, however, was far more complicated than it sounded.[2] Many of the toxic waste dumps had been managed by several different operators, so determining exactly who was responsible for what was nearly impossible. Many of the dumps had been closed or abandoned, making it difficult to identify precisely what toxic materials had been dumped. Some operators had gone bankrupt and were therefore unable to pay for any cleanup costs. Furthermore, many of the companies had disposed of the toxic wastes under government-approved procedures and argued that it was unfair to require them to pay for the cleanup.

Even in those instances where dumps were still operating, information on the toxic wastes was scarce. Records detailing what the substances were and where they came from were usually poor. In some cases different materials had mixed together into hard-to-identify substances, whose health effects were even harder to predict. Even when investigators could determine exactly what was in the sludge, health researchers could rarely give them precise estimates of the danger the substance caused. Scientists suspected that many of the dumped chemicals were capable of causing disease. The research, however, was often conducted by exposing laboratory animals to large amounts over short periods, while humans tended to be exposed to small amounts over long periods. The risks to humans were estimates, at best.

The many issues swirling around the dumps proved a recipe for government action. The hint of carcinogens even in small neighborhoods created irresistible political demands for a government program. Tracking down the companies responsible for the wastes and forcing them to pay for cleaning up the mess, even when it might be possible, would take years. During that time, innocent families would continue to be exposed to health hazards. They could not clean up

2. Jan Paul Acton, *Understanding Superfund: A Progress Report* (Santa Monica, Calif.: RAND Institute for Civil Justice, 1989), pp. 5–6.

the problem on their own and in most cases could not afford to move away from homes in which they had invested thousands of dollars and which had lost their value due to the proximity of the dump.

The realization that families with small children were living among, and sometimes drinking water contaminated by, toxic chemicals, made a major federal role politically imperative. Citizens and politicians alike were unwilling to wait for more detailed scientific investigation of the real risks from toxic wastes, or an assessment of whether other risks ought to have higher priority on the public agenda. The government could finance the cleanup and then seek to recover the costs from the companies that created the problem, thus avoiding the lengthy legal process that were delaying cleanups.

In December 1980, during the last days of the Carter administration, Congress passed the Comprehensive Environmental Response, Compensation, and Liability Act, known as Superfund. Its drafters intended Superfund to be an intensive, short-term program in which the federal government would set standards for cleaning up toxic waste dumps around the country. The government would also pay for the cleanup if the offending companies could not be found or if they could not afford the costs. From its original short-term focus, however, the program has grown into a near-permanent federal commitment expected to last generations and to cost hundreds of billions of dollars. The Reagan administration agreed to expand the program in 1986 and to quintuple its funding from the original $1.6 billion for the first five years to $8.5 billion for the second five years. In the process, Superfund created an unprecedented management burden for the Environmental Protection Agency (EPA).

Negotiating Market Behavior

Through Superfund, as well as through the other environmental regulations that followed EPA's formation in 1970, the federal government has stimulated the creation and growth of an enormous private market in environmental affairs. Spurred by government spending and, more important, by government regulations requiring expenditures from private pockets, private spending for pollution abatement has nearly doubled since 1970, to almost $60 billion a year (figure 5-1).

FIGURE 5-1. *Pollution Abatement Expenditures, 1972-87*

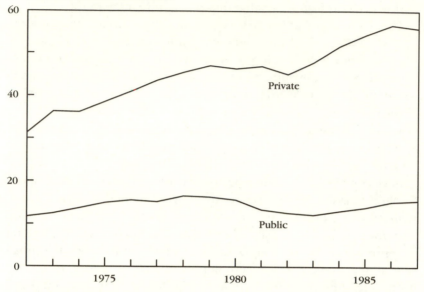

Billions of constant 1982 dollars

SOURCE: Kit D. Farber and Gary L. Rutledge, "Pollution Abatement and Control Expenditures," *Survey of Current Business,* vol. 66 (July 1986), p. 97; and Farber and Rutledge, "Pollution Abatement and Control Expenditures, 1984-87," *Survey of Current Business*, vol. 69 (June 1989), pp. 24-26.

Superfund shares certain characteristics with other federal programs, such as those that regulate and promote the nuclear power
industry, satellite technology, and defense systems that have an export
market. In all of these markets, private parties engage in a significant
amount of buying and selling. The government's participation, as a
regulator, a buyer, or both, prevents these markets from being completely private, however. Through its regulations, the federal government creates and structures the demand. Government restrictions
define what the products are, the standards they must meet, and in
some cases the prices that can be charged. Among private manufacturers of these products—the supply side—competition is often substantial and the market lively. Among buyers of the products—the
demand side—the market is far more constrained by the government's
standards and regulations. As sellers strive to accommodate themselves to the needs of the buyers, they frequently bargain with gov-

ernment over just what they can do and how. The Superfund program provides a lively example of this kind of negotiated market.

In implementing Superfund, EPA had to answer several questions that would shape the market for toxic waste cleanup. First, just how big was the overall problem? Congress had clearly intended the program to cover the cleanup of 400 sites. EPA's first pass at identifying sites produced a list of 418. By 1989 the list had grown to 1,200 sites and was increasing by 75 to 100 sites a year. William K. Reilly, the EPA administrator during the Bush administration, expected the list would reach 2,100 by the year 2000. EPA officials estimated that the number of sites eligible for cleanup under the Superfund program might eventually grow tenfold to 25,000. The Office of Technology Assessment (OTA) and the General Accounting Office (GAO) were even more pessimistic, predicting that the number could swell to 378,000 and ultimately cost $500 billion to clean up.[3] Making a good guess proved difficult, because EPA kept adding new substances to the list of what were considered hazardous wastes. "EPA does not know whether it has identified 90 percent of the hazardous waste that needs to be regulated or only 10 percent," GAO concluded. "This uncertainty is due to EPA's lack of focus and changing approaches in its waste identification efforts."[4]

The second question was which dump sites EPA should attack first. This question created an imposing political dilemma. Having recognized the risk from old toxic waste dumps and promised a cleanup, Congress had raised the political stakes around every waste dump in the country. Every citizen living near a potentially hazardous dump—and every member of Congress representing that citizen—wanted it cleaned up before the waste could cause any harm. At the same time EPA obviously could not clean up every waste dump immediately. Assigning priorities to competing sites not only created enormous

3. *Oversight of the Environmental Protection Agency's Management Review of the Superfund Program,* Hearings before the Senate Committee on Environment and Public Works, 101 Cong. 1 sess. (Government Printing Office, 1989), p. 20; Office of Technology Assessment, *Coming Clean: Superfund Problems Can Be Solved,* OTA-ITE-433 (October 1989), p. 27; and General Accounting Office, *Cleaning Up Hazardous Wastes: An Overview of Superfund Reauthorization Issues,* RCED-85-69 (March 29, 1985), p. ii.

4. General Accounting Office, *Environmental Protection Agency Issues,* OCG-89-20TR (November 1989), p. 9.

political risks for the agency, but also entailed exceptionally difficult technical problems. The relatively new science on which the priorities would be based could not answer with certainty a host of questions. Above what threshold would a carcinogen prove dangerous? What were the likely effects of different exposures to toxic chemicals, especially of low-level exposures over a lifetime? Were children more vulnerable than others? The technical uncertainties, in turn, worsened EPA's political problems.

Third, the debate over cleaning up toxic waste often proceeded as if everyone knew how to do it. The technical problems, however, proved far more difficult than anyone ever anticipated. Neutralizing toxic waste is a cutting-edge technology, and different waste sites posed different problems. Simply protecting the workers from exposure demanded development of new protective suits and equipment, as well as means to monitor the level of exposure. Finding ways to dispose of the sludge permanently and safely as cheaply and quickly as possible proved a daunting puzzle.[5]

Fourth, how clean was clean? The answer was simple if EPA only had to remove or neutralize the toxic waste, but in most cases the waste had leached into the soil or oozed into the water supply. Getting it all out was virtually impossible. EPA officials had to decide just what "cleaning up" meant. On one hand, they wanted to ensure that the cleanup removed enough of the hazard to prevent future health problems. On the other hand, they did not want to spend any more time or money on any one site than necessary, since that slowed progress on other sites. The technical uncertainties underlying the question made striking the proper balance difficult.

Because of these problems, the government could not rely on competition among private suppliers to structure the market. The government could not say with precision what it wanted to buy, and, in any event no off-the-shelf technology was available. Furthermore, without the stimulus of the Superfund program, it seemed unlikely that the private market, which had created the mess to begin with, would have produced the technology to clean it up.

With the prospect of billions of dollars of government business for years to come, however, private suppliers jumped into the market for

5. General Accounting Office, *Hazardous Waste: Uncertainties of Existing Data*, PEMD-87-11BR (February 1987).

cleanup technology. The Superfund program guaranteed these suppliers not only government contracts to clean up existing hazardous waste sites but also contracts with private manufacturers struggling to meet EPA's tough new antipollution standards. Competition among suppliers was lively. The Superfund market thus had a moderate level of imperfections on the supply side.

Imperfections on the demand side were relatively high, however. Without government regulation, demand for cleanup services by the polluters was low. Government itself stimulated the demand but lacked the basic expertise to know what job had to be done or how to do it. Congressionally mandated personnel ceilings, moreover, made it impossible for government to do the job itself. EPA therefore came to rely on contractors for nearly every phase of Superfund work. It structured the market, while private companies did the job. The peculiar structure of this market had important effects on the Superfund program's performance.

Controlling the Market

Before it was given responsibility for implementing the Superfund program, EPA was predominantly a regulatory agency that set pollution abatement standards. Private companies, as well as state and local governments, were responsible for meeting those standards, while state governments frequently were charged with administering them. With Superfund, however, EPA became not only a regulatory agency but also an agency with significant operational responsibilities. The program required the companies that had created the hazardous sites to pay for the cleanup. If the companies—called "responsible parties"—could not be located, if they could not pay, or if legal disputes dragged out questions of financial liability, EPA would engage a private contractor to remediate (clean up) the site and would pay for the cleanup with federal funds.[6] The agency, however, was unprepared in several ways to undertake the management necessary to ensure that the contractors acted efficiently and effectively.

6. State governments were responsible for 10 percent of costs when the Superfund program financed the cleanup. See OTA, *Coming Clean*, p. 7.

The Superfund Process

The administrative process for Superfund was complex (figure 5-2).[7] The first step entailed the discovery of possible hazardous waste sites. Through complaints by citizens and local officials, investigation by scientists, and other means, EPA was alerted to the presence of a potentially dangerous dump, which was then placed on an inventory of locations that might receive future attention. If the site appeared to pose imminent risks or if the hazard was likely to grow worse if cleanup were delayed, EPA could issue a "removal action," which would remove the site from the inventory and list it for closer scrutiny.

These sites now entered the second, preremedial, phase, the process of assessing whether the site required remedial action. Sites first received a preliminary assessment and, if the problem seemed serious enough, a site inspection. An elaborate scoring system rated the site's hazards and allowed EPA to compare it with other sites around the country. If the score assigned to the site was high enough, it went on a national priority list, the master catalog of the nation's most dangerous hazardous waste sites.

EPA then launched the remedial process for the worst sites. A "remedial investigation and feasibility study" examined the options for cleaning up the waste. In this stage neighbors and other members of the public had an opportunity to comment on the options. EPA then issued its decision about what method it had chosen, if any, for cleaning up the debris and why. The most critical step in the entire process, this "record of decision" was a kind of contract that detailed the government's pledge to make the site safe and identified the important problems to be solved and the technologies that would be used. EPA then typically hired a contractor to design the engineering steps required to neutralize the waste. The actual cleanup, known simply as a remedial action, followed. When the work was completed, the site was deleted from the national priority list.

This winnowing required EPA to choose from hundreds of thousands of candidates the few hundred sites that would go on the national priority list, and then to narrow down still further the number

---

7. This discussion is drawn from Office of Technology Assessment, *Are We Cleaning Up? 10 Superfund Case Studies—A Special Report of OTA's Assessment on Superfund Implementation*, OTA-ITE-362 (June 1988), p. 3.

FIGURE 5-2. *The Superfund Process*

Discovery of sites	Preremedial process	Remedial process
1. Identification of sites 2. Site placed on inventory for possible future action 3. Removal action to begin study for possible cleanup	4. Preliminary assessment to determine whether cleanup might be needed 5. Site inspection to continue investigation 6. Scoring of site's problems 7. Placement on national priority list (NPL) if score is high enough	8. Remedial investigation and feasibility study to identify options 9. Record of decision, EPA's policy determination 10. Remedial design to plan cleanup 11. Remedial action to conduct cleanup 12. Completion of work and removal from NPL

of sites that it actually could clean up. By the end of the program's first decade, EPA had spent most of its money on site studies, administration, and management. Of the 1,200 sites on the national priority list in 1989, EPA had completed the cleanup at only 41 sites and had started on another 204.[8] Sites were being added to the national priority list faster than EPA could clean them up.

Government's Manpower Problems

Because of the program's complexity, EPA would have had to turn to outside contractors in any event. But a provision in the 1980 Superfund act that capped the amount EPA could spend to administer the program ensured that private contractors would be involved. Underestimating both the magnitude and complexity of the problem, Congress enacted the cap to limit EPA's ability to increase its own staff instead of tending to the cleanup. Legislators did not want EPA to delay the cleanup by building up an operating unit that would not be needed after the cleanup was completed. Congress has continued the spending cap ever since.

8. *Oversight of the Environmental Protection Agency's Management Review of the Superfund Program,* Hearings, Testimony of Richard L. Hembra, p. 3.

FIGURE 5-3. *Superfund Program Appropriations, Fiscal Years 1982-89*

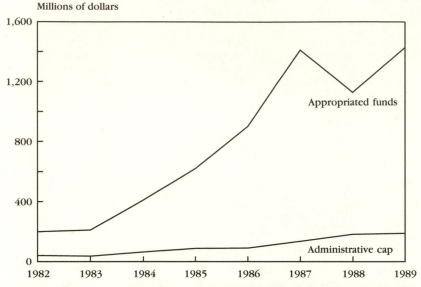

SOURCE: Office of Technology Assessment, *Assessing Contractor Use in Superfund:, A Background Paper of OTA's Assessment on Superfund Implementation,* OTA-BP-ITE-51 (January 1989), p. 11.

Congress initially allowed EPA to spend 21 percent of the program's budget on its own start-up administrative expenses. By fiscal year 1989 the cap had declined to 13 percent of appropriations (figure 5-3). Put differently, contractors spent nearly 90 percent of the Superfund budget. Over this period the total Superfund budget grew sevenfold, while EPA's administrative funds for Superfund grew only four and a half times.[9]

In addition to limited resources, EPA was also hampered by a lack of staff with expertise in toxic waste cleanup. One speaker at a 1986 conference on Superfund remarked, "There just aren't enough experienced people to do what EPA is being told to do."[10] Indeed, the demand, within both the government and private industry, for haz-

9. Office of Technology Assessment, *Assessing Contractor Use in Superfund: A Background Paper of OTA's Assessment on Superfund Implementation,* OTA-BP-ITE-51 (January 1989) p. 11.
10. OTA, *Assessing Contractor Use in Superfund,* p. 34.

ardous waste experts far outstripped the supply. Superfund was one of several government programs competing for such workers. The Department of Defense had found piles of toxic materials at military bases scheduled to be closed. These materials had to be neutralized before the bases could be converted to civilian uses. The Department of Energy had discovered a $100 billion (or more) problem in cleaning up its facilities for manufacturing nuclear weapons, as will be explored in the next chapter. Congress had also charged EPA with developing a program to clean up underground storage tanks that were leaking oil and gasoline into groundwater. Abandoned mines and mills had shafts, pits, and tailings that needed attention. Other public programs targeted substances such as asbestos and PCBs (polychlorinated biphenyls) for cleanup. All of these programs required people with technical expertise. To comply with government regulations and otherwise avoid potential problems, many private concerns launched their own cleanups; they too required experts to guide the work.

EPA's problems in cultivating the necessary expertise were made worse by unusually high turnover. The average tenure for Superfund remedial project managers, the officials responsible for supervising the cleanups in the field, was just eighteen months. Some contractors complained that they had had to deal with as many as four different project managers.[11] Annual turnover in some of EPA's ten regional offices reached as high as 30 percent of all staff. Turnover tended to be especially high in critical occupations, such as hydrologists and environmental engineers. Overall, the turnover rate among EPA workers detailed to the Superfund program was significantly higher than for federal employees as a whole.[12]

The high rates of turnover undermined EPA's ability to manage Superfund. "The high turnover of personnel," OTA argued in 1989, "robs the program of an ability to develop a sufficient, experienced core technical staff. The lack of a stable core of expertise prevents the program from attaining a high level of efficiency and from routinely making sound, consistent environmental decisions."[13] EPA's own in-

11. Acton, *Understanding Superfund,* p. 56.
12. General Accounting Office, *Superfund: Improvements Needed in Work Force Management,* RCED-88-1 (October 1987), pp. 42–43.
13. OTA, *Assessing Contractor Use in Superfund,* p. 31.

spector general, John C. Martin, acknowledged that high turnover tended to produce wide variances in program management among EPA's administration regions.[14] It also produced a bias in favor of funding cleanups through Superfund instead of attempting to force the industries who created the problems to remove them. EPA officials often found it easier to supervise private contractors doing the work directly for EPA than to negotiate complex agreements with the parties responsible for the dumps. High turnover thus led the government to pay more for the program.[15]

The primary cause of the high turnover rate was low salaries. EPA's frontline managers, who make the key decisions for each site, might earn less than $20,000 a year while supervising several multimillion dollar contracts.[16] Lack of advancement opportunities in the federal government, problems with regional managers, poor use of managers' skills, and disillusionment with the cleanup process also contributed heavily to the high turnover. Of those who left, nearly half took jobs in private industry, primarily in the hazardous waste field; on average, the job shift increased these workers' salaries by $7,000 a year.[17]

Lack of staff with adequate expertise makes it difficult for any government agency to assess contract proposals and to determine how well contractors are performing their work. In EPA's case those problems were exacerbated because the cleanup program has required the creation of technology at each step of the way.

Ironically, EPA has had to run training sessions for potential contractors, but it is the contractor, and not EPA, that then builds the expertise. "Because of the pull of the contractors," OTA noted, "instead of this expertise flowing *into* EPA, what expertise that does exist internally flows out. This leaves EPA personnel evaluating contractors who have at least some people with a better foundation in the basics and more experience."[18] Because most of that technological expertise

---

14. *Contracting at Environmental Protection Agency and Its Effect on Federal Employees,* Hearings before the House Committee on Post Office and Civil Service, 101 Cong. 1 sess. (GPO, 1989), Statement of John C. Martin, p. 41.

15. Acton, *Understanding Superfund,* p. 56.

16. OTA, *Assessing Contractor Use in Superfund,* p. 3.

17. GAO, *Superfund: Improvements Needed in Work Force Management,* pp. 51–57.

18. OTA, *Assessing Contractor Use in Superfund,* p. 34 (emphasis in original).

resides with Superfund contractors, there has been little opportunity for EPA personnel to acquire their own know-how.

In creating a large and expanding market for hazardous waste disposal, the government had created a serious imbalance in the market for hazardous waste experts. The demands of these programs were growing far more quickly than the supply of available technicians. This, in turn, produced inefficiencies. Cleanups were not always done well and had to be repeated. Inexperienced firms won contracts for work they could not adequately perform. Salaries in the private sector escalated, and the higher they went, the further behind the government, with its fixed civil service salaries, fell. Workers EPA had trained all too often left for higher paying and more rewarding jobs in the private sector, where they did the work that new and less skilled EPA employees would have to supervise. The agency's ability to supervise the program gradually eroded.

Role of the Contractors

EPA's lack of expertise meant that the agency had to rely on contractors to carry out virtually every part of the Superfund program. "Superfund could not exist without contractors," OTA concluded in 1989.[19] One OTA official captured the critical issue. "EPA signs the documents, the policy statements and the checks, and thus officially makes the decisions," he told a Senate committee. "But it really is another reality out there, and we raise the question: Is the Government really in control of Superfund when nearly all the important information, the analyses and ideas come from consultants and contractors?"[20]

Over time more and more of the key decisions flowed to contractors along with EPA's expertise. Superfund created "a huge new industry of environmental consultants," according to a report by the Hazardous Waste Treatment Council.[21] Within this industry contractors came to

19. OTA, *Assessing Contractor Use in Superfund*, p. 44.

20. *Examination of the Use of Consultants by the Environmental Protection Agency*, Hearings before the Senate Committee on Governmental Affairs, 101 Cong. 1 sess. (GPO, 1989), Testimony of Joel Hirschorn, p. 8.

21. OTA, *Assessing Contractor Use in Superfund*, p. 28.

decide which sites most needed to be cleaned up, how best to clean them up, and whether the cleanups were successful. The program's complexity and technical uncertainty put a high premium on the judgments of experts, and those experts were in the employment of contractors.[22] Representative Gerry Sikorski, the chair of the House Subcommittee on Civil Service, worried that EPA was "in serious danger of losing control over mandates which have been entrusted to it by Congress, and in danger of losing the remaining dedicated civil servants employed by the Agency."[23]

Moreover, contractors were involved not only in the actual business of cleanup, but in the minutiae of EPA management and policymaking. Contractors helped EPA respond to congressional inquiries, analyze legislation, and draft regulations and standards. Contractors even drafted records of decisions, the central documents guiding what would be cleaned up and how.[24] Contractors researched Freedom of Information Act requests received by the agency. They drafted memos, international agreements, and congressional testimony for top EPA officials. A geologist working for one contractor spent some of his time at EPA filing reports, answering the phone, updating lists, and preparing charts for EPA officials. Contractors trained and wrote statements of work for other contractors and then evaluated their performance. They even wrote the Superfund program's annual report to Congress. EPA did make occasional changes in the contractors' work, Senator David Pryor observed. For the annual report, for example, EPA replaced the contractor's letterhead with its own and replaced three words: two "ands" and one "the." "These consultants are not just editing and advising," Pryor said in 1989. "In fact, it is my belief that they are, in some cases, actually performing the basic work of the agency."[25]

22. OTA, *Assessing Contractor Use in Superfund*, p. 25.
23. *Contracting at Environmental Protection Agency and Its Effect on Federal Employees*, Hearings, p. 2.
24. *Examination of the Use of Consultants by the Environmental Protection Agency*, Hearings, Statement of Senator David Pryor and staff report, pp. 20, 31; *Contracting at Environmental Protection Agency and Its Effect on Federal Employees*, Hearings, pp. 33–37; and OTA, *Assessing Contractor Use in Superfund*.
25. *Contracting at Environmental Protection Agency and Its Effect on Federal Employees*, Hearings, p. 3; and *Examination of the Use of Consultants by the Environmental Protection Agency*, Hearings, p. 17.

Occasionally, EPA employees directed contractors to start work before the contracts had even been signed. In nearly a third of the contract actions that EPA's inspector general investigated, EPA officials told contractors to perform tasks before they had been approved and funded by contract supervision officials. As a result, in just a small sample of cases, contractors incurred costs of half a million dollars for work that had not been properly authorized. In another case, a contractor incurred costs of $800,000, 57 percent of the total for the project, before the project was finally approved. If EPA had found the original plan unacceptable or wanted to suggest changes, it probably would have had to pay for the unauthorized work anyway. In virtually all cases, the contractors were paid even though the sloppy procedures violated EPA's procurement regulations.[26]

Such problems grew over the years. EPA's reliance on contractors increased in part because of management changes in the late 1980s. A strategy intended to decentralize EPA management, increase competition among the contractors, and speed up the cleanup process replaced a handful of nationwide contracts with forty or more regional contracts. The strategy may have speeded the cleanup, but it placed the responsibility for monitoring contractors in EPA's regional offices, where staff turnover was highest and where the lack of clear central direction virtually guaranteed wide disparities in operations. The task of managing and monitoring the Superfund contracts was daunting, in part because of their sheer volume. By the late 1980s EPA had about 1,250 active contracts, most for Superfund, but that number understated the scope of contract activity. In its search for operating flexibility, EPA had begun to rely on "contract actions" rather than new contracts. When new problems with specific cleanups emerged, EPA negotiated contract actions—contract modifications, change orders, and funding increases—with the contractors. Although the number of active contracts actually declined from 1,482 in fiscal 1984 to 1,246 in fiscal 1988, the number of contract actions more than doubled from 4,530 to 10,912.[27] Each contract action required additional ad-

---

26. *Contracting at Environmental Protection Agency and Its Effect on Federal Employees*, Hearings, pp. 51–53.

27. *Contracting at Environmental Protection Agency and Its Effect on Federal Employees*, Hearings, p. 11.

ministrative work at EPA and imposed new oversight burdens on EPA officials.

Conflicts of Interest

With the supply of expertise so small and demand so great and growing, many contractors work simultaneously for both EPA and the industries that created the sites EPA is seeking to clean up. Furthermore, the network of contractors is a tangled one. A former employee of EPA's inspector general office noted that "there were problems identifying where contractors were subcontractors to other contractors on sites." In fact, she said, "Major contractors [were] subcontracting to other contractors all over the place. And if you tried to get the information, there was no index that you could go to that would let you know where the contractors were on site."[28] EPA did not know who was doing what where.

This tangled web led inevitably to many conflicts of interest. GAO, for example, found that a subcontractor at one Superfund site was also working for the company that had created the hazardous waste that contaminated the site. When preliminary hearings began to settle who would pay for the cleanup and what would be done, the subcontractor attempted to represent both sides. The subcontractor denied any conflict of interest, but EPA officials ruled that the subcontractor could not work for both sides. The subcontractor reluctantly agreed to drop part of its business and continue its Superfund subcontract. GAO, as well as congressional staff, found similar conflict-of-interest problems in other investigations.[29]

Some companies blatantly advertised their work with EPA in soliciting the business of private companies. A magazine advertisement placed by one of EPA's biggest contractors read: "Unlike other firms, we understand not only the technical engineering and remediation aspects of hazardous waste management, but also the framework of

28. *Activities of EPA's Office of Inspector General*, Hearings before the House Committee on Energy and Commerce, 101 Cong. 2 sess. (GPO, 1990), Testimony of Deidre M. Tanaka, p. 95. See also *Contracting at Environmental Protection Agency and Its Effect on Federal Employees*, Hearings, Statement of Richard L. Hembra, p. 24.

29. General Accounting Office, *Superfund Contracts: EPA's Procedures for Preventing Conflicts of Interest Need Strengthening*, RCED-89-57 (February 1989), p. 28. See also *Examination of the Use of Consultants by the Environmental Protection Agency*, Hearings, p. 42.

regulatory requirements, enforcement, and public involvement in which our clients must operate." Indeed, the company was in an especially good position to advise other parties on EPA's policies. It had EPA contracts to help write job descriptions for EPA employees, prepare statements of work for other EPA contractors, advise local citizens about how to get support on hazardous waste issues, analyze legislation affecting Superfund, draft documents, and write regulations.[30] Other firms actively recruited EPA employees who knew EPA's plans for future regulations.[31] Who better to advise on complying with federal regulations and to compete for upcoming contracts than the people who drafted the regulations and shaped the contracts in the first place?

Further complicating the conflict-of-interest problem were fundamental changes in the hazardous waste industry. Although hundreds of private contractors worked in the field, most of the business was highly concentrated; just six firms received 70 percent of Superfund's contract dollars. The limited expertise available in the private marketplace tended to favor those firms that could assemble a critical mass of experts. Once they received contracts, they could build greater expertise, which only increased their ability to win future business.

As the industry began to mature, it became vertically integrated.[32] Several firms that actively helped EPA write the regulations and determine which sites would be cleaned up and which technologies would be used also began to perform the cleanups as well. Clear conflicts of interest became harder to avoid. Initial studies could be written to favor certain regulations, certain regulations could favor particular technologies, and firms could then stand ready to offer those technologies, both to private companies, who had no choice if they were to comply with federal cleanup regulations, and to EPA who had the funding but no independent expertise to judge the effectiveness of the cleanup plan. EPA officials acknowledged the potential for conflicts of interest but maintained that the existing system worked well, since few actual cases of conflict of interest had been uncovered.

30. *Examination of the Use of Consultants by the Environmental Protection Agency,* Hearings, p. 18. The text of the ad appears on p. 86 of the hearings. The company is ICF Incorporated of Fairfax, Virginia.

31. *Examination of the Use of Consultants by EPA,* Hearings, p. 40.

32. OTA, *Assessing Contractor Use in Superfund,* p. 36.

GAO questioned those assurances: "Because of the weaknesses we found in the system, we question whether EPA can reasonably ensure that conflicts are not occurring." Without developing an adequate system for cataloging contracts and subcontracts, and without adequate in-house expertise to judge the work being done for the agency, EPA could not independently assess either the quality of the cleanups or the conflicts of interest that might occur, GAO said in a 1989 report.[33]

Program Oversight

If EPA faced problems in determining whether it was making the right decisions about specific cleanups, it had even more problems controlling costs and determining whether the contractors it hired were performing as promised. EPA, in fact, was spending billions of dollars on Superfund cleanups, with little information about what it was actually accomplishing. The agency had not set clear goals about what it wanted to achieve, nor had it developed adequate yardsticks for recognizing good program administration, either by its employees or by contractors. In one of its transition reports prepared during the 1988 presidential election campaign, GAO was especially blunt:

EPA does not know whether many multibillion-dollar environmental programs are effective in achieving planned goals, because its evaluation information is misleading, inadequate, or incomplete. Shortfalls abound in the basic descriptive information needed to establish and monitor environmental regulations, and the effects of some costly environmental programs that entail considerable compliance burdens are undocumented.[34]

EPA's cost control problems began with the type of contract it awarded. Nearly all Superfund contracts were of the cost-plus-award-fee type.[35] In the arcane world of government procurement, this meant

33. GAO, *Superfund Contracts: EPA's Procedures Need Strengthening*, p. 33.
34. General Accounting Office, *Program Evaluation Issues*, OCG-899-8TR (November 1988), p. 15.
35. General Accounting Office, *Superfund Contracts: EPA Needs to Control Contractor Costs*, RCED-88-182 (July 1988), pp. 18.

that EPA agreed to reimburse contractors for their costs plus a guaranteed profit, which for Superfund contractors, amounted to 3 percent of the reimbursed costs. Contractors were also eligible for an award fee of up to 7 percent of their costs, depending on EPA's assessment of their work. These cost-plus contracts had important advantages for EPA. They could be awarded quickly to get cleanups started, and they gave EPA great flexibility in working with the contractors, especially in adapting to the specific problems that individual hazardous waste sites produced. Instead of being held captive by the ceiling imposed through a fixed-price contract, in which a contractor agreed to accomplish the job for a price determined in advance, EPA could alter the work plans. The contractor would then bill the agency for its costs plus its fee. As jobs evolved, so too could the agency's agreement with its contractors. Faced with overwhelming incentives to move quickly, EPA found this flexibility attractive.

The cost-plus contracts were attractive to the contractors for even more obvious reasons. The higher the dollar amount of the contract, the higher the contractor's profit. If the contract amount for a project is fixed, contractors can increase their profits by becoming more efficient and reducing their costs. If the government agrees to reimburse a contractor for all of its costs, plus a fee on top of those costs, the contractor's incentives are to encourage cost increases.

Such contracts make sense when great flexibility is important, but they require stringent oversight by the government agency. EPA's problems in building expertise, however, made effective oversight difficult. GAO found, for example, that some contractors received substantial performance fees for clearly substandard performance. One contractor, with the lowest performance of any contractor examined in the GAO study, received a substantial award fee plus the full base fee. The study concluded that EPA did not gather enough information to make judgments about the contractors' performance, and that the award fee structure "does not sufficiently provide an incentive for . . . contractors to perform at satisfactory or better levels." In fact, GAO found, contractors received a substantial portion of their fees before enough of the work had been completed to assess its quality.[36]

36. GAO, *Superfund Contracts: EPA Needs to Control Contractor Costs,* pp. 18, 49–51.

Other indicators show that careful management of Superfund contractors and control of contractor cost was clearly not a top priority for EPA. Under federal procurement policy, agencies were required to report to a central data collection center on the use of contractors. EPA consistently underreported the number of contractors it used, in part because of governmentwide confusion over how to report the number and value of contracts. One year EPA made no report at all to the data center. EPA also tended purposely to embrace a narrow definition of just what constituted a contract to minimize the contractors' apparent role in managing the program.[37]

EPA also had difficulty tracking how Superfund monies were spent. GAO found, for example, that one contractor had billed EPA for the cost of tickets to professional sporting events among $2.3 million in unallowable costs and another $266,500 in questionable charges.[38] According to GAO investigators, EPA did not review most invoices submitted by contractors before paying them. EPA managers said they were reluctant to check the invoices closely because they viewed themselves as environmental specialists, not accountants, so careful checks of the invoices lay beyond their job assignments.[39] The program, as a result, was often managed according to what the contractors, not EPA, saw as proper activities.

The Audit Process

Some of EPA's difficulty in tracking Superfund spending stemmed from the complex audit process that all federal agencies used. The federal government for years has relied on "single focal point" audits, in which the government agency with the most business with a contractor is responsible for auditing all the federal money that contractor receives. The single focal point audit has two major advantages. With a single, comprehensive overview, contractors find it far more difficult to juggle funds among different accounts representing different federal agencies. Contractors, moreover, face only one round of audits

37. *Examination of the Use of Consultants by EPA*, Hearings, Testimony of Bernard J. Ungar, p. 34.

38. General Accounting Office, *Federally Sponsored Contracts: Unallowable and Questionable Costs Claimed by CH2M Hill*, T-RCED-92-37 (March 19, 1992), p. 2.

39. General Accounting Office, *Superfund: EPA Has Not Corrected Long-Standing Contract Management Problems*, RCED-92-45 (October 1991), p. 26.

instead of a ceaseless parade of investigators from every agency with which they do business.

For EPA the single focal point means that the Pentagon's Defense Contract Audit Agency conducts most of its audits, since most of its contractors do more business with the Department of Defense than with EPA or other federal agencies. The concentration of auditing, coupled with the overall manpower shortage of federal auditors, however, has produced huge delays in auditing EPA programs. By October 1990, GAO found 2,400 expired EPA contracts worth $4.1 billion that had not been closed out with a final audit. Many final audits, in fact, were often delayed four years.[40] Because EPA rarely has audit results while contracts are still active, it pays for costs that might be later disallowed in the audit. Once paid, disallowed costs are difficult to recover. Furthermore, ineligible costs can escalate without the government's knowledge.[41]

Such problems did emerge in the Superfund program. One audit found that $180,000 in labor costs had been incorrectly charged to the government over a three-year period. Another audit team could not locate more than half of a sample of a contractor's employees that the contractor claimed was working on an EPA project. The contractor was being paid, but its workers could not be found.[42] A GAO investigation discovered that poor subcontractor performance was increasing the cost of site studies in more than half of the sites in its sample. In most cases EPA had not challenged the costs. GAO worried that EPA was "conveying a message to contractors that it is willing to accept all costs regardless of the level of performance provided, thereby lessening the contractors' incentives to control costs."[43]

Even when problems were identified, there was no guarantee that they would be corrected. EPA had neither a solid system for following up on issues nor adequate staff to do the job. "A substantial investment in training and the development of new audit and investigative approaches" would be needed to curb Superfund's vulnerability to

40. *Activities of EPA's Office of Inspector General,* Hearings, Testimony of Richard L. Hembra, pp. 105–109.

41. *Activities of EPA's Office of Inspector General,* Hearings, Testimony of David J. O'Connor, p. 220.

42. *Activities of EPA's Office of Inspector General,* Hearings, p. 101.

43. GAO, *Superfund Contracts: EPA Needs to Control Contractor Costs,* p. 3.

fraud, waste, and abuse, EPA's inspector general once wrote.[44] Moreover, EPA's administrative structure made oversight even more difficult. Contracts were managed by ten regional offices, but the contractors operated throughout the nation, making it difficult, if not impossible, for a single regional office to monitor all of the activities of a single contractor. For the very reasons that prompted the federal government to move to the single focal point audit process, EPA's decentralized management structure is especially ill equipped to supervise the vast operations of its contractor network.[45]

Getting the Money Out

EPA's resources went primarily to getting the money out the door instead of examining how the money was spent. From fiscal 1984 to fiscal 1988, EPA's contract management staff (almost all assigned to Superfund contracts) grew 49 percent, more than twice as fast as the rate for all EPA employees. The contract management staff was charged with preparing the contracts and supervising payments. Responsibility for overseeing the *performance* of the contractors, however, rested with EPA's program staff, which did not enjoy nearly as large an increase in size, especially compared with the increased number of contracts they had to monitor. Half of all professional and administrative staff were involved in the contracting process, GAO estimated. Of all of these employees, EPA tended to view the contract management staff as the most important. Without these officials, contracts could not be signed, and without signed contracts, there could be no program.[46]

When EPA sought to determine what was happening with its money, it, like most federal agencies, relied on outsiders. To collect information on what its contractors were doing—often in response to congressional inquiries, local questions, or complaints by affected parties—the agency "often paid more money either to the original contractor to reexamine the work or to another contractor to repeat the work," OTA reported. "Although there are some very experienced

44. OTA, *Assessing Contractor Use in Superfund*, p. 9.
45. *Activities of EPA's Office of Inspector General*, Hearings, Testimony of Dennis B. Wilson, p. 7.
46. *Contracting at EPA and Its Effect on Federal Employees*, Hearings, pp. 11–12.

and expert staff at EPA, for the most part there is very little internal government capability, both [in] expertise and time, to *independently* check contested contractor work."[47]

Contractors who check their own work are clearly vulnerable to conflicts of interest. Contractors who check the work of other contractors might encounter one of two problems. On one hand, contractors who find fault with other contractors might be suspected of trying to undermine their competitors. On the other hand, contractors might well be reluctant to raise issues for fear of jeopardizing future relations with other contractors. This is a particular problem for Superfund contractors who frequently team up on projects.[48]

Moreover, because contractors have prepared most of the site studies and work plans, "EPA, in effect, has allowed the contractors to establish the parameters it uses in measuring the reasonableness of contractor cost proposals," GAO contended.[49] In other words, EPA has little capacity to judge for itself whether costs are reasonable.

Although EPA has acknowledged its problems, GAO contends that the agency has done little to solve them. In a report released in 1992, GAO concluded:

Despite several years of GAO's reporting on deficiencies in EPA's Superfund contract management, EPA has not adequately addressed most of GAO's recommendations to reduce the program's vulnerability to fraud, waste, and abuse. Controls over contractor costs, such as critical reviews of contractor cost proposals and invoices, are still not being fully used. In addition, contractor program management costs are excessive because EPA hired more contractors than it needed and then moved slowly to reduce its excess capacity. . . . Moreover, Superfund remains vulnerable to contractors' conflicts of interest because EPA contracting officials still need better guidance, and field checks of contractors' compliance with conflict-of-interest rules have not yet been performed.[50]

47. OTA, *Assessing Contractor Use in Superfund,* p. 24.
48. *Examination of the Use of Consultants by the Environmental Protection Agency,* Hearings, p. 9.
49. GAO, *Superfund Contracts: EPA Needs to Control Contractor Costs,* p. 19.
50. GAO, *Superfund: EPA Has Not Corrected Long-Standing Management Problems,* p. 5.

EPA simply was not looking hard enough, with enough people in the best ways, to determine how well Superfund and its contractors were working. When it did look, it engaged in what OTA called "over-simplified 'bean counting' of results instead of [evaluating] what those results mean technically and what they accomplish environmentally." When EPA did uncover problems, the program's high demands coupled with the limited supply of qualified contractors made it unlikely that poor quality work would cost contractors their reputations or business.[51]

EPA thus tended to be isolated from debate about its own performance. Although EPA officials retained final decisionmaking authority, they knew only what the contractors were telling them. They could consider only those options that contractors suggested and could assess only those technologies that the contractors developed. Formal authority without the technical base to use it effectively was hollow indeed.

Agency Cultures

Further weakening EPA's contract management were the cultures that grew up within the agency. Principal responsibility for managing the contracts was vested in EPA's lower-level professionals, who received little appreciation and few rewards for their work. Mid-level managers worried about performance but paid little attention to the contractors who were doing the work. Top officials were primarily concerned with politics. At the beginning of the 1980s several high EPA officials were caught in scandals that cost them their jobs. Their replacements concentrated in the latter part of the decade on restoring EPA's badly damaged reputation and political standing. The lack of a common focus among these three distinct cultures increased EPA's reliance on its contractors for substantive decisions and reduced the agency's ability to manage the contractors effectively.

Technical Managers

Internal EPA research revealed that half of EPA's professional and administrative employees were involved in some way with managing

51. OTA, *Are We Cleaning Up?* p. 1; and OTA, *Assessing Contractor Use in Super-fund,* p. 28.

contracts.[52] That was the natural result of policy decisions to increase the size of the programs EPA administered, especially Superfund, without a corresponding increase in employees. Project officers hired to handle the technical details of EPA projects found themselves managing contracts instead.[53] Few were trained for the shift in roles.

Although most of the staff working with contracts at EPA headquarters had substantial experience in government, little of it was in management. Two-thirds of these professionals had completed graduate work, but most of their studies were in the physical sciences. EPA found itself with too little of the right kind of expertise. The agency employees best equipped to perform technical oversight found themselves preoccupied with the administrative details of getting the contracts out the door.[54] There was thus a significant mismatch between their training and their work. EPA was "slow to recognize that different skills are needed to fulfill these changing roles," an internal EPA report concluded.[55]

The problem was worse in EPA's regional offices, where staff experience tended to be lower and turnover was often exceptionally high, especially for officials managing the Superfund program. These field officials had the frontline responsibility for administering the program, yet they had the least training in hazardous waste issues, little management experience, and short tenure at EPA. A majority of these frontline managers worried that they had little control over the program or its costs. What control there was lay in the hands of contract officers, and the concern of the contract officers was mainly with getting the contracts approved.[56]

Moreover, the technical people assigned to contract mangement had little incentive to do that job well. In an agency dominated by scientists, technical expertise, not administrative finesse, marked the fast track upward. Technicians and other scientifically trained contract managers thus had strong motivation to escape from the task—what one official called the "administrative stigma"—as quickly as possible.

52. Environmental Protection Agency, *Contracts Management: The People and the Process* (November 1988), p. 3.

53. EPA, *Contracts Managment*, pp. 47–48.

54. EPA, *Contracts Management*, app. A, p. 14.

55. EPA, *Contracts Management*, p. 48.

56. GAO, *Superfund Contracts: EPA Needs to Control Contractor Costs*, p. 38.

Sometimes, an EPA report said, "contracts management tend[ed] to be dumped on poor performers" because it was not a high-prestige task.[57] The culture of the lower-level contract managers thus only aggravated the erosion of authority to the contractors.

Senior Management

The views of EPA's senior managers could scarcely be more different from those of the contract managers they supervised. Senior managers believed that the contracting process was working well and liked the flexibility that the cost-plus contracts offered, especially given the agency's tight manpower situation. In reality, an EPA survey showed, "Most managers had only passing knowledge of the actual extent of contracting in their organizations." Except for occasional crises, they distanced themselves from the contracting process. Contracting, to them, was simply "a collateral duty" that took up relatively little of their employees' time. There was little understanding of the central role that contracting, and contract management, played in EPA's programs.[58]

Instead, as an EPA report explained, senior managers were interested in the product, not the process. They concentrated on tracking the budget, since overruns and other budgetary problems tended to cause them far greater and more immediate difficulty. They gave little weight to contract management in evaluating employee performance.[59] The key, as Superfund's manager put it, was thinking "in terms of getting the job done as well as management of the contracts."[60] Because EPA had not clearly defined its Superfund goals, holding senior managers accountable for the performance of their programs was extremely difficult. The annual appropriations process forced budget numbers into place as a proxy. Once focused on the numbers, however, senior managers became even more distant from the details of what actually was happening in the field.

The result was great flexibility in the program but little central direction. EPA's regions and their contractors had enormous maneu-

57. EPA, *Contracts Management*, pp. 3, 43, 44, 59.
58. EPA, *Contracts Management*, pp. 37, 39, 43.
59. EPA, *Contracts Management*, pp. 38, 40.
60. *Examination of the Use of Consultants by the Environmental Protection Agency*, Hearings, Testimony of Henry L. Longest, II, p. 19.

vering room, but that made Superfund "a loose assembly of disparate working parts," as OTA put it, "a system of divided responsibilities and dispersed operations."[61] Senior EPA managers in fact had relatively little management control over their programs.

Political Appointees

Scandals preoccupied EPA's political appointees for much of Superfund's first decade. Rita Lavelle, the program's first manager during the Reagan administration, was fired in 1983 for political manipulation of the program and conflicts of interest. She was convicted of having lied about her involvement in a case involving her former employer, Aerojet-General Corporation, and was sentenced to six months in prison and fined $10,000. She was also accused of withholding Superfund money from the Stringfellow Acid Pits in California to avoid helping the election campaign of Democratic gubernatorial candidate Edmund G. Brown, Jr., of shredding evidence about other political manipulations of the program, and of keeping a political hit list to target EPA employees who disagreed with the Reagan administration's philosophy. In all, more than twenty EPA officials, including EPA administrator Ann Burford, resigned following investigations into the scandals.

When William D. Ruckelshaus returned in May 1983 for a second stint as EPA administrator, he faced an enormous task in rebuilding the agency's once-shiny public image and in restoring the morale of its employees. Within a year, he had the Superfund program moving again, only to face in 1985 a difficult debate over the program's reauthorization. The first few years of site investigations had revealed the problem to be far larger and far more difficult to resolve than anyone had anticipated. Progress was slow and the agency's critics were still suspicious that EPA was deliberately dragging its feet to slow the cleanup and protect private business from the costs involved. Trying to decide just how big the problem was, how to try to solve it, how to win enough money to do the job, how to convince Congress that the agency could be trusted to spend it well, and how to regain support from the agency's important interest groups preoccupied

61. OTA, *Are We Cleaning Up?* p. 1.

EPA's top officials. The details of contract management did not even appear on this overwhelming agenda.

EPA's political appointees thus concentrated on EPA's big battles and left the details to lower-level officials. Senior managers grabbed the few handles that existed on the program, especially the budget issues, but that left them little leverage over the contractors. Faced with the overwhelming pressure for results from above, short-handed technical managers tried to keep the creaky machinery moving. They had little time, and sometimes inadequate expertise, to manage what was actually happening when shovels met the dirt at the sites. The cultures at each level produced behavior that, from the perspective of each level, was reasonable and predictable. Put together, however, these cultures distanced EPA from control of its programs.

An Imperfect Marketplace

Few government programs have ever begun with greater expectations, more uncertainty, or more troubled first steps than Superfund. The tales of red ice and purple dogs bred fears of cancer and demands for immediate cleanups. In response to those demands, government created a market—and funded its expansion—but had neither the expertise nor the manpower to assess how effectively that market was functioning. At the same time, the structure of the market posed substantial problems that the agency struggled constantly to solve.

On the supply side—the companies interested in supplying hazardous waste expertise to the government and to private industry, which had to comply with government regulations—there was far less expertise than the market demanded. Competition was high, but the ability of either the market or the government to punish poor performers was limited. The market also promoted complex relationships among contractors, where contractors sometimes served as subcontractors for each other. These ties in turn created serious conflicts of interest. The government's cost-plus contracts, furthermore, established irresistible incentives for driving costs up and keeping business coming in.

On the demand side—the government's ability to specify clearly what it wanted to buy and to manage those purchases effectively—other market imperfections hindered performance. The uncertain dimensions of both the problem and the technology to cure it made it difficult for the government to write clear contracts and to conduct vigorous competition for them. Personnel shortages and high turnover within EPA, especially in frontline field offices, made it impossible for the agency to escape dependence on its contractors or, once the contracts were signed, to monitor them effectively. The special cultures at each level of the agency further undercut EPA's ability to manage Superfund. Information failures were high and the appetite for correcting the problems meager.

Despite these problems, contracting out was the only sensible way to manage the Superfund program. The alternative, after all, was to create a huge government bureaucracy to duplicate what could be done, often more cheaply and usually more flexibly, in the private sector. The lesson of Superfund, however, is that contracting out does not ensure efficiency or effectiveness. Creating a market does not ensure that it will operate well. Especially in a market with such significant imperfections on the demand side, vigorous oversight, by a smart-buying government, is essential. In Superfund, however, the incentives—on both the supply and the demand sides—undermined government's capacity to buy smart.

6

Nuclear Weapons Production: Bombs and Bomb Makers

In late 1987 investigative reporters for the *New York Times* began filing stories about serious environmental and safety problems at the nation's nuclear weapons production facilities. The public outcry that ensued forced the Department of Energy (DOE), which managed the facilities, to cut back or shut down four reactors used in the production process because of concerns about their safety. Meanwhile, investigations by a host of government agencies revealed that residents living near some of the production facilities had been exposed to uncontrolled release of radiation and contaminated groundwater. In an echo of Superfund, the General Accounting Office (GAO) reported that 3,500 inactive DOE waste sites—most containing toxic chemicals from the manufacturing process, not radioactive materials—dotted the nation.[1]

News stories charged that DOE, intent on continuing the production of nuclear weapons, pressed ahead despite safety worries and mounting evidence of waste problems. In a blunt editorial headlined "The Bomb Maker Becomes a Bomb," the *New York Times* warned in September 1988 that "extended lack of maintenance and

1. General Accounting Office, *DOE's Efforts to Correct Environmental Problems of the Nuclear Weapons Complex*, T-RCED-90-47 (March 15, 1990), Statement of Victor S. Rezendes, p. 3.

pollution control now endanger both national security and the environment."[2]

On the environmental side, problems plagued every part of the DOE weapons complex. Toxic and radioactive wastes were leaking from underground storage tanks in Hanford, Washington. Radioactive wastes at the Savannah River, South Carolina, facility were leaking into the groundwater. Plutonium, americium, and toxic chemicals contaminated the soil around the Rocky Flats, Colorado, plant. Virtually everywhere investigators looked, they found serious environmental threats to both plant workers and area residents.

One count turned up more than 1,700 health and safety problems inside DOE facilities. Of these, 113 presented "clear and present danger" to workers or the public, and another 150 posed "significant risk." Threats to the environment outside the plants totaled nearly 1,300, including 192 posing a high risk to health. Some of these problems occurred at nonnuclear facilities, such as the strategic petroleum reserves used to store oil for national emergencies, but the vast bulk were the legacy of decades of production and testing of nuclear weapons.[3]

On the national security side, the problems threatened to shut down the nation's production of nuclear weapons. The *Times* editorial quoted a former Pentagon official as cautioning that "the U.S. is one crippling breakdown away from incipient structural nuclear disarmament."

"We have a moral obligation to rectify past sins," DOE Under Secretary Joseph F. Salgado said in 1988.[4] Rectifying those sins was likely to cost $160 billion or more over thirty years, according to GAO.[5] That would rank the cleanup as one of the biggest engineering and public works projects of all time.

Complicating the cleanup was an extraordinarily intricate public-private partnership that had grown up around nuclear weapons production. When the federal government set out to develop an atomic

2. "The Bomb Maker Becomes A Bomb," *New York Times,* September 22, 1988, p. A38.

3. General Accounting Office, *Nuclear Health and Safety: Need for Improved Responsiveness to Problems at DOE Sites,* RCED-90-101 (March 1990).

4. Cass Peterson, "Weapons Reactors to Remain Closed Over Safety Concerns," *Washington Post,* October 12, 1988, p. A1.

5. General Accounting Office, *Energy Issues,* OCG-93-13TR (December 1992), p. 4.

bomb during World War II, virtually every facet of the development and production was well past the cutting edge of knowledge in physics and chemistry. Manufacturing the bomb demanded the creation of new techniques of separating, purifying, concentrating, assembling, and testing exotic materials such as plutonium whose behavior to that point had only been modeled uncertainly by scientists. The Manhattan Project, as the effort to make the bomb was called, was driven by the "imperative of shortening the war." That meant breaking through the technological barriers as fast as possible—and doing so before Germany did.[6]

Both the speed and the many different kinds of expertise required to make the bomb led inexorably to a close linkage between the Army and industry, instead of the arm's-length relationship that characterizes competitive markets. Traditional means of contracting, with bidders responding to government specifications, was impossible.[7] The Army had, or could arrange the resources, but private contractors and academicians had the expertise. Pragmatism dictated a problem-solving approach that paid little attention to organizational boundaries.

The government obviously could not allow private companies to get into the business of manufacturing and selling the weapons. At the same time, the government did not want to create a large government bureaucracy to manufacture the weapons. The most expeditious way to manufacture the first atomic weapons was for the government to hire private contractors with the needed skills to build and operate the laboratories and productions facilities. This policy gave birth to "GOCOs" (government-owned, contractor-operated facilities), which provided the operational model for all future nuclear weapons production.

As a result DOE and its predecessor agencies were little more than an administrative shell over a vast empire of contractors.[8] Because of

---

6. McGeorge Bundy, *Danger and Survival: Choices About the Bomb in the First Fifty Years* (Random House, 1988), p. 58. Although many involved with the Manhattan Project thought Germany was also trying to develop an atomic bomb, it turned out to be untrue. Such an effort "could not have succeeded under German war conditions," one scientist later explained. (Bundy, *Danger and Survival*, p. 22.) Instead, German scientific expertise went into rocketry.

7. Vincent C. Jones, *Manhattan: The Army and the Atomic Bomb* (Washington: U.S. Army, Center of Military History, 1985), pp. 95–116.

8. The Department of Energy grew from a complex organizational parentage. After

security worries and reliance on the contractors' expertise, moreover, each facility operated like a mini-fiefdom, controlled only loosely, at best, from Washington. By 1992 the nuclear weapons complex consisted of fourteen major facilities in thirteen states. DOE employed about 20,000 workers, but its contractors, such as du Pont, General Electric, Martin-Marietta, and Westinghouse, employed 141,000 workers.[9] Fully 80 to 90 percent of DOE's budget was spent through contractors.[10]

The government had little choice but to rely heavily on contractors. Within the bureaucracy it had neither the technical expertise nor the manufacturing capacity to build nuclear weapons. Moreover, the weapons complex performed with distinction for more than a generation, consistently producing weapons that outperformed those of other powers. Pressured by the strategic challenges of the cold war, however, neither the government nor its contractors took time to deal with the side effects, or externalities, of that production—namely, the threats to safety and the environment that stemmed from the production operations themselves and from the huge quantities of radioactive and toxic wastes they generated.

The externalities arose out of a combination of supply- and demand-side imperfections. On the supply side, national security and technical problems had from the beginning limited the number of sellers

---

World War II the Manhattan Project was transformed into the Atomic Energy Commission. An administrative reorganization during the Ford administration, in response to the Arab oil embargo, broadened the commission's business to research and development, especially of nontraditional energy sources. Along with the broader mission came a name change, to the Energy Research and Development Administration (ERDA). Then, in 1977, the Carter administration combined ERDA with the Federal Power Commission and the Federal Energy Administration to form the Department of Energy.

DOE's research and development mission—promoting windmills, solar panels, and similar alternative energy sources—is perhaps the one the public most recognizes. The department has also promoted development of advanced nuclear power systems, including safer fission and new fusion reactors. Until the late 1980s, however, DOE devoted most of its personnel and budget to the production of nuclear weapons. With the discovery of safety and environmental problems throughout the weapons complex, cleanup replaced production as the department's main mission.

9. Thomas W. Lippman, "For the Energy Nominee, an Arms Gap," *Washington Post National Weekly Edition,* December 28, 1992–January 3, 1993, p. 15.

10. *Oversight of the Structure and Management of the Department of Energy,* Staff Report, Senate Committee on Governmental Affairs, 96 Cong. 2 sess. (Government Printing Office, December 1980), p. 310.

in the market. On the demand side, government could define the product only by working in close partnership with the sellers' technical expertise. The relationship was virtually a seamless alliance, a monopoly of many sellers with only one buyer, instead of a competitive market.

Huge externalities in monopolistic markets are unusual. While there is no direct theoretical connection between externalities and the level of market competition, the usual argument is that externalities can be better policed in monopolistic markets. When sellers are concentrated, it is frequently easier to observe their behavior. In the nuclear weapons case, however, national security demands cloaked production in secrecy; anyone interested in overseeing DOE and its contractors had a difficult time obtaining information about what was going on at the production facilities. A monopoly of production led to a monopoly of information.

DOE had surprisingly little information about what its contractors were doing. At most facilities, contract employees far outnumbered DOE employees, who in any event were trained to administer contracts and not to oversee the contractors' performance. Moreover, cultures within DOE and between DOE field workers and their counterpart contract employees had developed over the years; for different reasons each of these cultures minimized the importance of the growing safety and environment problems. When, after the Soviet nuclear threat ended, DOE shifted its focus from weapons production to environmental cleanup, the department continued to find its path hindered by these entrenched cultures.

These cultures, or "internalities," had also contributed to a sticky political problem for DOE. With each revelation of a new environmental mess at one of its facilities, the credibility of DOE and its contractors sank even lower. DOE could regain its credibility only by dealing with the externalities the market had created, but because few other contractors had the necessary expertise, DOE had to rely on many of the very same contractors to clean up the mess they had created. In addition to the imposing technical challenges of ridding the weapons complex of nuclear waste, the department thus faced significant problems in restoring public trust and confidence in its operations.

Trouble at Rocky Flats

Nothing exemplifies the government's difficulties in managing the shifting mission of its nuclear weapons facilities more than DOE's experiences at its facility in Rocky Flats, Colorado, just sixteen miles northwest of Denver. For forty years, Rocky Flats had manufactured the "pit," or the plutonium trigger, for the hydrogen bomb. Rocky Flats was, in essence, a precision machine shop, devoted to forming plutonium to the exact tolerances required to make the trigger work. One of the most toxic substances on earth, plutonium kills quickly if taken into the body even in minute quantities, and it remains lethal for tens of thousands of years. Plutonium wastes generated at Rocky Flats posed an environmental problem that the government and its contractors were slow to recognize—and to deal with.

The Primacy of Production

The pit production process had for decades produced huge quantities of plutonium-contaminated waste: everything from rags used to wipe machines to metal shavings from the production line. Over the years, the plant's operators had used commonly accepted practices to dispose of the material. Waste, for example, had been sprayed onto the ground to evaporate the liquid portion away. Other waste had been put into metal drums, but over time the drums leaked and the waste contaminated the ground around them. Because of inadequate storage and treatment, much of the land and groundwater surrounding the plant became contaminated with both plutonium and chemical wastes. After a major fire in 1970, the earth was tainted with plutonium at concentrations higher than measured at Nagasaki, Japan, after the first atomic bomb was exploded in 1945.[11] Some toxic solvents had leached into the groundwater in concentrations 1,000 times higher than the acceptable limits for drinking water. Inspectors had found 108 separate waste dumps in the plant, some containing unknown substances.[12]

11. Fox Butterfield, "Dispute on Wastes Poses Threat to Operations of Weapons Plant," *New York Times,* October 21, 1988, p. D21.

12. General Accounting Office, *Nuclear Health and Safety: Summary of Major Problems at DOE's Rocky Flats Plant,* RCED-89-53BR (October 1988); and Office of Technology Assessment, *Complex Cleanup: The Environmental Legacy of Nuclear Weapons Production* (February 1991), especially p. 26.

Many of the plant's buildings, furthermore, were old and deteriorating; some needed virtually nonstop maintenance. A DOE internal study revealed that many of the buildings could not withstand high winds or earthquakes. Some buildings were without earthquake bracing for the sprinkler systems and had antiquated fire alarms. Monitoring of air quality inside the plant was deficient. All told, DOE found 230 separate safety and health problems inside the plant that added another layer to the waste problem.[13]

The full extent of the waste problem at Rocky Flats was not known, despite several investigations, nor did effective means to clean up the pollution appear to exist. Previously unknown problems continued to surface; solving them frequently took DOE into new, untested technologies. To clean up the plant DOE had to remove the waste to safer, long-term storage sites away from populated areas. State and federal regulations about transporting radioactive and hazardous wastes, however, made it impossible to ship much of the material because it was combustible or otherwise unstable. DOE simply did not know how to solve the problem.[14] Rocky Flats had become one of the most dangerous sites in the entire DOE complex. In a classic of understatement, GAO concluded in 1988 that "the situation at the plant is not amenable to any quick solution."[15]

Despite the mounting evidence of problems, DOE officials continued to insist during the 1980s that the Rocky Flats plant was "being operated in a safe and environmentally acceptable manner at technically acceptable levels of risk to the public." Members of a House Energy and Commerce subcommittee sharply disagreed, saying in 1989 that these assurances "are simply not true."[16]

Tipped off about alleged illegal disposal of toxic wastes and other violations of federal environmental laws, seventy FBI agents in June 1989 raided the plant, operated under contract by Rockwell Interna-

13. GAO, *Nuclear Health and Safety: Summary of Major Problems*, p. 4.
14. General Accounting Office, *Nuclear Materials: Removing Plutonium Residues from Rocky Flats Will Be Difficult and Costly*, RCED-92-219 (September 1992).
15. GAO, *Nuclear Health and Safety: Summary of Major Problems*, p. 5. See also *Health and Safety at the Department of Energy's Nuclear Weapons Facilities*, Report by the House Committee on Energy and Commerce, Subcommittee on Investigations, 101 Cong. 1 sess. (GPO, June 1989), pp. 3–4.
16. *Health and Safety at the Department of Energy's Nuclear Weapons Facilities*, p. 3.

TABLE 6-1. *Evaluations and Bonuses at Rocky Flats, Fiscal Years 1986–88*

	Rating[a]			Fee	
Rating period	General management	Waste management[b]	Safety and health[b]	Bonus awarded (thousands of dollars)	Percentage of possible bonus
1986					
1st half	87 (very good)	· · ·	c	8,156	93.5
2nd half	90 (very good)	90 (very good)	c		
1987					
1st half	93 (excellent)	94 (excellent)	87 (very good)	8,658	81.5
2nd half	94 (excellent)	87 (very good)	87 (very good)		
1988					
1st half	90 (very good)	94 (excellent)	80 (moderately good)	9,973	79.7
2nd half	92 (excellent)	d	81 (good)		

SOURCE: General Accounting Office, *Nuclear Health and Safety: DOE's Award Fees at Rocky Flats Do Not Adequately Reflect ES&H Problems*, RCED-90-47 (October 1989), pp. 21, 23.

a. Highest possible rating is 100.
b. Includes environmental matters.
c. Not rated as separate functional area.
d. Dropped as separate category and included in general management or safety and health.

tional. The FBI supplemented the raid with "Operation Desert Glow," in which it undertook nighttime surveillance overflights by specially equipped spy planes. Citing an internal DOE memo, the FBI concluded that Rockwell's management of the wastes was "patently illegal."[17]

The FBI raid shook Rocky Flats management—both Rockwell and DOE—to its core. The attitude of top DOE managers toward field operations previously had been to "stay out of their business and let them run the show," DOE Inspector General John C. Layton explained in 1991. The theory "had been that we hire a contractor and make it [the contractor] responsible." Now, Layton said, "I don't think that sells" anymore.[18]

Rockwell, like other DOE contractors (and, for that matter, like most of the Superfund contractors) operated under cost-plus-fee contracts. The contractor was reimbursed for its costs, given an annual fee, and awarded a performance bonus, the size of which depended on the evaluations of DOE site managers. While toxic waste was being dumped outside the plant and safety conditions were worsening inside, DOE field officials continued to give Rockwell high marks, which led to high performance bonuses (table 6-1). From fiscal year 1986 through 1988, Rockwell consistently scored over 90 (out of a possible 100) in its overall performance, and it earned $26.8 million in award fees—84 percent of the total fees available. Even on environmental, waste management, and plant health and safety issues, its scores were consistently very high.[19]

These awards sent unmistakable signals: the standards set by DOE's field managers, and by the generous awards they made for Rockwell's performance, emphasized production far more than environmental and safety issues. Similar high awards for poor performance on environmental issues soon surfaced at other nuclear weapons facilities.[20]

17. T. R. Reid and Bill McAlister, "FBI Accuses Energy Dept. of Lying," *Washington Post*, June 10, 1989, p. A1.
18. General Accounting Office, *Meeting the Energy Challenges of the 1990s: Experts Define the Key Policy Issues*, RCED-91-66 (March 1991), Statement of John C. Layton, p. 108.
19. General Accounting Office, *Nuclear Health and Safety: DOE's Award Fees at Rocky Flats Do Not Adequately Reflect ES&H Problems*, RCED-90-47 (October 1989), pp. 1, 2, 5.
20. General Accounting Office, *Nuclear Health and Safety: Information on Award Fees Paid at Selected DOE Facilities*, RCED-90-60FS (October 1989).

The awards reinforced a long-standing commitment to production among workers in the field, both DOE and contractor employees. Whether the facility manufactured plutonium triggers or tritium gas, production goals took precedence over health, safety, and environmental issues. Even after DOE's top officials tried to turn the department's attention toward safety issues, the culture of production—what one internal report referred to as "the dominance of programmatic performance goals"—was slow to give way.[21]

"This is a big organization," Energy Secretary John Herrington explained in 1988. "There is an entrenched bureaucracy with a long-time defense role. You put somebody in the middle of it that wants to shut down their facilities," and you provoke "major battles." In fact, he said, he sometimes was looked on as a "revolutionary" in his own department for trying to force more attention to environmental and safety issues.[22]

Shifting Missions

In 1989 President George Bush named retired Navy Admiral James Watkins to replace Herrington, and Watkins devoted himself to changing DOE's organizational culture. The shift, however, proved far more difficult than he had anticipated.

At Rocky Flats, what was expected to be a short-term closure to clean up plutonium contamination soon stretched into months. The FBI raid convinced DOE officials to replace the contractor, Rockwell, with a different firm, EG&G. Secretary Watkins ordered a suspension of operations in November 1989 to give EG&G a few months before and after its January 1990 takeover of the plant to solve the problems and make Rocky Flats operational again. As EG&G began work, however, new problems, including plutonium contamination in ventilation ducts, continued to surface, and the plant remained closed indefinitely.

The breakup of the Soviet Union in 1991 once again scrambled plans for reopening Rocky Flats. The end of the Soviet threat meant that the United States would not need as many nuclear weapons and

21. Butterfield, "Dispute on Wastes Poses Threat," p. D21.
22. Keith Schneider, "Problems at Weapon Plants Conceded," *New York Times*, October 20, 1988, p. A16.

that disassembled weapons could provide all the nation's projected defense plutonium needs for the foreseeable future. The plutonium reserve was high enough that in July 1992 President Bush announced that the plutonium production network, including Rocky Flats, would be permanently shut down. Rocky Flats's basic mission changed radically, and almost overnight, from production to cleanup.

The change of mission, in turn, brought even more radical changes to the way Rocky Flats did business. In an effort to rebuild public trust and confidence, EG&G and DOE committed themselves to replacing the previous culture of secrecy with a new attitude of openness. Gone were the days when the plant's operations were shielded in secrecy and many of its employees refused to admit publicly even where they worked. Instead, DOE and EG&G launched a major public relations campaign. Rockwell had issued just five news releases in all of 1989. In 1990, EG&G's first year as a plant contractor, the company's public relations staff issued ninety-four press releases. "The most sound of technical operations in the world can't succeed without the people understanding it," explained Beth Brainard, director of public affairs for the DOE office at Rocky Flats.[23]

Rockwell often had not been forthcoming when bad news arose, which tended to make both reporters and area residents fear that the contractor was hiding even worse news. EG&G determined to tell the news, both good and bad. One EG&G official, Terry Smith, said that "when we started, Rocky Flats had zero credibility. We had to start by reestablishing that—by telling the bad news even when it hurts." The problem, Smith said, "is not really that complex or tough. You just have to talk with people. You have to work hard to be there all the time."[24]

EG&G's public affairs staff organized a major tour for the news media and, for the first time, brought them inside protected areas, not only with their notebooks but also with their cameras. The security staff was horrified at first, but EG&G and DOE were able to work out arrangements so that the television crews could obtain stock footage and newspaper photographers could take background pictures for

23. Interview with Beth Brainard, director of public affairs for Rocky Flats, Department of Energy, April 22, 1992.
24. Interview with Terry Smith, an EG&G official, April 22, 1992.

their files. The public affairs staff also established a "Breakfast with Bob" series, early morning meetings with acting DOE plant manager Bob Nelson. Nelson had been brought to Rocky Flats from DOE's Nevada Test Site to try to turn the plant's operations around. By meeting regularly with reporters, and by adopting an open, all-the-facts approach, he sought to demystify Rocky Flats's operations.

EG&G established five reading rooms at public facilities near the plant, where citizens could obtain information ranging from news clippings to historical radioactive exposure studies. The plant developed a detailed citizen participation plan. EG&G flooded the local news media with information and held public information meetings. So heavy was the saturation—and so big were the problems at Rocky Flats—that there were only seventeen days in all of 1990 when Rocky Flats was not in the news.[25] "What you do is less important than how you do it. You have to come across as caring and responsive," Smith explained. "You have to find common ground you can work on. You have to get them [local residents] to say, 'I don't agree with them [officials at Rocky Flats], but I do see them as responsible people.' "

The joint EG&G–DOE effort involved more than just public relations. An ageless strategy to solve public relations problems, of course, is to deluge reporters with so much information that they have to spend most of their time digging through it. That gives the provider of the information more control over both the agenda and the way stories are covered. There was some of that, one reporter who regularly covered Rocky Flats said. "They do blow smoke, in the volume of stuff they send me. They do a lot of over-information providing. But when I want something, I have access to the people at the plant. I think there's a real change—a real difference."[26]

That commitment to open access and communications could be measured by the negative stories that did not appear, said Brainard. To illustrate she described an incident involving a reporter who was checking out a rumor that senior plant officials were covering up serious problems. In the old days officials at the plant likely would have refused to talk to the reporter about the charges, thus reinforcing the perception that a cover-up did exist. But having spent time talking

25. Smith interview.
26. Interview with Gregg Todd, reporter, Boulder *Daily Camera*, April 24, 1992.

to Nelson before the rumor surfaced, the reporter was skeptical that the charge was true. When Nelson denied that any cover-up was going on, the reporter believed him and decided not to run the story. "I know Bob wouldn't have done that," he told Brainard. "No matter how different your views are," Brainard said, "as long as you talk to each other, everyone goes away changed."[27]

Virtually everyone in the communities around Rocky Flats agreed that communication with the plant had changed. "The level of cooperation is light years improved since 1989," noted Ginger Schwarz, executive director of the Rocky Flats Environmental Monitoring Council, a government-funded watchdog group.[28] Jean Jacobus, who followed Rocky Flats for Jefferson County, Colorado, agreed that there was "a complete turnaround."[29] The past president of a local chamber of commerce said, "It's been a positive partnership."[30]

Citizens' reports were not universally complimentary. Schwarz pointed out that there sometimes had been confusion between DOE and EG&G officials about who was handling which inquiries and how much EG&G could do on its own without clearance from DOE officials. Some citizens, moreover, wanted to know what DOE, not its contractor, thought. "It's difficult when a citizen wants information from DOE to be passed along to EG&G," Schwarz said.

Nor had EG&G been able to erase public distrust. "The public views them [EG&G] as the fox in the henhouse," with a vested interest in telling only the contractor's side of the story, Schwarz said.[31] A local businessman added, "There's a sense that they [DOE and EG&G] will say or do what you want to hear, but they go and do whatever they want. If they say it's going to be safe, how can you trust them? They've lied in the past."[32] A peace activist from nearby Boulder was harsher. "The new culture of safety that Watkins wants seems to be more imaginary than real," he said.[33] Even the plant's strongest critics, however, acknowledged that the atmosphere had changed dramati-

27. Brainard interview.
28. Interview with Ginger Schwarz, executive director of the Rocky Flats Environmental Monitoring Council, April 23, 1992.
29. Interview with Jean Jacobus, Jefferson County official, April 23, 1992.
30. Interview with Bob Dyer, local businessman, April 23, 1992.
31. Schwarz interview.
32. Dyer interview.
33. Interview with Le Roy Moore, Rocky Mountain Peace Center, April 23, 1992.

cally, and that there was a genuine effort at creating a new culture beneath the public affairs veneer.

If the relations among DOE, EG&G, the media, local governments, and the public were significantly different, changing the culture *within* the Rocky Flats plant proved more difficult. The department's own Advisory Committee on Nuclear Facility Safety concluded in 1991 that the "safety culture is not yet well-established at Rocky Flats." Not only did efforts at Rocky Flats lag behind progress at other DOE facilities, the committee said, but "much remains to be done to make safety and operations at Rocky Flats consistent with the standards being adopted at the Department of Energy's nuclear reactor facilities, and it is not clear that this will ultimately be achievable under the current program." That was because "operational personnel [were] willing to revert to older philosophies and to circumvent procedures in order to complete tasks," the committee said.[34]

The new culture toward which DOE and EG&G were working would scarcely have been possible even a few years earlier. Breaking down the reverence for secrecy would have been difficult, if not impossible, before the disintegration of the Soviet nuclear threat. Close DOE monitoring of contractor activities, moreover, was impossible in earlier days. Before the FBI raid, there were just 50 DOE employees on-site to oversee more than 8,000 contractor employees. Most of these DOE employees were contract administrators, in charge of processing the paperwork and not trained to oversee the contractor's performance. After the raid, DOE quadrupled its on-site staff to about 200 employees. Its staff devoted to environmental issues increased eightfold to about 40; for technical oversight, the increase was about tenfold.[35]

DOE, in short, aggressively sought to become a smarter buyer. DOE managers, supported closely by EG&G officials, tried to diagnose the problems they faced and solve them creatively. They had strong support from the community as well as from Secretary Watkins's highly publicized efforts to shift the department's focus to safety and cleanup. The local efforts could not have been sustained without support from

34. Advisory Committee on Nuclear Facility Safety, *Final Report on DOE Nuclear Facilities* (Department of Energy, November 1991), pp. 157, 139–40, 141.
35. Interview with David P. Simonson, deputy manager, DOE Rocky Flats plant, April 22, 1992.

the highest levels of the department, while the secretary's commitment to changing the culture would have been empty without supporting performance at the department's facilities.

Nagging Problems

Not all of the cleanup at Rocky Flats went smoothly, however. One snag, for example, involved a toxic, radioactive sludge at the bottom of evaporation ponds once used to separate water from liquid waste. The plan was to dispose of the sludge by mixing it with concrete, creating blocks called "pondcrete." The pondcrete would, in theory, be stable, provide a shield against the radioactivity, and be easily moved to long-term storage.

A contractor began work in 1985 and had moved more than 16,000 pondcrete blocks to a new location before DOE officials discovered that half of the blocks were cracking and crumbling. Disintegrating blocks posed new problems. Because they did not effectively shield the environment from radioactivity, they could neither be used for long-term storage nor moved. And because the storage site had not been monitored, no one knew how much radioactivity might have been released before the problem was discovered.

The cracked blocks had to be remanufactured. Meanwhile, as many as 20,000 additional pondcrete blocks had to be produced. DOE was unable to meet its first major targets for the cleanup, and costs soared, from an estimated $27 million in 1989 to $50 million soon thereafter, past $100 million in early 1991 to $169 million just nine months later. Nevada refused to allow DOE to ship any of the pondcrete to the planned storage facility at DOE's nuclear test facility. The longer DOE and its contractors struggled to produce the pondcrete blocks, the greater the chance that its permit to store the waste at Rocky Flats would expire. The department would then have no place to put it.[36] EG&G, meanwhile, stored the pondcrete under shelters at Rocky Flats

36. This case study is drawn from a series of GAO reports: *Nuclear Health and Safety: Problems with Cleaning Up the Solar Ponds at Rocky Flats,* RCED-91-31 (January 1991); *Managing the Environmental Cleanup of DOE's Nuclear Weapons Complex,* T-RCED-91-27 (April 11, 1991), Testimony of Victor S. Rezendes; *Nuclear Health and Safety: Problems Continue for Rocky Flats Solar Pond Cleanup Program,* RCED-92-18 (October 1991); and *Nuclear Weapons Complex: Major Safety, Environmental, and Reconfiguration Issues Facing DOE,* T-RCED-91-31 (January 25, 1992), Testimony of J. Dexter Peach.

while DOE officials negotiated an interim agreement with both the Environmental Protection Agency (EPA) and the Colorado Department of Health to meet federal and state waste requirements. DOE also worked to resolve problems with Nevada to produce a more permanent storage site.

EG&G was also running into problems with other cleanup projects. Costs for the plant's new "supercompactor," being developed to reduce the volume of waste, grew from an original estimate of $1.9 million to $10.5 million. Costs to upgrade the plant's waste transfer system increased from $1.5 million to $14 million. In both cases, project management problems delayed completion and drove costs up.[37]

The aftermath of the FBI raid produced even worse political problems. In March 1992, after a two-and-a-half-year grand jury investigation, the U.S. attorney managing the case announced that Rockwell had agreed to plead guilty to ten charges of violating federal environmental laws and to pay a fine of $18.5 million. Many local residents were astonished. The fine was the size of just two years' worth of Rockwell's performance bonuses. Local residents were even more stunned that, after hearing 110 witnesses and examining 760 boxes of documents, the grand jury did not return a single criminal indictment. "Why were individual Rockwell employees, and their supervisors at the Department of Energy, not going to be held accountable?" a local newspaper asked. Its answer: "What transpired behind the closed doors of the grand jury room sabotaged the will of the grand jury" and allowed DOE "to do business as usual at Rocky Flats."[38]

The grand jury had in fact proposed criminal indictments against three DOE officials and five Rockwell employees, but the U.S. attorney, allegedly at the direction of Justice Department officials in Washington, refused to sign them, which made them invalid. Members of the grand jury were furious and prepared a special report. The judge assigned to the case ordered the grand jury report sealed and warned jurors that they could be held in contempt of court if they spoke publicly. The grand jurors ignored the judge's warnings and leaked

37. General Accounting Office, *Department of Energy: Project Management at the Rocky Flats Plant Needs Improvement*, RCED-93-32 (October 1992), p. 2.

38. Bryan Abas, "Justice Denied," *Denver Westword*, September 30–October 6, 1992, p. 15.

the report to a reporter for *Westword*, a weekly Denver newspaper. Excerpts from the report then found their way into *Harper's*.

According to the report printed in *Harper's*, the grand jurors found "compelling evidence" that waste had been "illegally stored, treated, and disposed of." They also found "a culture of criminal misconduct, in which corporate bonuses were obtained through illegal means." Although the problems began with Rockwell, the grand jury charged that EG&G employees continued "to violate many federal environmental laws."[39]

In a report released January 4, 1993, congressional investigators found that the Justice Department had been reluctant to pursue the charges and that its prosecutors had surrendered to lobbying by senior DOE officials to drop the investigation. The investigators found "evidence of troubling behavior and attitudes" in the way that the Justice Department approached environmental crimes and said that the department "too quickly gave up" on broader policy issues. In addition, DOE's internal culture "created a situation in which no government official could be held culpable because the entire agency encouraged noncompliance with environmental laws. The result was a double standard in the administration of justice, where a government agency and its individual employees were allowed lesser standards of conduct than ordinary citizens," the investigators said. The Justice Department's decision meant that Rockwell probably would not be liable for millions of dollars in fines and that the employees alleged to have committed crimes would escape prosecution. The decision also helped protect Rockwell from civil lawsuits by the plant's neighbors.[40]

The government's lead prosecuter in the case, Kenneth Fimberg, defended his actions. "It was a watershed development in the enforcement of environmental law at DOE facilities," he said. In fact, the $18.5 million penalty was about five times higher than the previous record fine for violations of hazardous waste laws. The deal guaranteed success for the government and avoided the high risk of proving

39. "The Rocky Flats Cover-Up, Continued," *Harper's*, December 1992, p. 19.

40. "The Prosecution of Environmental Crimes at the Department of Energy's Rocky Flats Facility," Staff report, House Committee on Science, Space, and Technology, Subcommittee on Investigations and Oversight, 103 Cong. 1 sess. (January 4, 1993), p. 11. More broadly, see *Environmental Crimes at the Rocky Flats Nuclear Weapons Facility,* Hearings before the House Committee on Science, Space, and Technology, Subcommittee on Investigations and Oversight, 102 Cong. 2 sess. (GPO, 1992).

what "would have been an extremely difficult case, factually, legally, and scientifically," Fimberg said. Fimberg, furthermore, rejected the subcommittee's charge that he covered up the grand jury's investigation to protect DOE.[41]

Until the grand jury report was leaked, DOE and EG&G unquestionably had made great progress in dealing with the public and in beginning to turn the Rocky Flats operation around. But the leaked report, the news stories that it generated, and the congressional investigation that followed reminded local observers just how far DOE had to go to uproot the culture of production and the management problems it posed.

Changing the Bureaucratic Culture

The military imperative demanded by World War II, the great secrecy and technological excitement surrounding the Manhattan Project, and the enormous reliance of government on private contractors set a pattern for nuclear weapons production that was sustained throughout the cold war. "There was a military culture throughout the agency, a bunker mentality," a DOE assistant secretary during the Reagan administration told a *New York Times* reporter in 1988. "People saw their role as meeting the requirements for defense. Fundamentally, they saw completing the goals for materials production as their crucial mission." Other issues were secondary. "Every penny that went to safety programs was a penny taken from manufacturing nuclear warheads," the Reagan aide explained. Especially during the Reagan years, "what this Administration was all about was making warheads."[42]

From the beginning the managers of the production facilities assumed that the side issues, especially those concerning safety and health, would be addressed as soon as the national security crisis ebbed. When that finally happened, with the demise of the Soviet Union, the safety and environmental problems had themselves reached a state of crisis. At the same time, public scrutiny of DOE activities escalated, in large part because the government had for so

41. Michael D. Lemonick, "Sometimes It Takes a Cowboy," *Time*, January 25, 1993, p. 58.

42. Keith Schneider, "Defects in Nuclear Arms Industry Minimized in Early Reagan Years," *New York Times*, November 7, 1988, p. B12.

long glossed over the obviously growing safety and health problems. The political environment for solving the problems thus became far more difficult just as their enormous scale made them impossible to ignore any longer.

Periodic reorganizations of the federal agencies responsible for nuclear weapons production also weakened attention to health and safety problems. The nuclear complex had always been extremely decentralized, in part because security was more easily managed if the programs could be compartmentalized and because different facilities tended to be managed by different contractors doing different jobs. In 1977, when various agencies that supervised different forms of energy were combined and elevated to departmental status, individual facilities retained their autonomy as weapons production vied with energy exploration and research for the secretary's attention. The task of ensuring safety became fragmented at headquarters and weakened headquarters' oversight of field operations.[43]

DOE's oversight of weapons production was badly organized and poorly staffed. Personnel in the safety office, which was not even established until 1985, had weak authority and far less expertise than personnel in the operations it was charged with overseeing. A committee of the National Research Council chaired by Richard A. Meserve, a lawyer and physicist, studied safety issues concerning DOE's nuclear facilities and issued a series of reports in the mid-1980s. The committee found that "in the current system, the capacity to carefully balance programmatic needs against the safety needs of the reactors is modest. The structure tends to disperse responsibility for safety and seems to require decisions with safety consequences by organizations that are divorced from day-to-day safety responsibility."[44]

DOE, in short, had sacrificed safety to production. Those within DOE who knew about safety had little authority, and those who had authority knew or cared little about safety. What DOE did know it learned largely from its contractors.

When DOE finally began to recognize that it had to grapple with the growing safety and environmental problems, three distinct cul-

43. Committee to Assess Safety and Technical Issues at DOE Reactors, National Research Council (Meserve Committee), *Safety Issues at Test and Research Reactors* (Washington: National Academy Press, 1988), p. 30.
44. Meserve Committee, *Safety Issues at Test and Research Reactors*, p. 2.

tures within the agency hindered the flow of any information needed for effective management. Like political appointees at EPA, political appointees at DOE often lacked a full understanding of the issues that would have allowed them to make sense of what data they did receive. Senior managers often were bound up with contractors in the culture of performance, while technical managers concentrated on details to the exclusion of broader issues.

The Technical Culture

Like workers at the other weapons production facilities, workers at Rocky Flats relied on long-established routines to complete their tasks. As in any shop, managers had a difficult time convincing workers to take safety seriously; workers balked at virtually all safety precautions, from the wearing of hot, uncomfortable respirators to developing new work habits. "You'll still find there are lots of people in the plant saying you don't have to be concerned about safety," a senior DOE plant official explained in 1992. "It's very, very tedious to implement these processes. People see the down-side [such as the discomfort from wearing respirators] far more easily than the benefits."[45] Managers put people with a safety-first attitude into the plant as models for other workers to follow and launched safety training programs for workers. In some operations training occupied nearly 40 percent of the workers' time.

Changing the technical culture proved difficult, however, because of the many factors that reinforced existing patterns. Technicians around the weapons complex spent their days focusing on the details of controlling the reactors and operating the production machinery. Working behind tall fences, surrounded by armed guards, and wearing security badges reinforced the culture of secrecy. Technicians for DOE and its contractors shared a culture oriented to the critical importance of their work in maintaining national security, the need to keep it confidential, and the imperative to keep the facilities working. DOE and contractor employees worked so closely together that DOE Secretary Herrington, on a visit to the department's Savannah River facility in 1988, complained that he could not tell who worked for whom.[46]

45. Simonson interview.
46. Matthew L. Wald, "Nuclear Arms Plants: A Bill Long Overdue," *New York Times*, October 23, 1988, sec. 4, p. 1.

Because they possessed the expertise, the technicians tended to be the group that defined the problems and the way they were characterized to senior department officials. Because their focus was almost exclusively on production, the rising tide of environmental damage simply did not register as a major issue for the technicians. Operators tended to assume that the waste products were not problems or that, if they were, a new technology could be developed to ease the cleanup. Seldom did DOE's technicians warn higher-level officials of brewing problems. As a result, when DOE's headquarters staff began to look into the cleanup problems at Rocky Flats, they were constantly surprised by new revelations that surfaced not through the department's chain of command but in the newspapers.

The Managerial Culture

The critical broken link in the information chain proved to be the department's field managers. Their job was to make the system work to serve the department's customer, the Department of Defense. The Pentagon's demands created clear incentives for field managers to produce, and the incentives were overwhelming to ignore anything—including health and safety problems—that got in the way.[47]

As Representative John Dingell put it, the Defense Department demands created "a mentality of production over all else."[48] Representative Mike Synar added that DOE's field managers "were rewarded for making up great reports when obviously conditions at these plants were miserable. They've been rewarded for not telling the truth. And it's a dangerous practice, because what we now see at the Department of Energy can be summarized in one sentence: the top guys at the Department of Energy have no idea what is going on within their agency."[49]

47. Committee to Provide Interim Oversight of the DOE Nuclear Weapons Complex, National Research Council (Meserve Committee), *The Nuclear Weapons Complex, Management for Health, Safety and the Environment* (Washington: National Academy Press, 1988) p. 2.

48. Fox Butterfield, "Trouble at Atomic Bomb Plants: How Lawmakers Missed the Signs," *New York Times,* November 28, 1988, p. B10. See also Government Accounting Office, *Better Oversight Needed for Safety and Health Activities at DOE's Nuclear Facilities,* EMD-81-108 (August 4, 1981), p. 35.

49. Keith Schneider, "Operators Got Millions in Bonuses Despite Hazards at Atom Plants," *New York Times,* October 26, 1988, p. B9.

A few workers who tried to attract their superiors' attention to potential safety problems found themselves punished instead of praised. For example, four employees at the Hanford, Washington, facility who complained about health and safety violations reported that they had been demoted, threatened with the loss of their security clearances, and ordered to see a therapist.[50] Anyone who raised questions about safety threatened to disrupt the close working relationships between contractors and government officials. These complaints upset routines that had gradually developed over decades, routines that gave contractors great flexibility in their operations and that narrowly constrained the roles of government officials. The avalanche of internal investigations, GAO studies, FBI probes, newspaper reports, and congressional hearings that began in the 1980s struck to the very core of the managerial culture. Implicit in these challenges was an imperative to change completely the way the managers had, for years, gone about their business. It was little wonder that change was painfully slow and difficult.

The Political Culture

Although safety in the end is the product of the behavior of the technical staff actually operating the equipment, the way that technicians approach safety is set by top managers. A culture devoted to health and safety issues must come from the top, and in DOE there was for a decade precious little attention paid to these concerns.

President Reagan stirred the lasting enmity of many DOE staff members in 1981 by appointing James B. Edwards as secretary. Edwards was a dentist who had been active in the 1964 Goldwater presidential campaign, had run unsuccessfully for the House of Representatives, and had served as governor of South Carolina in the mid-1970s. Senior DOE staff members sometimes wondered how a dentist could effectively oversee the highly technical world of weapons production. For Reagan, the appointment had symbolic value. He had pledged to eliminate the department altogether, and the appointment signaled that he did not want an activist energy policy. For many DOE insiders, it symbolized a neglect of the critical issues that then were arising.

50. Matthew L. Wald, "Retribution Seen in Atom Industry," *New York Times*, August 6, 1989, p. 1.

The first important internal DOE report on the emerging health and safety issues—the Crawford committee report—was issued in 1981 about the same time that Edwards took office. It called for "close attention at the most senior levels of management" to safety concerns. Had the office of the secretary, in particular, followed the issues more carefully in the past the problems "might not have developed or might have been corrected."[51]

The Crawford committee report languished without serious top-level attention. Six years later the Meserve committee echoed almost precisely the same advice. "Within even a large, properly structured organization, safety is a reflection of institutional commitment and capability. Leadership at the policy-making level is essential, and dedication to safety must permeate the Department of Energy," the committee wrote.[52]

Inattention to environmental, health, and safety issues was compounded by a lack of expertise, which crippled top-level DOE decisionmaking. Many decisions that could have been made at lower levels were passed up the chain or command to top officials. The deluge of memos sometimes created "delay and paralysis in decisionmaking," the Meserve committee noted.[53] Meanwhile, top officials failed to make the critical decisions about health and environmental issues. The attention paid to issues that mattered relatively little, and the lack of attention to issues that did, set the stage for the problems that DOE encountered at the end of the 1980s.

When important decisions reached Washington, decisionmakers were often at a disadvantage because they knew far less about the critical issues than the contractors they were supervising. James S. Kane, who headed a special study for DOE published in 1985, explained, "We found that the level of excellence in technical understanding was much less in Washington than among the contractors. A regulator has to be smarter than those he regulates. Otherwise you're just counting beans."[54] In fact, Kane found that bean count-

51. Department of Energy, Nuclear Facilities Personnel Qualification and Training Committee, *A Report on a Safety Assessment of Department of Energy Nuclear Reactors* (March 1981), introduction, pp. 46, 47.
52. Meserve Committee, *Safety Issues at the Defense Production Reactors: A Report to the U.S. Department of Energy* (Washington: National Academy Press, 1987), p. 83.
53. Meserve Committee, *The Nuclear Weapons Complex*, p. 22.
54. Schneider, "Defects in Nuclear Arms Industry Minimized in Early Reagan Years."

ing—a check of the paper trail instead of a thorough review of the operations themselves—was the extent of most DOE safety reviews by headquarters staff.[55]

George Bush tackled the problem head-on by naming James D. Watkins his energy secretary. A protégé of Admiral Hyman G. Rickover, Watkins had established himself for a generation in Washington as a powerful supporter of safe nuclear energy. He took personal charge of establishing a new management system in the department devoted to safety. Watkins developed new ways of collecting intelligence about the nuclear weapons complex's operations and sought to end the department's production-first mentality. Watkins's tenure was plagued by a series of new revelations, notably at Rocky Flats, concerning health and safety problems and possible departmental misconduct in handling them. His leadership was marked, nevertheless, by a remarkable change in the department's culture, especially at the very top, that set the stage for a concerted attack on the department's environmental problems.

The Intelligence of Government

DOE's painful discovery was that its top officials must know and understand what the department's contractors are doing in its behalf if they are to manage them effectively. The government, however, had gradually allowed what expertise and institutional memory it possessed to flow away into the contractors until it had become completely dependent upon them. Many of the department's technical experts were relegated to contract management, while the contractors were "by default . . . becoming the intelligence of government."[56] The government, in short, had structured the market from the beginning by abandoning any effort to solve the monitoring problem at the core of principal-agent relationships.

55. James S. Kane, "Report and Recommendations on the Department of Energy's Management Activities in Environment, Safety, and Health," special study for Energy Secretary Herrington (Department of Energy, 1985) p. 8.

56. *Use of Consultants and Contractors by the Environmental Protection Agency and the Department of Energy,* Hearing before the Senate Governmental Affairs Committee, Subcommittee on Federal Services, Post Office and Civil Service, 101 Cong. 1 sess. (GPO, 1989), pp. 63, 79.

Meanwhile, the culture of production that pervaded the entire department only worsened the problem. When senior officials protested that they had not been warned about the growing issues, even cursory investigations showed years of warnings. Bureaucratic cultures within DOE, formed by the culture of production and strengthened by a decade of neglect by top officials, aggravated the information problems and made it difficult for later DOE secretaries to attack the crisis aggressively. Horizontal cultures linked workers across organizational boundaries, so that some DOE workers had more in common with their contractor colleagues than with higher-level supervisors. As a result, the government was ill equipped to detect, understand, and correct the difficulties plaguing the nuclear weapons complex.

More than anything else, DOE's struggles demonstrate that buying goods and services from contractors is far more than just a transaction between buyers and sellers. Good management of the relationship is fundamental to the nation's governance, and special capacity is required to manage effectively. Chapter 7, which explores the growth of contracting at the state and local levels, shows that these issues extend across the fabric of American federalism.

7

Contracting Out in State and Local Governments

S tate and local governments certainly have not been strangers to the privatization movement. During the late 1970s a widespread popular movement to limit taxes, spurred by Proposition 13 in California, forced state and local officials to search for tactics to deliver government goods and services at lower costs. Privatization proponents advocated contracting out, using much the same rhetoric that was heard at the national level: lack of competition had allowed state and local governments to grow too big and lazy; replacing government monopolies with private competition was the key to improving efficiency. Contracting out, following the competition prescription, was a natural solution, and state and local governments moved aggressively to contract out more and more of their services. In doing so, they discovered many of the same problems that plagued the federal government. Contracting out proved to be not an antidote to government but a strategy that transformed government, often in unanticipated ways.

For more than a century before the privatization movement of the 1980s, state and local governments had contracted with private companies to provide a range of services, from road construction to social

An earlier version of this chapter was commissioned by the National Commission on the State and Local Public Service (the Winter commission). Portions were previously published in Frank Thompson, ed., *Revitalizing the State and Local Public Service: A Foundation* (San Francisco: Jossey-Bass, 1993). Permission to use some of that material in this chapter is gratefully acknowledged.

services. Worried that corruption was undermining the efficiency and integrity of government, Progressive reformers at the beginning of the twentieth century developed formal procedures for government contracts. These procedures included careful specification of what was to be contracted out and a bidding process to eliminate favoritism. The aim of those reforms was to *decrease* private competition and *increase* government power, to reduce the pernicious effects of the market on public services. Today's debate over public-private relations is proceeding in reverse.

State and local contracting began its most recent expansion in the 1950s in response to new federal programs. State governments used federal funding to pay private contractors to build the interstate highway system. Local governments managed federal urban renewal programs the same way. In both cases, governments did most of the program planning, while private contractors did most of the actual work. Federal social programs of the 1960s and 1970s spurred a new breed of public-private partnership, this one with nonprofit organizations. Programs such as model cities, community development block grants, and the Comprehensive Employment and Training Act had as their primary goal the empowerment of citizens and neighborhood organizations. Local governments thus quickly found themselves trying to sort out and manage complicated new relationships, founded on a presumption of their own incompetence and unrepresentativeness. Partnerships with nonprofit organizations at the state level started a bit later and moved a bit more slowly. But with the enactment of new social service grants to the states under title XX of the Social Security Act, these governments too encountered parallel problems in managing their contracts.[1]

Ironically, when the tax revolts of the late 1970s sparked new demands for privatization, state and local governments had already developed substantial public-private partnerships. From 1972 to 1982 the value of the contracts let by local governments to private organizations had tripled, from $22 billion to $65 billion. Some experts estimate that contracting out has been growing at a rate of 16 percent

---

1. Martha Derthick, *Uncontrollable Spending for Social Services Grants* (Brookings, 1975).

a year.[2] These new partnerships, in another irony, were the product of *expanding* governmental ambition, not the *shrinking* of governmental power that privatization's advocates recommended.

The debate over state and local contracting has often been feverishly ideological. Conservatives have argued that government has grown too fat and must be reduced.[3] Liberals have contended that the conservatives' campaign for efficiency is really intended to do away with the welfare state.[4] Government employee unions have sensed in the privatization arguments an effort to eliminate their jobs.[5]

The Evidence on State and Local Contracting

Despite the often contentious debate over contracting out, a consensus has developed on several points.

Almost Everything Can Be—And Has Been—Contracted Out

Enthusiasts of contracting argue that "virtually every service provided or function performed by local government conceivably could be farmed out."[6] Scottsdale, Arizona, for example, contracted out its fire service. Some state and local governments have turned over their prisons, libraries, police service, and parole programs to private contractors. For many privatization advocates, these examples suggest the ideal form of government: a mayor to administer contracts, a bookkeeper to pay the contractors. Some communities are not far from

2. National Commission for Employment Policy, *Privatization and Public Employees: The Impact of City and County Contracting Out on Government Workers* (Washington, 1988), p. 8.

3. E. S. Savas, *Privatizing the Public Sector: How to Shrink Government* (Chatham, N.J.: Chatham House Publishers, 1982); and New York State Senate Advisory Committee on Privatization (hereafter Lauder Commission), *Privatization for New York: Competing for a Better Future* (Albany, 1992).

4. Sheila B. Kammerman and Alfred A. Kahn, eds., *Privatization and the Welfare State* (Princeton University Press, 1989), especially Paul Starr, "The Meaning of Privatization," pp. 15–48.

5. American Federation of State, County, and Municipal Employees (AFSCME), *Passing the Bucks: The Contracting Out of Public Services* (Washington, 1984); and AFSCME, *When Public Services Go Private: Not Always Better, Not Always Honest, There May Be A Better Way* (Washington, 1987).

6. James L. Mercer, "Growing Opportunities in Public Service Contracting," *Harvard Business Review*, vol. 61 (March–April 1983), pp. 178–88.

this target. In La Miranda, California, a city of 41,000, just fifty-five government employees managed the contracts for more than sixty services. Lakewood, another California community with a population of 60,000, had only eight city workers. One Dallas suburb came close to the ultimate in privatization: it had just one secretary to manage the paperwork for its fully contracted-out service system.[7]

Almost Everyone Contracts Out Something

Not only is virtually every service imaginable contracted out, but contracting out has become a near-universal phenomenon. According to the Mercer Group, which conducted a survey of privatization in 1990, "Virtually all local governments surveyed contracted out at least one service to a private company."[8] The gospel of privatization's efficiencies has many converts. Contracting's promise of cost reductions and administrative flexibility lures both large and small governments.

Everyone Contracts Out Different Things

Even though almost everyone contracts out something, and almost everything can be contracted out, there is little consensus among local governments about what services to contract out. According to the International City Management Association (ICMA), only two services—vehicle towing and storage and legal services—were contracted out by more than half of the 1,681 local governments surveyed in the mid-1980s. Most of the nearly seventy-five goods and services identified by ICMA were contracted out by fewer than a third of all the governments surveyed (table 7-1). (Similar figures for state governments are not available.)

The Mercer Group survey found that local governments were most likely to contract out engineering, management consulting, major construction, food services, and legal and architectural services. More than one-fourth of the communities surveyed contracted out janitorial services, solid waste collection, building maintenance, security services, towing services, management and maintenance of parking garages, landscaping and grounds maintenance, human resources, food

---

7. John D. Donahue, *The Privatization Decision: Public Ends, Private Means* (Basic Books, 1989), p. 135.
8. The Mercer Group, "The 1990 Privatization Survey" (Atlanta, 1990).

TABLE 7-1. *Services Local Governments Contract Out Most and Least Often*

Services contracted out most often	Percent of local governments contracting out the function	Services contracted out least often	Percent of local governments contracting out the function
Vehicle towing and storage	80	Operation of libraries	1
Legal services	55	Prisons and jails	1
Street light operation	46	Police and fire communication	1
Hazardous materials disposal	44	Fire	1
Operation of homeless shelters	43	Traffic control and parking enforcement	1
Fleet management and vehicle maintenance	41	Parole programs	3
Commercial solid-waste collection	38	Water treatment	3
Residential solid-waste collection	36	Sanitary inspection	3
Street repair	36	Water distribution	4
Tree trimming and planting	36	Crime prevention and control	4
Operation of mental health facilities	35	Sewage collection and treatment	6
Drug and alcohol treatment programs	34	Payroll	7
Day care facility operation	34	Secretarial services	7
Labor relations	33	Personnel services	8
Utility billing	32	Operation of museums	8
		Recreation services	8

SOURCE: Derived from International City Management Association (ICMA), *Service Delivery in the 90s: Alternative Approaches for Local Governments* (Washington, 1989), pp. xii–xiii.

and medical services, services for the aging, consulting, landfill, data processing, and wastewater services.[9]

Sifting through the long catalog of services that governments provide their citizens uncovers some important patterns in what is contracted out and what is not. First, the programs *most likely* to be contracted out are those for which the services are already available

9. The Mercer Group, "1990 Privatization Survey."

in the private market. Towing services work the same way, whether the drivers are towing cars for the city or for a private garage. Tree trimmers, street repairers, planners, and data processors do not differentiate according to whether their customers are in the public or private sector. An important exception to this first generalization are social service programs, for which there is no significant market apart from government programs. I will return to that point a bit later.

Second, local governments are *least likely* to contract out programs at the core of their missions. Prisons, police, fire, water and sewage treatment, and emergency communications are all fundamental programs that protect the public health and safety. Some government somewhere has contracted out each of these programs at some time, but for both programmatic and political reasons, most local governments have been reluctant to turn such basic responsibilities over to the private sector. The costs of service disruptions could be high, and the political fallout from problems with services such as police and fire would be fatal.

Contracting Out Saves Money

Almost every local government that tried contracting out reports having saved money, both the ICMA and Mercer Group surveys report. The ICMA survey revealed that 40 percent of local governments saved more than 20 percent from previous outlays; another 40 percent saved 10 to 19 percent. The much-advertised savings available through contracting out appear to be real—although savings are never guaranteed and some contracting-out efforts are aborted because of performance problems.[10] According to a 1987 survey by Touche Ross, an accounting and consulting firm, cost savings ranked as the top advantage, by far, of contracting out (table 7-2). Moreover, local government officials generally find that contracting out produces good quality service. A

10. The Mercer Group, "The 1990 Privatization Survey"; and International City Management Association (ICMA), *Service Delivery in the 90s: Alternative Approaches for Local Governments* (Washington, 1989), p. 3. See also Harry P. Hatry, *A Review of Private Approaches for Delivery of Public Services* (Washington: Urban Institute Press, 1983); Eileen Brettler Berenyi and Barbara J. Stevens, "Does Privatization Work? A Study of the Delivery of Eight Local Services," *State and Local Government Review*, vol. 20 (Winter 1988), pp. 11–20; Lauder Commission, *Privatization for New York*; and National Commission for Employment Policy, *Privatization and Public Employees*.

TABLE 7-2. *Advantages to Local Governments in Contracting Out*

Advantage cited	Percent of respondents
Saves money	74
Solves labor problems	50
Shares risk	34
Offers higher quality service	33
Provides services not otherwise available	32
Shortens implementation time	30
Solves local political problems	21

SOURCE: Touche Ross, *Privatization in America* (Washington, 1987), p. 5.

1989 survey showed that 72 percent of local officials said that the quality of services contractors provided was "very favorable."[11]

Private contractors reduce costs through three principal techniques. First, because they are free of government rules and civil service requirements, they have more flexibility than public agencies. They use incentive pay systems and have greater freedom to hire and fire workers. They employ more part-time workers, have less absenteeism, and use employees for more than one task. Second, private contractors tend to pay lower wages than government agencies. Third and most important, contractors tend to pay their workers substantially lower fringe benefits, especially retirement benefits. The difference in fringe benefits is "the largest difference between the government and the private contractor," according to the National Commission for Employment Policy.[12]

The cost-savings argument masks a genuine anti–government worker sentiment underlying the privatization prescription. Labor costs account for more than half of state and local government spending, compared with just 14 percent of the federal government's outlays. With so much of state and local spending concentrated on personnel costs, any argument to reduce that spending inevitably is an argument

11. David Osborne and Ted Gaebler, *Reinventing Government: How the Entrepreneurial Spirit Is Transforming the Public Sector, from Schoolhouse to Statehouse, City Hall to the Pentagon* (Reading, Mass.: Addison-Wesley, 1992), p. 89.

12. National Commission for Employment Policy, *Privatization and Public Employees*, pp. 2–3.

to reduce the number of employees as well.[13] Some of the savings from contracting out comes from improved management. Most of it, however, comes not from superior workers, but from greater flexibility in managing those workers—and from less generous compensation of their work.

The evidence shows that what matters most is not who performs government services but how they are performed. Policy analyst John D. Donahue observed that "*public versus private* matters, but *competitive versus noncompetitive* usually matters more."[14] One study, for example, found, that in communities where there was competition to provide electric service, costs were reduced by about 11 percent, regardless of whether the service provider was government or a private concern.[15] Private monopolies are just as subject to inefficiencies as is the government monopoly. It is the presence of competition, not the locus of power, that matters.

Some state and local governments have introduced competition into their own operations, much as the federal government does through the A-76 process. Phoenix requires its municipal workers to bid against private contractors for selected local services. In Rochester, New York, city officials decided not to sign a contract with a private garbage collection firm after city employees proposed to reduce their crew size from four to three, which made their costs considerably cheaper than the private contractor's.[16] Workers at a Los Angeles county health clinic formed a private company and bid successfully for a county contract.[17] In Newark, New Jersey, information the city gained from the bidding process for a refuse collection contract helped improve the productivity of city refuse workers.[18] Analysts

13. Donahue, *The Privatization Decision,* p. 131; and John A. Rehfuss, *Contracting Out in Government: A Guide to Working with Outside Contractors to Supply Public Services* (San Francisco: Jossey-Bass, 1989), p. 201.
14. Donahue, *The Privatization Decision,* p. 78 (emphasis in original); see also Osborne and Gaebler, *Reinventing Government.*
15. Walter J. Primeaux, "An Assessment of X-Efficiency Gained Through Competition," *Review of Economics and Statistics,* vol. 59 (February 1977), pp. 105–13.
16. Hatry, *A Review of Private Approaches for Delivery of Public Services,* p. 22.
17. E. S. Savas, "Introduction," in Lauder Commission, *Privatization for New York,* p. 8.
18. ICMA, *Service Delivery in the 90s,* p. 4.

contend that such competition might produce the biggest benefits of all in local education.[19]

Savings through contracting are not inevitable. Some jurisdictions, in fact, contract out specifically because they can bypass government regulations and pay contractors *more* than they can pay civil servants. Contracting therefore can actually cost more than government-operated programs. When savings result, however, they are most likely to come from the pressures of competition.

Competition Is Not Always Easy to Develop or Promote

The Mercer Group survey reported that local governments nearly always use competitive bids in awarding contracts and that the governments could usually, but not always, rely on sufficient competition among contractors to have confidence in the process. Sometimes there are not enough potential contractors available to create a truly competitive bidding process. For some services, such as code enforcement, it is almost impossible to find private suppliers. For other services private concerns might not be interested in bidding on jobs in small jurisdictions, where the size of the contract and potential profits would also be small. Many contractors, furthermore, complain about red tape and the slow pace with which governments often pay vendors. Nearly 10 percent of all jurisdictions surveyed said that they had difficulty finding sufficient contractors. The number rose to 30 percent among special-district governments such as water and sewage treatment authorities. The problem was most serious for governments of small jurisdictions, where there often were few contractors for some services.[20]

Competition, moreover, is costly to create and sustain. To manage a contract competition, government officials first must define precisely what they want to buy. Contract solicitations must be detailed and specific, for they shape the transaction that is to occur. Government officials must advertise the solicitation and review the bids, resolve technical disputes among bidders and between government officials

19. John E. Chubb and Terry Moe, *Politics, Markets, and America's Schools* (Brookings, 1990).

20. Mercer Group, "The 1990 Privatization Survey"; see also ICMA, *Service Delivery in the 90s,* pp. 16–17.

and potential contractors, and oversee the contract once it is awarded to ensure both the cost and quality of the services provided. Perhaps most important, they must ensure that the winning contractor does not grow into a monopolist, to which the government would find itself captive and from which the promised efficiencies might soon evaporate. Critics argue, for example, that privately managed mass transit systems are frequently monopolies that share the same limited incentives to control costs as governments.[21]

Contracting Out Creates Risks as Well as Advantages

Market competition, of course, poses significant problems as well as potential benefits.[22] Corruption can occur throughout the contracting process. A principal reason for the bureaucratization of state and local governments at the turn of the twentieth century was to insulate government from private corruption. Since then, bid rigging, bribery, and kickbacks certainly have not been eliminated; opponents of privatization suggest that such problems are rampant.[23] It is impossible, of course, to determine just how widespread such problems are, but they are undoubtedly real and will continue, at least to some degree.

Conflicts of interest are a constant problem. San Francisco, for example, hired a private consulting firm to manage its public works programs. The city also hired from this firm a new manager to oversee its budget and personnel policies. The manager awarded contracts to his own firm—and the city soon decided to replace him.[24]

Services provided by private contractors can also be disrupted if the contractor does not perform well, if equipment breaks down, or if the contractor suffers its own labor problems or goes bankrupt. "Shifting to contracting for at least some major activities is a major move and is not easy to reverse," privatization expert Harry Hatry points out.[25] Contractors may be less flexible than governments. New York City switches its garbage trucks to snow plow duty when bad weather threatens. Such options might not be available if a community be-

21. James L. Perry and Timlynn T. Babitsky, "Comparative Performance in Urban Bus Transit: Assessing Privatization Strategies," *Public Administration Review*, vol. 46 (January–Feburary 1986), pp. 57–66.

22. Donahue, *The Privatization Decision*, pp. 146–48.

23. AFSCME, *Passing the Bucks;* and AFSCME, *When Public Services Go Private.*

24. Donahue, *The Privatization Decision*, p. 148.

25. Hatry, *A Review of Private Approaches for Delivery of Public Services*, p. 27.

comes dependent on private garbage haulers who do not own snow plows. Transferring responsibility to the private sector can also reduce a government's own capacity both to provide services and to manage them. It can lose an important source of information about what works how, and that can undercut its ability to manage contractors effectively. How have jurisdictions responded to this problem? Often by hiring other contractors to supply what the government has lost.

Finally, governments that contract out risk becoming subject once again to monopoly power. Contractors in fields as far ranging as day care and garbage collection have often lobbied aggressively to restrict competition.[26] Not all market forces are self-policing.

Contracting Out for Social Services

As with the market for federal goods and services, there is considerable variation in contracting out for state and local goods. Existing suppliers and a relatively high level of competition characterize some markets, such as snow removal and building services. These markets have relatively low levels of market imperfections—and they are, not surprisingly, the ones most often cited as examples of the benefits of privatization. In other markets, however, supply-side imperfections can be relatively high even though demand-side imperfections are not. As in federal contracting, the more market imperfections there are, the more problems there are for public management (figure 7-1).

In data processing, for example, the market is dominated by a handful of suppliers. The waste disposal business is dominated by just two companies, Browning Ferris Industries and Waste Management Inc. In some markets, the demand-side imperfections are relatively high. In the emerging private prison industry, for example, governments are obviously the only buyers. There would, in fact, be no market for the service without the government's police power. Some markets, notably the market for social services, are highly cooperative. State and local governments hire an extensive network of contractors. The social service arena, however, is a notoriously difficult one in which to define goals and measure results. Thus it is an espe-

26. Osborne and Gaebler, *Reinventing Government,* p. 106.

FIGURE 7-1. *Market Imperfections in State and Local Government Contracting*

	Snow removal	Data processing	Prisons	Social services
Supply-side imperfections	Low	High	High	Very high
Demand-side imperfections	Low	Moderate	Very high	Very high

cially useful setting in which to examine the information problems in state and local governments.

The Market for Social Services

Quite apart from the privatization rhetoric, state and local governments have been moving steadily for a generation toward increasing contracting out for social services. According to one national survey, the share of all social services that governments contracted out climbed from 25 percent in 1971 to 55 percent in 1979.[27] No comparable survey has been conducted since then, but the impressionistic evidence indicates that the share has continued to grow. Most public money spent on social services is funneled through private and nonprofit contractors. Governments directly manage relatively few programs.[28]

Massachusetts has contracted out day care services to more than 600 providers, for example. Other state governments have contracted out the management of hospitals, employment programs, mental health programs, adoption services, child care support enforcement, and medicaid.[29] A 1984 survey of fifty-seven welfare agencies in the San Francisco Bay area showed that over 70 percent of them contracted out at least one social service. "Contracting today is far more than an anomaly on the periphery of the welfare state; it is a core

27. Keon S. Chi, Kevin M. Devlin, and Wayne Masterman, "The Use of the Private Sector in Delivery of Human Services," in Joan W. Allen and others, *The Private Sector in State Service Delivery* (Washington: Urban Institute Press, 1989), pp. 95–96.

28. E. S. Savas, *Privatization: The Key to Better Government* (Chatham, N.J.: Chatham House Publishers, 1987), p. 206.

29. Chi, Devlin, and Masterman, "Use of the Private Sector in Delivery of Human Services"; and Lauder Commission, *Privatization for New York.*

TABLE 7-3. *Contracting Out for Social Services by Local Governments*

Percent

Service	Provided by local government employees	Provided by contract	
		In part	Completely
Homeless shelters	43	32	4
Mental health and retardation programs	35	40	14
Drug and alcohol treatment programs	34	41	14
Day care facility operation	34	27	25
Food programs for the homeless	26	43	5
Operation and management of hospitals	24	19	36
Programs for elderly	19	57	22
Public health programs	19	37	32
Child welfare programs	17	44	33
Public and elderly housing	14	28	22

SOURCE: ICMA, *Service Delivery in the 90s*, p. 96.

feature of ground-level social welfare administration in many service areas," wrote the scholars who conducted the study. They concluded that "the mingling of public and private funds and functions pervades the welfare state."[30]

The ICMA survey revealed a wide range in the contracting practices of local governments for social service programs (table 7-3.) Although contracting is widespread, it is not the only management strategy state and local governments use. Most rely on a mixed strategy, using their own employees to deliver some services directly and contractors to deliver other services.

Contracting out, furthermore, is most common in the largest jurisdictions, as table 7-4 shows. Although the evidence on the reason is unclear, it is unlikely that smaller jurisdictions provide more services themselves. Rather, larger local governments tend to provide more social services, and many social services tend to be contracted out. This tendency to rely on a mixed public-private-nonprofit system to

30. National Commission for Employment Policy, *Privatization and Public Employees*, p. 9.

TABLE 7-4. *Contracting Out, by Size of Locality*
Percent

Population of locality	Food programs for the homeless	Programs for the elderly	Day care facility operation
Under 10,000	0	14	20
10,000–49,000	15	12	22
50,000–249,000	31	27	42
250,000 and over	46	46	59
All cities and counties	26	19	34

SOURCE: ICMA, *Service Delivery in the 90s*, p. 96.

provide the increasing number of social services has made the sectors more interdependent and steadily eroded the boundaries separating them.

The reasons for this growing interdependence are complex. The federal government itself has fueled much of the trend, by providing state and local governments with grants and then mandating that much of the money be funneled through nonprofit community organizations.[31] This mandate became common in the 1960s, largely because the federal government distrusted state and local government. The federal government also directly funded community organizations as a strategy to enfranchise them. In the second generation of programs, during the 1970s, the federal government gave grants to state and local governments with the expectation that they would build upon and strengthen the community organizations that had been created the decade before. Much of the money for job training and community development was spent through neighborhood organizations.[32] Federal grants to state governments for social services encouraged many states to expand their purchase of services from nonprofit

31. Steven R. Smith and Michael Lipsky, *The Age of Contracting: Nonprofit Agencies and the Welfare State* (forthcoming); and Michael O'Neill, *The Third America: The Emergence of the Nonprofit Sector in the United States* (San Francisco: Jossey-Bass, 1989), especially chap. 6.

32. Donald F. Kettl, *Managing Community Development in the New Federalism* (Praeger, 1980); Richard P. Nathan: *Block Grants for Community Development* (Housing and Urban Development Department, 1977); and Richard P. Nathan, *Public Service Employment: A Field Evaluation* (Brookings, 1981).

organizations.[33] They also encouraged the use of contractors by allowing local welfare agencies to receive three dollars for every one dollar a state or local government contributed for social services provided by a contractor. Such matching proved irresistible.[34]

By the third generation of programs in the 1980s, the federal-state-local-private-nonprofit partnership had been firmly established. The Job Training Partnership Act, as its title suggested, relied explicitly on public-private ties to prepare workers for employment. Even though federal funding for such programs decreased, the administrative patterns for the programs that remained became increasingly intertwined.[35] They challenged managers to develop innovative tactics for coordinating and effectively managing community-based programs.[36]

The federal government's medicaid program also contributed to state governments' reliance on private contractors. Medicaid proved to be one of the fastest growing areas of state expenditures in the 1980s. To rein in cost growth, some states turned to private contractors, such as Electronic Data Systems (EDS), to improve their claims management. Kentucky state officials estimated that they saved $1 million to $1.2 million a year through its EDS contract. EDS, they said, achieved a 99 percent accuracy rate while processing claims in an average of three to four days; before EDS was hired, claims processing had taken two weeks.[37] Other states have turned to private contractors to provide home health care and "managed care" to reduce the program's medicaid's costs.[38]

State-local relations have also played a heavy role in stimulating the nonprofit sector. Many states require local governments to provide social services, from child welfare to health programs, sometimes without financing the mandates. Faced with expanding state programs, local governments unsurprisingly have turned to nonprofits.

33. Derthick, *Uncontrollable Spending for Social Services Grants.*

34. Donald Fisk, Herbert Kiesling, and Thomas Muller, *Private Provision of Public Services: An Overview* (Washington: Urban Institute Press, 1978), pp. 52–53.

35. Allen and others, *The Private Sector in State Service Delivery.*

36. Harry P. Hatry and others, *Excellence in Managing: Practical Experiences from Community Development Agencies* (Washington: Urban Institute Press, 1991).

37. Chi, Devlin, and Masterman, "Use of the Private Sector in Delivery of Human Services," pp. 88–89.

38. Edwin S. Rubenstein, "Medicaid," in Lauder Commission, *Privatization for New York*, pp. 44–76.

The nongovernmental social service system is a varied one, composed in part of for-profit concerns such as EDS that provide managerial help and some services (such as health care) and of nonprofit organizations that provide most of the service delivery. For governments, reliance on nonprofits has several advantages. The ICMA survey showed that government officials believe that nonprofits tend to put the welfare of their clients first and that they are responsive to the needs of local citizens. The costs of nonprofits often are lower than the costs of other service providers, because they rely heavily on volunteers. Because nonprofits often pool different sources of funds, government officials believe that they can leverage additional support through grants to the organizations.[39]

Nonprofits have grown rapidly over the last few decades. One study of the nonprofit sector in New York state discovered that between 1981 and 1987 nonprofit employment grew twice as fast as employment in the for-profit world and three times as fast as government employment.[40] Most nonprofits providing social services tend to be relatively small.

What kind of system does this produce? For service providers, it is a system dominated by nonprofits. In New York, for example, these organizations receive about 40 percent of their funding from government and the rest from voluntary contributors and organizations such as the United Way. The financial footing of nonprofits is therefore often uneasy. Moreover, they must not only meet the stringent financial and managerial standards required by federal programs, but serve the needs of their other funding sources as well. As a result, their goals are diverse. Serving public goals is an important, but not the only, part of their mission.

From governments' viewpoint, the system is diverse, extremely complicated, and only partially under their control. Governments seek control of the programs they fund, but other constituencies simultaneously vie for control as well. Governments want to ensure that the money is spent well, but they must struggle with the sometimes bare-bones competence of nonprofit organizations. They seek to co-

39. ICMA, *Service Delivery in the 90s*, p. 97.

40. Avner Ben-Ner and Theresa Van Hoomissen, *A Study of the Nonprofit Sector in New York State: Its Size, Nature, and Economic Impact* (Albany: State University of New York, Rockefeller Institute of Government, 1989).

ordinate their programs with services provided by other organizations, but establishing workable links is difficult. Increasingly, state and local governments have become little more than holding companies, providing public funding for a loosely knit conglomerate of nonprofit and private providers whose behavior ultimately determines the effectiveness of social services.[41]

From an analyst's viewpoint, social services present special problems of privatization. Privatization advocates preach the benefits of competition, but competitive contracting is relatively rare in social services. Most social service contracts tend to be negotiated, not put up for bids.[42] Goals are hard to define, and results are hard to measure. Indeed, social service contracting is justified far more by the pragmatic and complex demands of service delivery than by the cost-saving rhetoric of the competition prescription.

Competition

Finding suppliers for social services, especially qualified nonprofit organizations, is often difficult. A survey of mental health contracting in Massachusetts found that, on the average, each request for proposals issued by the state mental health department received just 1.7 responses. In two-thirds of the "competitively" bid contracts, only one vendor had responded; only two vendors had responded in another 15 percent of the contracts. When state managers encountered problems in finding enough interested contractors, they obtained a waiver of the requirement for competitive bids. The easy way was to declare that a given contract required "unique capabilities" that only one vendor could meet. Three-fourths of the state's contract administrators said that the lack of qualified providers inhibited competition.[43] A study of mental health contracting in Arizona found a similar pattern. The level of contractor competition was so low that the authors of the study described the system as "provider-dominated."[44]

41. For a detailed analysis of these problems, see H. Brinton Milward, Keith Provan, and Barbara Else, "What Does the Hollow State Look Like?" in Barry Bozeman, ed., *Public Management Theory* (San Francisco: Jossey-Bass, forthcoming).

42. Savas, *Privatization*, p. 206.

43. Mark Schlesinger, Robert A. Dortwart, and Richard T. Pulice, "Competitive Bidding and States' Purchase of Services: The Case of Mental Health in Massachusetts," *Journal of Policy Analysis and Management*, vol. 5 (Winter 1986), pp. 251–52.

44. Milward, Provan, and Else, "What Does the Hollow State Look Like?"

In North Carolina, the "availability of suppliers" was a significant problem for 42 percent of county officials.[45] Because of the small number of contractors for Michigan social service programs, "officials were often forced to give contracts to the only available providers, even though they did not always conform to the government's priorities."[46]

The result is less a competitive market than a negotiated network. Neither side in the transaction, in fact, *wants* competition. For the contractors dependent on government contracts for a large portion of their income, competition is a threat to be avoided. Social service contractors frequently become important political forces. When budget cuts have threatened local social service programs, the contractors have frequently been the most active in the battle to save the programs.

For the local government, competition and the potential for changing contractors threatens the consistency of the programs. In dealing with persons in need, as is the case by definition in most social service programs, continuity of care is important. "You might compete at the front end to get in," one county social service manager said, "but once you get in, it tends to be a network. There has to be a stability in the system."[47] Massachusetts scholars found the same thing: "Many programs may therefore, to protect what they perceive as quality care, act to discourage competition."[48] The desire for continuity promotes a tendency to develop long-term relationships with contractors that social service managers know and trust. Dependence becomes mutual.

To the degree that social service contracting produces lower costs, it is by replacing government workers with lower-paid contract workers. Because wage and fringe benefits rates are open to competition, moreover, state and local governments have a difficult time judging the relative bids of contractors. Work tends to be labor-intensive, so

45. Beverly A. Cigler, "County Contracting: Reconciling the Accountability and Information Paradoxes," *Public Administration Quarterly*, vol. 14 (Fall 1990), pp. 285–301.

46. Ruth Hoogland DeHoog, *Contracting Out for Human Services: Economic, Political, and Organizational Perspectives* (State University of New York Press, 1984), p. 130.

47. Interview with Carol Lobes, director, Dane County, Wisconsin, Department of Human Services, June 11, 1992.

48. Schlesinger, Dortwart, and Pulice, "Competitive Bidding and States' Purchase of Services," p. 252.

most differences between competing bids—when there are competing bids—rest on differences in wage and, especially, fringe benefit rates. Local officials worry about whether they should reward low bidders with contracts when the bids are lower because of a thin fringe benefits package.

Competition is by its very nature disruptive to social services. It imposes high transaction costs on both the buyer (the government) and the seller (the contractor).[49] If social service contracting is a child of the privatization movement, with its reverence for competition, it is a prodigal child. Virtually no one directly involved in the social service system—government, contractor, or client—has any incentive to disrupt the system once it is established. The monopolistic behavior of government, which lies at the core of the privatization arguments, has been replaced by monopolistic behavior on the part of its contractors.

Defining Goals

The very nature of social services, with their fuzzy objectives and uncertain technologies, makes it difficult for governments to write crisp, enforceable contracts. Contractors naturally resist goals that are too specific or that hold them to levels of performance they doubt they can achieve. Governments cannot prescribe in advance exactly what outcomes they want or, if they know the outcomes, they cannot explain how to get there. This inability to articulate precise goals can be a severe problem. In fact, in a survey of North Carolina counties, respondents rated the problem of what should be written into contracts as the top information problem they had to solve.[50]

State and local governments typically attempt to solve the problem in two ways. First, instead of setting out the goals to be achieved, contracts typically define units of service to be performed. A contract might specify, for example, the number of hours of consultant time to be provided or the number of persons to be served. Contracts thus have tended to define input or process measures, not outcome measures. Given the nature of the activity, the contract mechanism, and

49. Ruth Hoogland DeHoog, "Competition, Negotiation, or Cooperation: Three Models for Service Contracting," *Administration and Society*, vol. 22 (1990), p. 323.
50. Cigler, "County Contracting," p. 296.

the small work force devoted to contract management, however, definition of inputs is about as well as the government can do.

Second, because governments usually manage their relationships with contractors through process measures, they have a hard time knowing what *results* the programs actually produce. It is a maxim in the social service business that activity alone cannot guarantee results. It is one thing to bring children to a day care center and pick them up unharmed at the end of the day. It is quite another for the day care center to provide solid nutrition and a nurturing learning environment for the children in its care. Simply counting the number of children in day care tells little about what happens to them during the day. Without much competition in the social services market, moreover, there are precious few sources of information about what the government's alternatives might be: how other contractors might operate differently and produce different results. Thus governments have difficulty not only defining and communicating what they want, but also knowing what they are getting and what their options might have been.

Monitoring Performance

State and local governments typically devote few staff members or other resources to oversight. In one Wisconsin county, for example, just 11 workers must supervise 143 contractors managing 360 separate contracts accounting for $60 million—two-thirds of the county's social services budget. In circumstances like these, government workers have time for little more than processing paper. Tracking how contractors are spending public money, let alone whether it is being spent effectively, is nearly impossible. In such cases oversight consists of self-reporting by contractors.

In fact, if there is any overriding consensus on social service contracting in state and local governments, it is that oversight is virtually nonexistent. "Actually, most agencies do not know what their costs are, and others do not consider it worth the cost to find out," public management expert John Rehfuss observed.[51] In Arizona, according to one report, "There was no attempt by the state department of health services to monitor the performance of the local providers. The

---

51. Rehfuss, *Contracting Out in Government,* pp. 45–46.

department of health services stated that they did not have the administrative capacity to engage in performance evaluation."[52]

Nearly two-thirds of North Carolina county administrators reported that "difficulty in managing the performance of contracts" was the "greatest disadvantage" in contracting out.[53] Two Michigan state departments charged with managing social service programs generally failed to conduct on-site inspections and relied instead on self-reporting by the contractors. In Massachusetts, the level of oversight was so low that the state embarrassed itself by paying contractors who delivered no service at all.[54]

Thus it is no exaggeration to say that state and local governments tend not to know what results their social service contracts are buying. Because competition is low, they have little opportunity to test the market to see what alternatives they have. Few resources are spent to look past what the contractors themselves report. The political system has few incentives for digging deeper and many more incentives to maintain the status quo. In fact, without effective monitoring, contracts "may degenerate into what are effective monopolies for the private vendors."[55] The problems with oversight underline earlier observations: whatever advantages contracting out for social services might produce, greater efficiency through market-tested competition is not one of them. State and local governments are engaging in the equivalent of a shopping trip while blindfolded, with little effort spent to squeeze the tomatoes or thump the watermelons.

Accountability in Service Networks

In traditional public administration, the basic players are elected officials, administrators, and citizens. With the addition of contractors, the players increase to four. As public administration scholar John Johnston has pointed out, that means that "the number of relationships has doubled and the complexity has increased exponentially."[56]

52. Milward, Provan, and Else, "What Does the Hollow State Look Like?"
53. Cigler, "County Contracting," p. 293.
54. DeHoog, Contracting Out for Human Services, pp. 101–12.
55. Schlesinger, Dortwart, and Pulice, "Competitive Bidding and States' Purchase of Services," pp. 254, 248.
56. John Johnston, "Public Servants and Private Contractors: Managing the Mixed Service Delivery System," Canadian Public Administration, vol. 29 (Winter 1986), p. 550.

FIGURE 7-2. *Accountability in the Social Service Network*

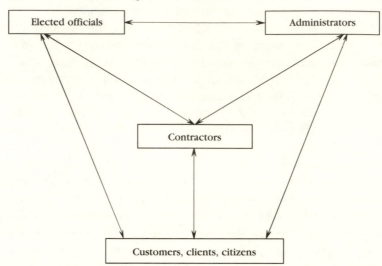

SOURCE: John Johnston, "Public Servants and Private Contractors: Managing the Mixed Service Delivery System," *Canadian Public Administration*, vol. 29 (Winter 1986). p. 550.

Contractors assume a critical position as intermediaries in the governmental system, standing between the governmental apparatus—elected officials and administrators—and citizens (figure 7-2). Their ability to make direct links to each of the other three players gives contractors a great deal of autonomy from any one of them.

The philosophy of contracting out presumes that the basic relationship between government and contractor will be that of principal and agent. The contractor's job is to act as agent of the government's policy. The relationship is fractured, however, if contractors create independent political ties with policymakers and thus outflank their administrative overseers. In such cases contractors are less agents than partners, helping to shape the very design of the program, free of any significant oversight, and beneficiary of state and local governments' dependence on their performance.

As was the case in federal contracting, the demands on state and local managers increase as imperfections in the market for goods and services increase. The areas of fastest growth and most significance in state and local contracting—indeed, perhaps in all of state and local administration—are precisely those where the market is least able to supply its discipline. The experience of state and local governments underlines the lessons of the case studies in this book: government's growing reliance on contractors has created complex interwoven networks that not only do not manage themselves but impose new and often greater demands on its public managers. Beneath the veneer of privatization rhetoric have grown administrative challenges of astounding size and variation.[57]

Government must manage well to ensure effective services at the lowest possible cost. But effective management is not enough. Government must also govern to secure the policy interests adopted by elected officials and, more generally, to promote the welfare of citizens as a whole. The government's interests—the public interest—transcend those of all other participants in the market. I turn to that issue in the next chapters.

57. A helpful study of pragmatic approaches to the problems of contracting out, at all levels of government, is Susan A. MacManus, *Doing Business With Government: Federal, State, Local and Foreign Government Practices for Every Business and Public Institution* (Paragon House, 1992).

8

The Smart-Buyer Problem

Put together, the four federal case studies and the study of state and local contracting lead to one overwhelming point. The rhetoric of the competition prescription is that greater reliance on private markets can solve many of the problems of public monopoly. Governments often do save money through contracting. Recurring market imperfections, however, make it hard to produce good results consistently or to ensure that governments, in contracting out, do not simply shift problems to another setting that will have to be managed at another time. Even in markets with the fewest imperfections, such as the federal government's A-76 contracting program, barriers to competition reduced many of the advantages of a competitive market. As market imperfections increase, so too do the problems. As the study on the telecommunications market illustrated, a market dominated by a handful of firms presents substantial supply-side imperfections, which can make it difficult for the government to strike a good deal. Most important, as demand-side—that is, the government's own—imperfections increase, problems with contracting grow exponentially, as the study of nuclear weapons procurement showed. These problems are mirrored in state and local contracting for social service programs.

It would be tempting to point to these very cases as evidence supporting the competition prescription. Privatization advocates might contend that the market would have solved many of the problems described in the case studies if the government had only allowed it to function without interference. The evidence, however, is that the prob-

179

lems are based fundamentally on the nature of the goods and services the government is buying. Defects in the market are inescapable.

I am not attacking either privatization or competition. Indeed, contracting out makes eminent sense for many governmental programs because there are many goods and services that the government cannot, or should not, produce on its own. Rather, the evidence of the case studies suggests two points. First, not all contracts are equal. The difference between contracting out a government cafeteria and contracting out the production of nuclear weapons could scarcely be greater.

Second, these contracts do not manage themselves. The much-praised self-discipline of the market exists only when competition can reward success and punish failures. If market imperfections hinder such self-discipline, problems ranging from conflicts of interest to fraud can simmer. These two points lead to one clear conclusion: as market imperfections increase and market self-discipline decreases, the more important it is for the government to act as a smart buyer.

The Government as Smart Buyer

To act as a smart buyer, the government—whether federal, state, or local—must know how to answer three questions suggested by the principal-agent theory laid out in chapter 2: what to buy, who to buy it from, and what it has bought.

What to Buy

First, the government must know *what it wants to buy*. It must be able to define its goals independently of its private partners. Considerable collaboration is possible, even inevitable. In the end, however, if the government is to maintain its sovereignty, it alone must make the decision about what to buy. A smart car buyer does not allow the salesperson to dictate what kind of car to buy. The risks are obvious. The incentive for the salesperson is to sell a bigger, more expensive car than the buyer wants and that may be the wrong car for the buyer's needs. Only smart buyers, who know what they want to buy, can ensure that they get what they want at the best price.

As the cases showed, competitive markets can help the government define the product. The A-76 contracts were for commercially available goods and services, so the market presented federal managers with many options. Indeed, the market itself helped define the goods and services, as it does, for example, for car buyers. As market imperfections multiplied, however, defining the product became harder. When supply-side imperfections increased, such as in the FTS-2000 oligopoly, the market's capacity to frame the government's choices diminished. The government and its contractors gingerly felt their way into brand new technology. When demand-side imperfections grew, such as in Superfund, the government's capacity to frame precisely what the program ought to accomplish shrank. And when imperfections on both sides multiplied, as in the Department of Energy (DOE) case, the smart-buyer problems were the greatest. Competitive markets help define options; without good markets, government has very little independent information on which to base its purchasing decisions.

Who to Buy From

Second, smart buyers must know *who can sell them what they want*. Even in the A-76 process, government agencies frequently struggled to find competent contractors. In contracting for a new telecommunications system, the government's most fundamental task was choosing which of the competing companies could best provide the new generation of services it wanted. Assessing whether suppliers could actually deliver what they promised was even more difficult in the Superfund and DOE cases. As market imperfections increase, the harder it is for the government to know from whom to buy. Without competitive markets to shake out the better from the worse suppliers, the government-as-buyer struggled to make its own judgments independent of the information that markets might otherwise have provided.

What Has Been Bought

Third, smart buyers must know *how to judge what they have bought*. This is the core of principal-agent theory and the critical step in the smart-buying process. To continue the example, car buyers have a number of ways to judge the quality of what they have bought. They can turn to magazines and radio shows that rate the relative quality of different vehicles. Mechanics can provide information about individual cars, helping consumers balance their driver's seat view with an under-the-hood perspective. If the intricacy of each car's innards makes it difficult for car buyers to really know what they are buying, the competitive market helps solve the problem by presenting consumers with many choices. If consumers do not like one car, they can trade it in for another. The accumulation of such decisions—measured in the marketplace, in buyer-satisfaction indexes, and in word-of-mouth recommendations—provides broader information about which cars are good and which are not.

The markets in which the government buys goods and services, however, do not provide nearly as effective a check on quality. Even goods and services bought through the A-76 process can be amorphous enough in nature to muddy signals about success and failure. Competing suppliers may be enmeshed in conflicts of interest so that feedback is more a sign of eagerness for business than quality product offered by a superior supplier. As market imperfections increase, the government's difficulty in gaining feedback grows. Because the government often has a hard time knowing what to buy, it has a hard time judging the quality of what it has bought. The federal government's usual approach is to assume that the market knows best. Given the alleged advantages of the market over government, whatever the market produces is often believed to be superior. This assumption can lead to disappointment and new problems—witness the contamination from nuclear weapons facilities and conflicts of interest among Superfund contractors.

Mutual Dependence

The actual markets in which the federal government buys its goods and services are thus very different from the assumptions and arguments embodied in the competition prescription. The federal government's reliance on private contractors predates the theory of privatization by decades; the government's connections with its private contractors have evolved quite apart from the theory; and its oversight of its contractors raises critical questions that the theory of privatization does not anticipate. Most fundamentally, the federal government's relationships with its private contractors are not those required by the competitive market. Instead of arm's-length transactions among many buyers and sellers for undifferentiated goods and ser-vices, the relationship between government and its contractors is frequently one of mutual dependence.

The case studies help focus three important questions. First, what are the basic relationships between the government-as-buyer and the contractors-as-sellers? Second, how do these relationships vary? Third, what lessons do these relationships teach about managing mutual dependence?

Relations among Buyers and Sellers

Market imperfections have three important and overlapping effects on the relationships between buyers and sellers: convergence of in-terests, eroding boundaries, and more tightly coupled relationships among them.

CONVERGENCE IN INTERESTS. As market imperfections grow, the government's market alternatives shrink. As alternatives diminish, in-terdependence between contractors and the government grows. Gov-ernment contracts have allowed many contractors to expand their businesses and brought others into existence. The toxic-waste cleanup business is unlikely to have developed, at least on its existing scale, without federal law. Without the government-as-buyer, a nuclear weapons complex like the one that DOE and its predecessors devel-oped simply would not exist.

As Murray Weidenbaum pointed out, "government-oriented corpor-ations" such as defense and aerospace companies, try to hold on to their government business by creating a "tendency for a convergence" in interests between government and its contractors. As a result, some private contractors have become "virtual appendages of the government."[1]

Likewise, because of the government's own limited capacity, its dependence on private contractors has grown. Without private con-tractors, many federal programs simply could not exist. From medicare

1. Murray Weidenbaum, *The Modern Public Sector: New Ways of Doing the Gov-ernment's Business* (Basic Books, 1969), pp. 34, 33. See also Clarence H. Danhof, *Government Contracting and Technological Change* (Brookings, 1968); and Thomas L. McNaugher, *New Weapons, Old Politics: America's Military Procurement Muddle* (Brookings, 1989).

to space, from defense to environmental cleanup, the government does not have enough employees in-house to perform the work that legislation demands. Hiring private contractors is a pragmatic necessity. In some programs, such as the A-76 process, the government often has choices. As supply-side imperfections grow, however, the government's market choices shrink. In the FTS-2000 competition, the government had trouble maintaining even an artificial marketplace. Even fewer alternatives existed for nuclear weapons production. Not surprisingly, as supply-side imperfections increase, the government's interdependence with its contractors increases as well. That suggests the following proposition: *As market imperfections increase, interdependence among buyers and sellers increases.*

ERODING BOUNDARIES. The growing interdependence has often tended to blur the boundaries between buyer and seller, government and contractor—indeed, between public and private. "In effect," Clarence H. Danhof pointed out long ago, "the government has reinterpreted the nature of the public interest, moving and blurring the boundaries between what is public and what is private."[2] This erosion of boundaries has several important effects on the behavior of government and its contractors.

First, the boundaries of an organization help define what it is and what it does.[3] Organizations take in resources across these boundaries, process them in some way, and export them back across the boundaries. The boundaries define an organization's domain, its technical core, and the functions that are required to link that core with the larger environment in which it operates.[4] As boundaries blur, it becomes harder to determine with confidence where one organization, such as the government, ends, and where another, such as the contractor, begins.

Second, the government-as-buyer faces enormous uncertainty, especially about the technical aspects of its programs and the political

2. Danhof, *Government Contracting and Technological Change*, p. 13.
3. See, for example, Philip Selznick, *TVA and the Grass Roots: A Study of Politics and Organizations* (University of California Press, 1949); Daniel Katz and Robert L. Kahn, *The Social Psychology of Organizations* (Wiley, 1966); James D. Thompson, *Organizations in Action* (McGraw Hill, 1967); and Mayer Zald, "The Social Control of Industries," *Social Forces*, vol. 57 (September 1978), pp. 79–102.
4. See Thompson, *Organizations in Action.*

environment in which they must function. It must deal with those uncertainties at its boundaries. That is where government organizations exchange inputs for outputs: where they take in the public's tax money and produce the programs with which they have been entrusted.[5] When boundaries are blurred, the job of absorbing that uncertainty—of drawing information from the environment, processing it, and transmitting it in ways the organization can use—becomes far more difficult.[6] Blurred boundaries increase uncertainty, and greater uncertainty complicates the jobs of government managers.

The boundary of the organization thus is the locus of the smart-buyer problem. Because contracting out tends to blur organizational boundaries, it tends also to increase the problems the government faces in absorbing uncertainty. Where market imperfections are the greatest, organizational boundaries are the fuzziest and the problems of absorbing uncertainty are the greatest. Thus: *As market imperfections increase, the problems of absorbing uncertainty increase.*

TIGHTLY COUPLED RELATIONSHIPS. When relations among participants in a marketplace are at arm's length, the behavior of one participant does not necessarily affect others. In a market with many auto dealerships, for example, the bankruptcy of one is unlikely to have a great effect on the other dealerships or on consumers. The same is roughly true in the government's most competitive marketplaces, such as the A-76 contracting process. As relationships become more tightly coupled, however, disturbances in one part of the market can quickly spread throughout it. In the FTS-2000 case, where there were only two competitors, Sprint's aggressive marketing practices quickly disturbed AT&T's market share and the General Service Administration's management of the entire contract. Conflict-of-interest problems multiplied through Superfund contracts because of the high interdependence of the contracting system. DOE's ties to its nuclear weapons contractors were so close that it often was impossible to discern differences between them. The interests of buyer and seller became

5. Talcott Parsons, *Structure and Process in Modern Societies* (Free Press, 1960), p. 18.
6. James G. March and Herbert A. Simon, *Organizations* (Wiley, 1958), p. 165. See also Gary Wamsley and Mayer N. Zald, *The Political Economy of Organizations* (Lexington, Mass.: Lexington Books, 1973), p. 59.

indistinguishable. In short: *As market imperfections increase, buyers and sellers become more tightly coupled.*

Organizational Learning

To survive and prosper, organizations must be able to conquer the uncertainties that surround them. They must learn which organizational structures and which behaviors work best in the particular environments they face.[7] If they are to be smart buyers, organizations need to learn: they need to detect and correct errors if they are to avoid repeating them. If they do not, they will fall victim to "wooden-headedness," as historian Barbara Tuchman calls it, "the refusal to benefit from experience."[8]

At best, wooden-headedness can lead to slow organizational decline. At worst, it can have catastrophic implications for both the organization and for the citizens it serves.[9] Both conflicts of interest and bureaucratic cultures can make learning difficult.

7. On the importance and role of organizational learning, see Richard M. Cyert and James G. March, *A Behavioral Theory of the Firm* (Prentice-Hall, 1963); Aaron Wildavsky, "The Self-Evaluating Organization," *Public Administration Review*, vol. 32 (September–October 1972), pp. 509–20; James G. March and Johan P. Olsen, "The Uncertainty of the Past: Organizational Learning under Ambiguity," *European Journal of Political Research*, vol. 3 (March 1975), pp. 147–71; Chris Argyris and Donald A. Schon, *Organizational Learning: A Theory of Action Perspective* (Reading, Mass.: Addison-Wesley, 1978); Robert Duncan and Andrew Weiss, "Organizational Learning: Implications for Organizational Design," in Barry M. Staw, ed., *Research in Organizational Behavior*, vol. 1 (1979), pp. 75–123; Bo Hedberg, "How Organizations Learn and Unlearn," in Paul C. Nystrom and William H. Starbuck, eds., *Handbook of Organizational Design* (Oxford University Press, 1981), pp. 3–27; C. Marlene Fiol and Marjorie A. Lyles, "Organizational Learning," *Academy of Management Review*, vol. 10 (October 1985), pp. 803–13; Warren Bennis Warren and Burt Nanus, "Organizational Learning: The Management of the Collective Self," *New Management*, vol. 3 (Summer 1985), pp. 7–13; Ronald J. Burke and Catherine Bolf, "Learning within Organizations: Sources and Content," *Psychological Reports*, vol. 59 (December 1986), pp. 1187–96; Laurence E. Lynn, Jr., *Managing Public Policy* (Little, Brown, 1987); Richard L. Daft and George P. Huber, "How Organizations Learn: A Communication Framework," *Research in the Sociology of Organizations*, vol. 5 (1987), pp. 1–36; Robert B. Behn, "Management by Groping Along," *Journal of Policy Analysis and Management*, vol. 7 (Fall 1988), pp. 643–63; Barbara Levitt and James G. March, "Organizational Learning," *Annual Review of Sociology*, vol. 14 (1988), pp. 319–40; and James G. March and Johan P. Olsen, *Rediscovering Institutions: The Organizational Basis of Politics* (Free Press, 1989).

8. Barbara W. Tuchman, *The March of Folly: From Troy to Vietnam* (Knopf, 1984), p. 7.

9. Harold L. Wilensky, *Organizational Intelligence: Knowledge and Policy in Government and Industry* (Basic Books, 1967), p. 7.

CONFLICTS OF INTEREST. The competitive market is a wonderful learning device. It creates strong incentives for adaptation, rewards those who succeed, and punishes harshly those who fail. As market imperfections nudge aside competition, however, the ability of the market to police itself declines. New problems rise as competition declines. As the case studies showed, conflicts of interest among contractors undercut the ability of the market to produce reliable information. In Superfund, for example, contractors hired to evaluate the performance of other contractors had strong incentives to underrate their competitors to win a piece of the business. Government itself did not have the capacity to evaluate the contractors' performance independently. Thus: *As market imperfections increase, conflicts of interest reduce the quality and quantity of information the market supplies to the government.*

BUREAUCRATIC CULTURES. An organization's ability to learn depends, obviously, on the flow of information. How well that information flows depends on how various cultures within the organization distort the processing of the information and on the ways that these cultures influence communications among organizations. A quick survey of how organizations process information suggests important implications for how organizations learn—in particular, the problems that government agencies managing contracts must solve if they are to learn effectively.

The smooth flow of information is inherently problematic. Information may simply be *omitted* as it is passed up the bureaucracy from the bottom to the top. The sheer volume of information can overwhelm managers, so lower-level officials may filter out many of the details. Crucial information may be buried simply because lower-level officials do not realize its importance. Information can also be *distorted.* Its meaning can be changed, or information can be systematically slanted, most often by passing along good news and suppressing the bad.[10] From his career working both in the Pentagon and as the

10. See Donald T. Campbell, "Systematic Error on the Part of Human Links in Communication Systems," *Information and Control,* vol. 1 (1958), pp. 334–69; March and Simon, *Organizations;* Cyert and March, *A Behavioral Theory of the Firm;* Harold Guetzkow, "Communications in Organizations," in James G. March, ed., *Handbook of Organizations* (Rand McNally, 1965), pp. 534–73; and Anthony Downs, *Inside Bureaucracy* (Little, Brown, 1967).

executive of a major defense contractor, Norman Augustine observed that managers "quickly learn to fear bad news with even greater fervor than they covet good news."[11] Bad news can bring retribution from superiors, threaten an agency's budget, and weaken a program's political support.

The ways in which information is condensed and distorted depend on the lenses through which individuals view that information. Such lenses create frames of reference that influence how individuals relate to other members of their organization (and to members of other organizations). Individuals with different lenses view data differently and sometimes tend to talk past each other. Individuals who see through the same lenses tend to process information in similar ways.[12] Such shared perceptions can lead in turn to a kind of "groupthink" phenomenon in which consensus matters more than discriminating analysis.[13]

Each organization tends to breed its own culture. Some culture building occurs through recruitment of new members, since officials doing the hiring tend to select individuals with some values more than others. If certain professions come to dominate the organization, moreover, the norms of those professions can shape the organization's culture.[14] Lawyers, for example, tend to see problems as legal ones, while engineers define tasks in engineering terms. Once on board, individuals tend to pick up the organization's norms, which are reinforced by social interactions among the organization's members.

These norms, in turn, shape the way that individuals and organizations learn. They provide a way of understanding a complex environment. They help rationalize what has happened in the past, which then provides a mechanism for making sense of the future. Such norms reinforce the organization's culture and simplify communica-

11. Norman R. Augustine, *Augustine's Laws* (Viking, 1986), p. 328.
12. See March and Simon, *Organizations;* Katz and Kahn, *Social Psychology of Organizations;* Thompson, *Organizations in Action;* Michael L. Tushman, "Special Boundary Roles in the Innovation Process," *Administrative Science Quarterly,* vol. 22 (December 1977), pp. 587–605; and Duncan and Weiss, "Organizational Learning," pp. 75–123.
13. Irving L. Janis, *Victims of Groupthink* (Houghton Mifflin, 1972).
14. Paul Shrivastava and Susan Schneider, "Organizational Frames of Reference," *Human Relations,* vol. 37 (October 1984), p. 801.

tion, by reducing the vast uncertainty that clutters the organization's environment.[15]

In addition to cultures that affect whole organizations, layers of different cultures tend to build up within them. Typical analysis of bureaucratic structure tends to assume a continuous chain of command from top to bottom. Talcott Parsons argued, however, that there are three levels within a bureaucracy and that important distinctions characterize the behavior of employees at each level, independent of their functions. At the *technical* level, he said, employees concentrate on competently handling the basic job of the organization, processing inputs into outputs. At the *managerial* level, employees concentrate on making the technical functions work, by securing the resources that the technical workers need. At the *institutional* level, employees serve as mediators between the organization and the broader political environment in which the organization operates.[16]

What is the significance of these different levels? Two variants on the following proposition, richly illustrated by the DOE case study in chapter 6, suggest themselves: *As market imperfections increase, internal organizational cultures become more important than market incentives. (1) Different cultures at different levels of the same organization inhibit the flow of information up the chain of command. (2) The same culture in different organizations often produces a flow of information across organizational boundaries but not up the chain of command.*

As the DOE case study illustrated, these cultures can create three different blocks to the flow of information and, thus, to organizational learning. The technicians tended to *see no evil*. They saw their jobs narrowly, in terms of solving the technical problems at their workbenches. Broader issues, such as environmental concerns, were not seen as problems because their technical lenses did not allow them to see the issues that way. The managers tended to *speak no evil*. With a narrow focus on production, they tended to define away issues

15. See Terrence E. Deal and Allan A. Kennedy, *Corporate Cultures: The Rites and Rituals of Corporate Life* (Reading, Mass.: Addison-Wesley, 1982); and Edgar H. Schein, *Organizational Culture and Leadership* (San Francisco: Jossey-Bass, 1987).

16. Parsons, *Structure and Process in Modern Societies,* pp. 60–65. See also Thompson, *Organizations in Action,* pp. 10–12; and Paul H. Appleby, *Policy and Administration* (University of Alabama Press, 1949).

that did not relate directly to production. The institutionalists, finally, tended to *hear no evil*. In the constant struggle to ensure political support, they had little time and less incentive to pay attention to problems bubbling up from within the agency.

Thus information about environmental problems tended to be ignored; when the information was recognized, it tended not to be passed up the chain of command; and when it was passed up, it tended to be interpreted as a minor issue that could be dealt with at some point in the future. At each level within DOE, organizational cultures tended to condense and distort the flow of information in ways that kept the bad news from flowing up. In the end, these cultures prevented DOE from learning—until the costs of failing to learn became so large and catastrophic that they no longer could be ignored. In the long run, the failure to learn also undercut DOE's political support. The department lost the trust and confidence of the political communities with which it had to work.

These cultures are present to some extent in almost every government organization, but the pathologies they create are worse where the market imperfections are highest. The tight coupling between DOE and its contractors exaggerated the effects of the bureaucratic culture. The Superfund case study demonstrated some evidence of the culture as well, although problems were much less severe. In FTS-2000 and A-76, the bureaucratic culture problem was virtually invisible. Barriers to organizational learning tended to be highest when market imperfections, especially demand-side imperfections, were greatest.

The explosion of the space shuttle *Challenger* on a cold January morning in 1986 provides further evidence that agencies operating in markets with high imperfections struggle to learn. Just seventy-three seconds after launch, a fiery hole in one of the shuttle's solid-rocket boosters ignited the external fuel tank, full of hydrogen and oxygen. The shuttle exploded, killing the seven astronauts on board and horrifying millions of viewers watching on live television.[17]

The subsequent investigation revealed that National Aeronautic and Space Administration (NASA) officials had been alerted about the risk

17. For an excellent analysis of the leadership issues involved in the *Challenger* disaster, see Barbara S. Romzek and Melvin J. Dubnick, "Accountability in the Public Sector: Lessons from the Challenger Tragedy," *Public Administration Review*, vol. 47 (May–June 1987), pp. 227–38.

of launching the shuttle on such a cold morning. The night before the launch, technicians from Morton Thiokol, the contractor that built the *Challenger*'s solid-rocket booster, had warned officials that launching in the cold weather predicted for the next morning could prove disastrous. The solid-rocket boosters had developed holes in the past, and some technicians feared there was a connection between cold weather and the booster's seals. The weather predicted for Cape Kennedy was more than 20 degrees below the previous low temperature for a shuttle launch, 53 degrees. At even higher temperatures, the O-ring seals had partially failed. "We should not fly outside of our data base," these technicians warned NASA.[18]

Both NASA officials and Morton Thiokol engineers fully understood the potentially catastrophic implications of a failure of the booster's seals. What they fundamentally disagreed on was the *likelihood* of failure: the odds that the cold temperature predicted for the next morning would cause the seals to fail. According to the report on the disaster by a presidential commission, Lawrence Mulloy, NASA's solid-rocket booster manager, was furious with Thiokol. "My God, Thiokol, when do you want me to launch, next April?" he said. George Hardy, NASA's Marshall Space Flight Center deputy director, added, "I'm appalled at your recommendation."[19] The mission was already a week late, having been plagued by weather, equipment problems, and a wrench that would not work right. Newspaper and television correspondents were joking that NASA could not seem to do anything right. There was, moreover, heavy pressure to move toward an ambitious "operational" launch schedule of twenty-four flights a year, and the problems NASA continued to encounter getting the *Challenger* into the air threatened that goal.

Caught between their own engineers and the government agency that hired them, Thiokol's managers met privately to decide whether to support their engineers or to accept Mulloy's argument. The managers were acutely aware of proposals to add a new contractor for the solid-rocket boosters and possibly to replace Thiokol as contractor. Reliability problems with Thiokol's rockets could spur such a change. Overruling their engineers, Thiokol's managers cleared the

18. Presidential Commission on the Space Shuttle *Challenger* Accident (hereafter Rogers Commission), *Report to the President* (1986), p. 90.

19. Rogers Commission, *Report to the President*, pp. 94, 96.

launch. Their contract provided "far greater incentives for minimizing costs and meeting schedules than for features related to safety and performance," a House committee report later concluded.[20] Thiokol engineer Allan McDonald argued that, if anything went wrong, he did not want to have to explain the decision to a board of inquiry. Seconds after the explosion, which Thiokol's technicians and managers watched live on television, many of its engineers guessed what had happened.

In arguing that the launch should be delayed, Thiokol technicians rose above the "see no evil" posture. Thiokol managers, however, overruled the engineers with a "speak no evil" judgment. Top NASA officials, including the directors of the launch team—the institutionalists—did not learn about the engineers' worries until the inquiry had begun. They did not have a chance to rule on whether the shuttle should be launched in cold weather because the managers never presented them with the decision.

The institutionalists were not blameless in the disaster, however. Top NASA officials had been briefed on the O-ring problem, including the potential that they could fail, but "always in a way that didn't communicate the seriousness" of the risk, a House committee report concluded. "The existing communication system is disseminating too much information, often with little or no discrimination in its importance. Accordingly recipients often have difficulty 'separating the wheat from the chaff.' "[21] At the institutional level, the flood of information from below gave few clues about which problems were really important. The relative lack of technical expertise at the top, coupled with officials' need to shore up NASA's dwindling political base, blinded them to the problem until it was too late.

Some months after the disaster, Lawrence Mulloy explained why it happened in terms that underline how bureaucratic cultures can block information:

In hindsight, obviously, more should have been done. The turning, I think, we started down a road where we had a design deficiency.

20. *Investigation of the Challenger Accident*, Report of the House Committee on Science and Technology, 99 Cong. 2 sess. (Government Printing Office, 1986), p. 179.
21. *Investigation of the Challenger Accident*, pp. 172, 6.

When we recognized that it had design deficiency, we did not fix it. Then we continued to fly with it, and rationalized why it was safe, and eventually concluded and convinced ourselves that it was an acceptable risk. That was—when we started down that road, we started down the road to eventually having the inevitable accident. I believe that.[22]

A competitive market might have made both Thiokol and NASA managers more open to dealing with problems as they arose. Suppliers that produce troublesome goods or services can be replaced in a competitive market, and potential competitors can be trusted to put their case forward aggressively. The less the competition and the greater the interdependence, however, the less likely the market's self-discipline is to work—and the more likely the market is to be blinded to the lessons that an effective system of learning might teach.

In the end, therefore, market imperfections tend to promote interdependence. In the short run, the tight coupling between buyers and sellers can reduce the uncertainties—both political and technical—with which they must deal. In the long run, however, the reduction of uncertainty by stifling organizational learning creates the potential for instability. Pressures must be released sooner or later. They can be released gradually, by detecting or correcting problems when they are small. If pressures are allowed to build up, they tend to erupt, like a volcano, in ways that may be costly and uncontrollable. Hence: *As the ability to learn decreases, the interdependence among buyers and sellers increases but the potential for instability increases as well.*

Management Issues for Contracting

The more the government has come to rely on contractors, the more it has encountered the smart-buyer problem. The logic of contracting out makes eminent sense for those markets in which there is reasonable competition, that is, where the imperfections on both the demand and supply sides do not block the discipline on which the privatizers build their case. In many, perhaps most, markets in which

22. *Investigation of the Challenger Accident*, p. 161.

the government buys its goods and services, however, these assumptions simply do not hold. Supply-side imperfections, as the FTS-2000 case illustrates, can limit the government's choices. Even worse, demand-side imperfections—the government's capacity to act as smart buyer—cripple the model. A smart buyer could manage supply-side imperfections. Imperfect markets cannot compensate for demand-side imperfections; indeed, they aggravate them. If *caveat emptor* is the watchword in the marketplace, what happens if the *emptor* cannot *caveat*?

The simple answer is that the government must improve its capacity to act as a smart buyer or settle for ineffective programs. Contracting out can save money, but at the same time it imposes new, and often significant, costs, what economists call "transaction costs."[23] Contracting can result in two kinds of transaction costs. The first is the cost of investing in the capacity to act as smart buyer. Too often, however, the government has underinvested in that capacity, and its ability to act as a smart buyer has suffered as a result. If the government does not develop its capacity to act as a smart buyer, it incurs costs of second kind: inefficient and ineffective programs, which can produce substantial side costs such as pollution and can undermine public trust and confidence in government itself. Thus: *As market imperfections increase, the government's transaction costs increase.*

Instead of developing its own capacity to determine what to buy, government has turned to contractors. In many cases government agencies have given some of their fundamental functions over to contractors. A 1991 review by the General Accounting Office of 108 randomly selected contracts at the Department of Transportation, the Department of Energy, and the Environmental Protection Agency showed that in 28 of them, the contractors were performing "inherently governmental functions"—functions that by law and policy ought to have been left to the government. Contractors helped these government agencies write testimony, determine whether security clearances were required for a particular project, and develop policy. Contractors even helped EPA develop its own definitions for what an inherently governmental function was. In most cases, the agencies

23. See Ronald H. Coase, "The Nature of the Firm," *Economica*, vol. 4 (November 1937), pp. 386–405; and Oliver E. Williamson, *Markets and Hierarchies: Analysis and Antitrust Implications* (Free Press, 1975).

relied on contractors because congressionally imposed personnel ceilings did not allow them to hire government employees to do the job. GAO found

> serious problems with various government programs in which the government may have placed substantial reliance on contractors and with that lost its capacity to manage the contracts effectively. The problems in the examples we found suggest that the government should not relinquish its control over important projects involving contractor support. When the government allows contractors to assume control over key functions, situations that are not in the government's best interest and that may be costly to correct could result.[24]

In fact, situations "that are not in the government's best interest" and that have proved "costly to correct" *have* resulted. That is the evidence of the case studies. Hence: *As market imperfections increase, the government-as-buyer's ability to act as a smart buyer decreases.*

Government could eliminate some of its problems in determining what to buy if it invested more in monitoring and evaluation. If the government cannot independently determine what to buy, it could at least develop the expertise to determine what it has bought. As reliance on contracting has grown, however, the government's investment in such oversight has actually diminished. Shrinking funds allocated to management and program evaluation have lowered the government's capacity and led to a series of well-publicized management problems, from the savings-and-loan debacle to the expensive myopia developed by NASA's Hubble space telescope. "Fewer program evaluation units were in operation" by the mid-1980s, "and both budgetary and human resources were reduced," GAO reported in 1987. The number of evaluations needed did not decrease, however, and so fewer evaluators had to do more work. As a result, evaluations tended to be smaller in scale, lower in cost, shorter in time, and less probing in technical rigor.[25] OMB's own 1992 study of federal agen-

---

24. General Accounting Office, *Government Contractors: Are Service Contractors Performing Inherently Governmental Functions?* GGD-92-11 (November 1991), p. 60.

25. General Accounting Office, *Federal Evaluation: Fewer Units, Reduced Resources, Different Studies from 1980,* PEMD-87-9 (January 1987).

cies' auditing of their contracts conceded that oversight had long been inadequate.[26]

Instead of relying on market competition, government has bound itself into tight interdependence with its contractors. This interdependence is very much like the vertical integration that occurs in the private sector when a large organization seeks to minimize uncertainties by bringing suppliers into its organizational structure. A similar integration of government and supplier reduces day-to-day transaction costs by blurring the boundaries, allowing easy transfer of cultures, and promoting interdependence between organizations in the market. It increases the chances that goverment and suppliers will speak with one voice. It also, however, undermines the government's independent ability to behave as a smart buyer. That problem would be big enough for an individual who cannot independently assess what kind of car to buy or how well one works. It is bigger for organizations, which must protect themselves from becoming captives of their partners. It is most serious for government, which is charged with not only effectively managing programs but also protecting the public interest. The question is whose voice dominates: the government's or the contractor's?

This "mixing or sharing of powers," Frederick C. Mosher observed, "has further confused the problem of governmental accountability."[27] The vertical integration of government and private suppliers makes it difficult to determine who is responsible for which decisions and to ensure that public, not private, goals ultimately guide public programs. David Bell, President Kennedy's budget director, anticipated the smart-buyer problem in 1962:

> The management and control of such programs much be firmly in the hands of full-time Government officials clearly responsible to the President and the Congress. With programs of the size and complexity now common, this requires that the Government have on its staff exceptionally strong and able executives, scientists, and engineers, fully qualified to weigh the views and advice of technical

26. Office of Management and Budget, *Interagency Task Force Report on the Federal Contract Audit Process* (December 3, 1992).

27. Frederick C. Mosher, *The GAO: The Quest for Accountability in American Government* (Westview Press, 1979), p. 237.

specialists, to make policy decisions concerning the types of work to be undertaken, when, by whom, and at what costs, to supervise the execution of work undertaken, and to evaluate the results.[28]

That is the central question raised by the smart-buyer problem. In short: *As market imperfections increase, the tendency toward vertical integration increases. As vertical integration increases, the problems of public accountability grow as well.*

28. Bureau of the Budget, *Report to the President on Government Contracting for Research and Development*, S. Doc. 87-94, 87 Cong. 2 sess. (GPO, 1962), pp. 192, 216.

9

Managing Versus Governing

The vigorous debate about whether government should turn over more of its activities to the private sector often misses critical points. The rhetoric of the competition prescription has spread an ideological veneer over governmental practice, but the prescription itself speaks little to the very real problems of making contracting work.

The reality is that American government has long been steadily increasing its reliance on private contractors. Practice developed far in advance of the rhetoric, for largely pragmatic reasons: to provide expertise and capacity that the government did not possess and could not, or did not want, to build; to supply flexibility that traditional governmental procedures did not permit; and to reduce government's costs. In fact, the two major policy thrusts of post–World War II American government have been the growth of entitlement programs and increasing dependence on contractors.

In his farewell address in 1961 President Dwight D. Eisenhower warned that overreliance on the "military-industrial complex," the network of contractors and government procurement officials who were building the nation's cold war defenses, threatened democratic processes. The years since have not only justified Eisenhower's concern but broadened the significance of his warning, as contracting has been extended into virtually every cranny of American government.

The cases in this book underline the warning. They are not failure stories; each case produced at least some positive results. Instead, they

199

teach an important lesson: the competition prescription is scarcely a cure-all for government's problems of size and inefficiency.

Competition's capacity for reducing the size of government and increasing its efficiency is exaggerated on three scores. First, the competition prescription envisions free, open competition for the goods and services that government buys. Many, if not most, of the goods and services that government buys are specialized, however, and purchased in markets full of imperfections. The government often cannot know precisely what it wants to buy, who to buy it from, or what the purchase has produced. Its own capacity for answering these questions has been reduced over the years, and market competition does not replace this information. The competition prescription thus starts from assumptions about the way the market works that do not apply to government.

Second, the competition prescription tends to misrepresent the role of competition even in private transactions. Most transactions are full of uncertainty.[1] How much should a buyer pay? How good are the products the supplier is offering? Could a buyer get a better deal elsewhere? Could a supplier charge more for the same product? Neither buyers nor sellers in private markets fully welcome competition because the uncertainty it produces complicates their lives. The lesson of complex private markets, Oliver Williamson observed, is that large organizations seek to reduce their uncertainty more than they seek low prices. The search for stable patterns that allow companies to produce acceptable goods at acceptable costs is far more often the priority in private markets than dog-eat-dog, survival-of-the-fittest competition.[2]

Furthermore, as Steven Kelman pointed out, "government shows more competition than private-sector purchasing does." By setting specifications—even if imprecise—for what it wants to buy, collecting sealed bids, and awarding contracts to the lowest bidder, government imposes more competitive rules than most private marketers ever do. Consistently awarding contracts to the lowest bidder in sealed-bid competitions "is virtually unknown in the business world itself," Kel-

---

1. James G. March and Herbert A. Simon, *Organizations* (Wiley, 1958).
2. Oliver E. Williamson, *The Economic Institutions of Capitalism: Firms, Markets, Relational Contracting* (Free Press, 1985).

man noted.[3] The government's competitions do not always produce the best goods and services, however, and they certainly have not protected government from the very problems that the privatizers want to use more competition to solve.

What privatization advocates do not realize or acknowledge is that uncertainty—not lack of competition—is the fundamental problem for government and business alike. Business, no less than government, operates in a world of substantial complexity. An automobile manufacturer that cannot count on the quality of glass in its windshields or the price of the steel in its frames cannot reliably and predictably produce cars. The threat is not marginal differences in cost but uncertainty in supply and quality. Long-term relationships between buyers and sellers are the rule, not the exception, in private business. What matters is not so much efficiency but the reality that suppliers who do not perform up to the buyer's satisfaction can be replaced.[4] That is the real meaning of competition.

Third, common problems afflict all contracting relationships between buyers and sellers, in both the public and private sectors. Conflicts of interest and monitoring problems are endemic to all transactions between principals and agents. The basic model underlying the competition prescription itself suggests that agents will have many goals besides those of the principal and that principals will have difficulty detecting which missions their agents are carrying out. There is no escaping, even in the private sector, the problems that the case studies illustrate.

My arguments are scarcely an *apologia* for government and the inefficiencies with which it sometimes is plagued. They constitute, rather, a warning that a too-enthusiastic embrace of the competition prescription might produce the wrong medicine for a misdiagnosed disease. Government's problems are manifest, but they are not fundamentally ones of sloppiness encouraged by monopoly practice. Rather, government's problems are rooted in its struggle to act as a smart buyer in the public-private partnerships on which it has come to rely.

3. Steven Kelman, *Procurement and Public Management: The Fear of Discretion and the Quality of Government Performance* (Washington: American Enterprise Institute, 1990), pp. 62, 63.

4. Kelman, *Procurement and Public Management;* and Williamson, *Economic Institutions of Capitalism.*

Coping with Uncertainty

As the case studies show, government officials have developed four responses to cope with the conflict-of-interest and monitoring problems they face: competition, bureaucracy, cultural change, and leadership.[5] These responses are often helpful, but none of them—alone or in combination—can solve the problems inherent in the contracting relationship.

Coping Strategies

In both the A-76 and FTS-2000 programs, the government relied on *competition* to deliver the best service at the lowest price. Whether the competition was for a relatively small contract, as in A-76, or for a huge one, as in FTS-2000, policymakers were convinced that putting the contracts out to bid would allow the self-correcting behavior of the market to select the best performers. Competition did indeed eliminate those who could not perform. It also supplied the government—usually—with goods and services. Competition, however, could not always tell the government just what to buy, could not prevent conflicts of interest, and could not inform the government about just what it had bought.

In these cases, but even more in the other two cases, government officials also resorted to *bureaucratic* fixes to cope with conflict-of-interest and monitoring problems. Under heavy pressure from the General Accounting Office (GAO), the Environmental Protection Agency (EPA) implemented procedural reforms, including additional auditing of its Superfund contractors. GAO and EPA also put more pressure on the contractors to produce quicker results. Officials at the Department of Energy (DOE) reorganized their supervision of their nuclear weapons contractors, putting far more emphasis on health and safety issues than they had in the past and, in the Rocky Flats case, reducing the number of bureaucratic levels between the

---

5. For a different analysis of how managers attempted to cope by adopting strategies of bureaucratization, professionalization, and culture-building, see John J. DiIulio, Jr., *Principled Agents: Leadership, Administration, and Culture in a Federal Bureaucracy* (Oxford University Press, forthcoming). Many of the same behaviors DiIulio observed occurred in the four cases studied here, but professionalization was notably absent. Professional expertise was largely the province of the contractors, not the government, in these cases.

field and headquarters. These procedural and organizational reforms changed the incentives of the contractors and improved the flow of information to the top, but they could not resolve the fundamental problems in the contracting relationship. EPA still struggled with abuses by contractors that signaled continuing conflict-of-interest problems. Despite the best efforts of top DOE officials, performance problems continued to plague the nuclear weapons program.

Intertwined with DOE's efforts to make bureaucratic changes were its efforts to *change the culture* within the weapons complex. DOE officials acted forcefully on their pledge to replace the old culture of production and secrecy with a new culture of safety and openness. The changes within the complex were dramatic, from new public hearings on cleanup problems to altered financial awards for contractors. The department, however, could not simply create a new culture through fiat or expect to turn around overnight decades of distrust among local citizens. The new culture of openness and decentralized authority, moreover, sometimes conflicted with other departmental imperatives. Many top officials who had to answer to Congress and the media for problems in the field were reluctant to delegate authority for which they might later have to apologize. New attitudes did not come easily either to government employees or to contractors.

Finally, in all of the cases, *political leaders* emphasized the importance of performance. Support for the A-76 program came from both Republican and Democratic presidents. The Reagan administration, in its effort to downsize the federal government, proved an especially enthusiastic cheerleader. The administration's enthusiasm for the competition prescription spilled over into the FTS-2000 procurement. When problems developed along the way, this enthusiasm pushed the procurement along. To ease constant congressional attacks, top EPA officials pressed for Superfund results. Senior DOE officials were determined to change the department's culture, and this support from the top made possible the reforms at the bottom. In all four cases, this leadership proved important, but in the end it was never determinative. Leadership lost its force as it descended the chain of command within the government's bureaucracy and especially in the often troubled relationship between the bureaucracy and the contractor.

Each of these coping strategies helped address the basic problems inherent in contracting relationships but did not eliminate them. This does not mean that the government, acting directly, could have managed the programs better; it only would have had to cope with a different set of problems. Nor does it mean that the competition prescription makes no sense. Given the staggering technical complexity of many of these programs and the government's own limited capacity, contracting out makes pragmatic sense. It does mean, however, that coping strategies, however aggressively pursued, cannot overcome the problems inherent in a principal-agent relationship. The only sure way for the government to deal with these unavoidable problems is to learn to be a smart buyer.

The Cost to Government

Whatever efficiencies competition might create, it increases uncertainties, which can prove disruptive and costly. If the government cannot define clearly what it wants to buy, and if government cannot judge well what it has bought, it surrenders a measure of its authority to its private partners. Without the capacity by government to act as a smart buyer, increased competition is meaningless.

Government has relied on contractors not only to provide it with goods and services, but also to tell it what it ought to buy, to evaluate what it has purchased, and to manage many of the steps in between, including writing testimony for government officials to present to Congress explaining the transactions. If the government is not a smart buyer, the critical responsibility for the performance of public programs passes to its contractors. Government cannot be sovereign if it cannot buy smart.

Surrendering sovereignty to its contractors entails more than just transferring power from the political arena to the marketplace. It risks undermining the accountability of government. Voters elect officials to make policy, and elected officials delegate power to administrators. It is one thing for these administrators to delegate the delivery of goods and services to private partners. It is quite another for those private partners to have such an advantage in expertise over government officials that they, not government, are, in effect, the authors of public policy. In an ever more complex world, government must have an independent, smart-buyer capacity if it is to govern.

The erosion of capacity matters in several ways. First, government is presumed capable of carrying out the programs it creates. That is a keystone of the republican system of government in the United States. Second, the bureaucracy is presumed capable of exercising responsibly the discretion that elected officials delegate to it. If that presumption is invalid, the delegation of authority is troublesome—constitutionally, politically, and pragmatically. Third, in day-to-day operations, the government's legitimacy often hinges on the presumption that government agencies are expert and employ that expertise to guide their actions. The courts, for example, have long cited this presumption of the bureaucracy's expertise in upholding their actions. The government does not need to do everything itself, or to know everything itself, to uphold these presumptions. It does, however, need to be in a position to make intelligent judgments on the information it receives from those who supply the expertise on which it acts; in other words, it needs to be a smart buyer. To the degree that the government is not a smart buyer, it inevitably shares its sovereignty and risks undermining its legitimacy.

If American government does not develop the capacity to behave as a smart buyer, it is doomed to two predicaments. First, it will surrender governmental authority to its private partners. Second, it will lose its ability to see the big picture and know how the pieces fit together.

Unfortunately, as government's reliance on contracting out has increased, so too has its disinvestment in its own capacity. At one time, scholars of public administration celebrated the fact that the government employed world-class experts on virtually every issue: mapmakers, chemists, engineers, attorneys, housing economists, librarians, agricultural analysts, food safety specialists. The government no longer has such a range of in-house expertise. In part, that is because of quantum leaps in the complexity of governmental programs. No organization, public or private, can hope to be master of all of the knowledge that lies behind society's major post–World War II innovations. In part, the government's expertise has dwindled because the demand for expertise is far greater than the supply of experts, and private employers can almost always outbid the government, leaving the government no choice but to enlist private partners to help it in the day-to-day conduct of its work. In part, the loss of expertise has resulted from the enthusiasm of some elected officials, especially in the Reagan and Bush administrations, for shrinking the government. The bureaucrat-bashing campaign of the late 1970s and 1980s supported that movement.

Finally, among practitioners and analysts alike, policymaking has often received far more attention than policy execution. Elected officials find it more attractive to take symbolic stands on new programs than to deal with the myriad details that translate symbols into results. Practicing policy analysts and academics alike have indulged in the conceit that shaping policy is a higher calling than implementing it. Electoral and professional imperatives have often conspired to emphasize policymaking over management, under the false assumption that once the right decision is made, the administrative details will take care of themselves.

Indeed, that is the critical flaw in the competition prescription. Its champions simply assume that the competitive process rewards winners, punishes losers, and produces optimal results. The market is a way of managing scarcity, however, and all decisions under conditions of scarcity have both benefits and costs. In their enthusiasm, competition advocates have forgotten this essential cornerstone of economics.

Effects on Governance

The government's growing reliance on private contractors not only has posed a new breed of public management problems but has also fundamentally transformed governance in four important ways.

First, the extensive reliance on contractors has changed the relationship between government program managers and program outputs. Instead of dealing directly with the recipients of government goods and services, program managers deal with the contractors who deliver the goods and services. The change in mission also changes the requirements for government bureaucrats, often in ways that the civil service system does not anticipate. Instead of using their substantive knowledge of the policy area, government employees find themselves dealing with the procedural features of contract monitoring and compliance. As a result, government workers are often doing jobs for which they were not trained, while their expertise goes unused.

Second, contracting has changed the relationship between political appointees and the programs they are charged with managing. High-level officials in many government agencies find themselves sitting on top of complex public-private relationships whose dimensions they may only vaguely understand. Because they spend much of their time mending political fences in the capital, these administrators frequently have even a fuzzier knowledge of what the contracting system is doing and what problems need to be solved. The contracting system, moreover, puts an extra link in the chain from policymaking to policy execution. Top officials frequently become frustrated by their relatively loose leverage over contractors' behavior and, hence, over the programs they are charged with managing. They are responsible for a system over which they have little real control.

Third, contracting has changed the relationship between elected officials and citizens. If political appointees have loose control over programs managed through contracts, the programmatic connection between elected officials and citizens is even looser. Contracting out has great symbolic appeal to officials trying to shrink government. Problems with contractors, however, can dull the shine of the idea, and elected officials are often woefully unprepared to solve them. They frequently have little sense of what happens between invocation of the market model and the problems that the resulting complex partnerships produce. The tendency is to see the problems that do emerge as isolated instances of mismanagement or program abuse, instead of as a generic thread that winds its way through contracting relationships.

Finally, contracting has changed the fundamental relationship between citizens and government. Because it puts an extra link in the chain, it extends and complicates the relationship. Contract incentives make contractors responsive to the goals the contract sets—and to the government officials who are charged with determining if the goals are met. The "customers" in the contracting relationship thus tend to be contract managers more than citizens, even if citizens are the recipients of services. Involving citizens in the oversight process is possible, of course, but involving them in drawing up contract incentives is complex—substantially more complex, in fact, than the already difficult task of incorporating a citizen-centered approach in direct service delivery. The same is true for coordination of services. As chapter 7 demonstrated, contracting for social services can easily become a fragmented, compliance-centered enterprise instead of an integrated, citizen-focused service. In the process of defining goals and measuring contract compliance, the citizen can ultimately become lost.

It is worth repeating that problems of implementing policy and responding to citizens would occur even if the government were to provide services directly. The rhetorical support for the competition prescription grew out of profound dissatisfaction with the performance of directly managed government programs. Indeed, given the increasing interrelationships of the public and private sectors, inter-sectoral and intergovernmental partnerships make much sense. The lesson, rather, is that invoking the virtues of competition does not cast a spell that magically makes problems disappear.

Market competition substitutes one set of problems, revolving around conflicts of interest and monitoring, for the manifest problems of direct government administration. The problems associated with the market must be managed, not chanted away with the competition mantra. Most of all, they must be recognized by all the players. The competition prescription has been an irresistible idea for which enormous promises have been made, but whose full dimensions have been seen only dimly at best. Without a full recognition of the costs as well as the benefits of the competition prescription, no careful judgment can be made about it. The risk, moreover, is that ambitious promises will be undercut once again by the inevitable problems, and that, in the process, public trust and confidence in government will erode even more.

Building a Smart-Buying Government

The competition prescription can be a valuable part of America's governance mix, but only if the government builds the capacity to act as a smart buyer. Building a smart-buying bureaucracy need not be expensive. A handful of government employees, in fact, can supervise millions of dollars of contracts. A smaller bureaucracy, however, must be a smarter bureaucracy. What is needed is not *more* bureaucracy but a *different kind* of bureaucracy. What, then, are the elements of a smart-buying government?

—Hire and reward front-line bureaucrats trained to manage contracts. The government has tended to hire individuals who know a great deal about the substance of the contract but then has required them to handle the contract's procedural aspects. All too often, the

result has been frustrated workers poorly trained for the jobs they actually perform. Government needs to recognize that its reliance on contractors has created the need for a new class of government officials, and then it needs to find and hire them. These new contract managers should be skilled at drafting clear and enforceable standards, managing information, auditing, and, above all, negotiating.

—*Retrain mid-level bureaucrats.* Frontline contract managers who perform well typically are promoted to mid-level management, where their job is to serve as a buffer between task-oriented lower levels and policy-oriented top officials. Hiring individuals for substantive knowledge and employing them as procedural watchdogs provides a weak background for this critical middle role. To solve the problem, government agencies must adopt aggressive training programs for officials who play the critical middle role.

—*Make political appointees aware of the issues involved in contracting.* It is a truism that many political appointees have little knowledge of the substance of the programs they manage.[6] They also have little understanding of the administrative system that produces the programs they run, or of the typical problems that such a system generates. Top managers need be neither experts in the field of their department's work nor experts in contract management. They must, however, develop a keen sense of the substantive issues and a process that ensures that the public interest is paramount. The problems will appear on their desks one way or another. If top officials do not anticipate them, the problems inevitably will surface at the most inconvenient time, in a way guaranteed to be difficult and politically embarrassing to attack. Unless government's political appointees are committed to building a smart-buying bureaucracy, moreover, an organizational culture committed to buying smart is unlikely to develop.

—*Tone down the political rhetoric.* Touting the advantages of market competition over government monopoly is irresistible to many politicians. Given American's lasting reverence for individual choice over government power, how could it be otherwise? And given the disappointing results of many government programs since the Great

6. For a discussion of these issues, see James W. Fesler and Donald F. Kettl, *The Politics of the Administrative Process* (Chatham, N.J.: Chatham House Publishers, 1991), chap. 7.

Society, the rhetoric rings clearly. Adopting market competition as a palliative, however, works about as well as cutting waste, fraud, and abuse to balance the budget. In principal, both make unarguable sense; in practice, both promise more than they can deliver—and further undermine confidence in government institutions. Leavening the enthusiasm for the competition prescription with a measure of the real problems that must be solved to make it work would help avoid this problem.

—Avoid contracting for core governmental functions. Effective contract management—management alert to risks of conflicts of interest and the need for monitoring—requires at least a minimal foundation of government expertise. Just where the line should be drawn between functions that are inherently governmental and those that can be legitimately contracted out is perhaps the most difficult puzzle of the public-private relationship. The Office of Management and Budget tautologically has determined that government agencies should not contract out work of a policymaking nature that is the direct responsibility of agency officials. Two meetings that GAO conducted with experts in the field produced agreement on little more than the belief that the definitional question needed more study.[7] GAO itself has concluded that some functions should never be contracted out: "presenting testimony, holding hearings, representing an agency before the public, and supervising federal employees."[8]

More difficult is the problem of generating and interpreting information. The government cannot be a smart buyer unless it has the information to offset the contractors' manifest advantage. Contractors inevitably will produce some of that information and analysis. The government, however, must have at its core the capacity to know what to make of the information. Otherwise, it is simply increasing, not reducing, the asymmetries on which the problems of the principal-agent relationship rest.

—Recognize that market methods raise new issues for governance. Government officials, at every level and in every branch, need to

---

7. General Accounting Office, *Government Contractors: Are Service Contractors Performing Inherently Governmental Functions?* GGD-92-11 (November 1991).
8. GAO, *Government Contractors,* pp. 5–6.

recognize that conducting the business of government in new ways brings new questions that they must consider. What does it mean for a president or governor to be chief executive of a branch much of whose work is done by nongovernmental workers? How do the levers of legislative oversight work when frontline workers are beyond the direct reach of legislative committees? How should the judiciary resolve disputes if the primacy of federal expertise can no longer be taken for granted? The constellation of issues generated by the growth of government contracting spill over onto the most basic questions of American governance.

Governing through Leadership

These recommendations are tough and can be implemented only with strong and aggressive political leadership. Only political leaders can make and win the case for investing in the resources needed to make government a smart buyer. Only political leaders can shape the bureaucratic culture to make buying smart the central imperative.

Investment in smart buying is an investment in quality programs and in the country's future, but it will not happen of its own accord. Bureaucrats who make the case for more of the right kind of resources might well seem to be attempting to maximize their power and budgets, which is precisely the charge that privatizers make in arguing for contracting out. Only forceful political leaders can make the case for enhanced government capacity—and point out the far greater costs that would accrue if the investment is not made. Without such an investment, the government will not be able to manage its programs effectively. Moreover, political leadership itself will become impossible, for leaders will not have the foundation of data and analysis with which to chart their course. An investment in smart buying, in a bureaucracy of a different kind and capacity, is the keystone of political leadership for the future.

Political leadership must extend to more than simply building support for the needed resources. As the progressively more complex case studies illustrate, only political leadership from the top of an agency can begin to change the culture *inside* it: to underline the importance of information to learning; to emphasize careful review and communication of critical information; to create an atmosphere that accepts, even encourages, the reporting of bad news; and to emphasize the values that promote the agency's goals. Both in building external political support and in changing the internal bureaucratic culture, political leadership is the foundation for creating a smart-buying bureaucracy.

Index

213